ISBN: 9781314522952

Published by:
HardPress Publishing
8345 NW 66TH ST #2561
MIAMI FL 33166-2626

Email: info@hardpress.net
Web: http://www.hardpress.net

THE LIBRARY
OF
THE UNIVERSITY
OF CALIFORNIA
LOS ANGELES

A
TREATISE
ON
THE REFORM ACT,
2 WILLIAM IV. CHAP. 45,

WITH

PRACTICAL DIRECTIONS TO OVERSEERS AND TOWN-CLERKS,

AND

A COPY OF THE ORDER IN COUNCIL
Of the 11th July, 1832;

ALSO

An Appendix,
CONTAINING A COPY OF THE ACT,

AND ALSO

THE BOUNDARY ACT, 2 & 3 WILLIAM IV. C. 64.

BY

WILLIAM RUSSELL, ESQ.
OF LINCOLN'S INN, BARRISTER AT LAW.

LONDON:
SAUNDERS AND BENNING, LAW BOOKSELLERS.
(SUCCESSORS TO J. BUTTERWORTH AND SON,)
43, FLEET STREET.

1832.

LONDON:
PRINTED BY C. ROWORTH AND SONS, BELL YARD,
TEMPLE BAR.

TO

THE RIGHT HONOURABLE

LORD JOHN RUSSELL,

&c. &c. &c.

HAVING been entrusted by His Majesty's Ministers with a share in the task of preparing the REFORM BILL, and having consequently had an opportunity of becoming acquainted with the principles on which its Provisions were founded, and the views with which its Enactments were framed, I have ventured to consider myself in some degree qualified to attempt, now that it has passed into a Law, a Treatise in explanation of it.

Independently of any public grounds, motives of private affection and esteem alone would be sufficient to induce me to wish for the sanction of your name; but, apart from any such considerations, I

iv DEDICATION.

am satisfied that all will agree that there is no one to whom a Work on the Reformed Law of Election could with greater propriety be addressed than to yourself.

Regretting my inability to offer upon a subject of such general importance a more sufficient Commentary than that which I now address to you,

I remain,

Ever yours with affectionate Regard,

WILLIAM RUSSELL.

28, Lincoln's Inn Fields,
July 20th, 1832.

"Certain abuses and corruptions grow into the law as close as the ivy unto the tree, or the rust to the iron, and in a little tract of time gain the reputation of being part of the law: so that a great and considerable part of that reformation that is pleaded for, is not so much of the law as of abuses and corruptions, and wens and excrescences, that do adhere to the law, and will in time strangle and stifle it with their close adherence to it."

"But yet farther—I do not think that the only things fit to be reformed in the law are the abuses and corruptions of it; but there are some things, that are really and truly parts of the law, as necessary to be reformed as the errors and abuses of it."

SIR MATTHEW HALE.

PREFACE.

It has been the object of the Author to present in the following Treatise, a careful Commentary upon the whole of the Reform Act, arranging its Provisions in the order that seemed most favourable to perspicuity, and offering a particular explanation of those parts of the Statute which appeared to require it. Such points of the Old Law and Practice of Elections have been noticed, as it seemed proper to refer to for the purpose of showing how they are affected by the Act.

To this have been added, in the Three last Chapters of the work, Practical Directions, somewhat in detail, which it is hoped may be found convenient for the use of those who are to carry the Provisions of the Act into effect.

The Author gladly avails himself of this opportunity of acknowledging the great assistance he has received from his friend Mr. Gregson, with whom,

viii PREFACE.

and with Mr. Henry Roscoe, he had the pleasure of being associated in preparing the Reform Bill for Parliament: But for that assistance this Treatise would have fallen far short of any pretension to accuracy that it may possess.

CONTENTS.

CHAPTER I.

NUMBER OF KNIGHTS OF THE SHIRE TO SERVE FOR ENGLAND AND WALES.

	Page
Number of Knights of the Shire	1
Counties of York and Lincoln	1, 2
What Counties to be Divided	3
What Counties to return Three Knights	4
What Counties in England and Wales to return Two . .	*ib.*
What Welsh Counties will return One Knight only . .	*ib.*
Isle of Wight to be a County returning One Knight . .	5
Certain Counties of Cities and Towns incorporated with Counties at large	*ib.*

CHAPTER II.

NUMBER OF MEMBERS TO SERVE FOR CITIES AND BOROUGHS IN ENGLAND AND WALES.

	Page
Classification of Cities and Boroughs returning Members	6
What Cities and Boroughs in England to return Two Members	7, 8, 9
What Cities and Boroughs in England and Wales to return One Member	9, 10
Welsh Contributory Boroughs	11, 12, 13, 14
Boundaries of all Cities, Boroughs, &c. settled by Boundary Act	14

x   CONTENTS.

CHAPTER III.

ELECTORS FOR COUNTIES.

Page

Classification of County Electors 15
1st. As to Freeholders :—
   Freeholder's Qualification defined . . . . 15 to 17
   No Person to Vote for a County in respect of any
     Freehold Property occupied by himself in a Bo-
     rough which might confer a Vote for the Borough
     under the 27th Section 18, 19
2dly. As to Copyholders :—
   County Right extended to Copyholders 20
   Right defined . . , ... 21
   Where Property might confer Right for a Borough it
     will not for a County 21, 22
3dly. As to Tenants in Ancient Demesne :—
   Previous State of the Law as to them 22, 23
   How their Right of Voting will be regulated in
     future 23, 24
4thly. As to Leaseholders :—
   Definition of Leasehold Right—Value of 10*l. per
     Annum* required if term originally created for not
     less than Sixty Years. 24, 25
   Value of 50*l. per Annum* required if term originally
     created for Twenty Years at the least 26
   No Leaseholder to Vote for County in respect of
     Property which might confer a Vote for a Borough *ib.*
5thly. As to Occupying Tenant, (without reference to
     length of term) :—
   Occupying Tenants at Rent of 50*l.* to Vote . . . 27
   Right defined . . . . *ib.*
   Property not to give a Vote for a County if it might
     confer one for a Borough 28
   Provision as to Equitable Estates 28, 29

CONTENTS.

xi

CHAPTER IV.

ELECTORS FOR CITIES AND BOROUGHS.

Page

Classification of Rights for Cities and Boroughs . . . 30
  1st. As to New Rights:—
    New Qualification defined by Sect. 27. What re-
      quisite to constitute it . . . . 30 to 39
  2dly. Old Rights Reserved in Perpetuity:—
    What they are 39
      1st. Freeholders and Burgage Tenants in certain
        Counties of Cities and Towns . . . . 40 to 42
      2dly. Burgesses and Freemen, and Freemen and
        Liverymen of the City of London 42, 43
  3dly. Old Rights Reserved for a time:—
    What they are . . . . 45 to 50

CHAPTER V.

PROCEEDINGS WITH REGARD TO THE REGISTRATION OF VOTERS FOR COUNTIES.

General Outline of Process of County Registration . 54, 55
Details of County Registration 56, 71

CHAPTER VI.

PROCEEDINGS WITH REGARD TO THE REGISTRATION OF VOTERS FOR CITIES AND BOROUGHS.

General Outline of Borough Registration . . . 72 to 74
Details of Borough Registration . . . . . . 74 to 89

CHAPTER VII.

PROCEEDINGS PREPARATORY TO AND DURING COUNTY ELECTIONS.

Duty of Returning Officer as to Notice of Election, Erecting Booths, Mode of Polling, &c. . . . . . 90 to 93

xii   CONTENTS.

                                                                Page
Expenses of Booths, Deputies, &c. 93
Duration of Poll   94
Duties of Poll Clerks . . . . *ib.*
Final Declaration of the Poll . . . · 95

CHAPTER VIII.

PROCEEDINGS PREPARATORY TO AND DURING BOROUGH ELECTIONS IN ENGLAND.

Notice of Election 97
Provisions as to Booths, Polling, &c. . . . . . . 98 to 100
Expenses of Booths, &c. 99
Duration of Poll . . . . *ib.*
Duties of Poll Clerks 101
Final Declaration of the Poll . . . . *ib.*
Returning Officers for New Boroughs . . . . 101 to 103

CHAPTER IX.

PROCEEDINGS PREPARATORY TO AND DURING ELECTIONS FOR BOROUGHS IN WALES.

Provisions as to Polling, &c. at Elections for Monmouth,
    and for the Welsh Boroughs 104, 105, 106

CHAPTER X.

POINTS COMMON TO ALL ELECTIONS, WHETHER FOR COUNTIES OR BOROUGHS.

Subjects of Inquiry at the Time of Polling 108
Oaths to be taken at Elections 108, 109
Tender of Votes at Election by Party excluded from
    Register 110
Scrutiny before Returning Officer abolished 111
Register Questionable before Committee of House of Com-
    mons . . . . *ib.*
Adjournment of Poll in case of Riot 112

CONTENTS.   xiii

CHAPTER XI.

EXPENSES INCIDENT TO REGISTRATION IN COUNTIES AND BO-
ROUGHS, AND PENALTIES FOR NEGLECT OF DUTIES UNDER THE
ACT.

Page

Remuneration of Barristers 113
Expenses of Overseers, Clerks of the Peace, &c.   114 to 116
Penalties for neglect of Duties 116

CHAPTER XII.

PROCEEDINGS UNDER THE ACT FOR THE YEAR 1832.

Dates for First Registration 118
Order in Council   . . . .   121 to 131

CHAPTER XIII.

DUTY OF OVERSEERS WITH REGARD TO MAKING OUT LISTS
OF COUNTY ELECTORS . . . .   132 to 145

CHAPTER XIV.

DUTIES OF OVERSEERS WITH REGARD TO THE LISTS OF
ELECTORS FOR CITIES AND BOROUGHS . . .   146 to 167

CHAPTER XV.

DUTY OF TOWN CLERKS IN PLACES WHERE FREEMEN HAVE
A RIGHT TO VOTE . . . .   168 to 176

Appendix.

THE REFORM ACT, 2 Wm. 4, c. 45.

THE BOUNDARY ACT, 2 & 3 Wm. 4, c. 64.

INDEX.

b

ERRATA.

Page 9, " Wolverhampton" should be in *Italics*, as having acquired the Right of Sending Members to Parliament under
the Act.

Page 59, *for* " before the 25th of August," *read* " on or before, &c."

TREATISE

ON

THE REFORM ACT,

2 WILLIAM IV. CAP. 45.

CHAPTER I.

NUMBER OF KNIGHTS OF THE SHIRE TO SERVE FOR COUNTIES IN ENGLAND AND WALES.

THERE will in future be 159 Knights of the Shire to represent the different Counties in England and Wales.

These may be classed as follows:

There will be

1 County returning 6 Knights of the Shire	6
26 Counties will return 4 each	104
7	will return 3 each	21
9	will return 2 each	18
10	will return 1 each	10
		159

1st. The County of York will return Six Knights of the Shire; that is to say, Two for each of the

Number of Knights of the Shire in future Parliaments.

County of York to return Six Knights.

B

KNIGHTS OF THE SHIRE.

Each Riding to be as a separate County.

Three Ridings ; and for all Election purposes each Riding is to be considered as a separate County ; therefore the Qualifications arising in each separate Riding will confer a Right of Voting in the Election of the Knights to serve for that particular Riding alone. *2 W. 4, c. 45, s. 12.*

It is to be observed that the North Riding of Yorkshire will, for the purpose of electing Knights of the Shire, include the City of York and the Ainsty; and the East Riding of Yorkshire will comprehend the County of the Town of Kingston upon Hull. *See S. 17, and Sched. (G.)*

County of Lincoln to return Four Knights.

2dly. The County of Lincoln will in future return Four Knights of the Shire ; that is to say, Two for the Parts of Lindsey, and Two for the Parts of Kesteven and Holland ; and, for the purposes of Elections, the Parts of Lindsey are to be considered as one distinct County, and the Parts of Kesteven and Holland together as another distinct County; and, as has already been explained with regard to the several Ridings of Yorkshire, the Qualifications arising in the Parts of Lindsey will confer Rights of Voting as to those Parts only, and the Qualifications arising in the Parts of Kesteven and Holland as to the Parts of Kesteven and Holland alone. *S. 13.* The Parts of Lindsey will comprehend, for the purposes of Elections, the County of the City of Lincoln. *See S. 17, and Sched. (G.)*

KNIGHTS OF THE SHIRE.

3dly. Each of the following 25 Counties will, in future Parliaments, be represented by Four Knights of the Shire; but they are to be divided each into Two Divisions, and each of such Divisions is hereafter to return Two Knights of the Shire: *(Certain Counties to be divided, each Division to return Two Knights.)*

Cheshire,	Northumberland,
Cornwall,	Northamptonshire.
Cumberland,	Nottinghamshire,
Derbyshire,	Shropshire,
Devonshire,	Somersetshire,
Durham,	Staffordshire,
Essex,	Suffolk,
Gloucestershire,	Surrey,
Hampshire,	Sussex,
Kent,	Warwickshire,
Lancashire,	Wiltshire,
Leicestershire,	Worcestershire.
Norfolk,	

These Counties are enumerated in the Schedule (F.) annexed to the Act; and each of their Divisions is, for all the purposes of Elections, to be considered as a distinct and separate County, so that the Qualifications arising in each Division will confer a right of voting for that Division only. *S.* 14. *(Each Division to be as a separate County.)*

The Division is to be effected by a separate Act to be passed for the purpose, which is, however, immediately upon its passing to become virtually a part of the Reform Act. The precedent for this prospective incorporation of an Act not yet passed *(Division to be effected by Boundary Act.)*

B 2

KNIGHTS OF THE SHIRE.

with one which has actually become a Law, is to be found in the Act of Union with Scotland. *See* 5 *Ann, c.* 8, *art.* 22.

Certain Counties to return Three Knights.

4thly. Each of the following Counties will in future return Three Knights of the Shire, viz.

Berkshire,	Herefordshire,
Buckinghamshire,	Hertfordshire,
Cambridgeshire,	Oxfordshire.
Dorsetshire.	

These are enumerated in the Schedule (F. 2.) *See S.* 15.

Counties to return Two Knights.

5thly. The Counties which will each return Two Knights of the Shire are as follows, viz.—

IN ENGLAND.	IN WALES.
Bedfordshire,	Caermarthenshire,
Huntingdonshire,	Denbighshire,
Middlesex,	Glamorganshire.
Monmouthshire,	
Rutlandshire,	
Westmoreland.	

Welsh Counties which are to return One Knight only.

6thly. The following Counties in Wales will return one Member only as heretofore:—

Anglesea,	Merionethshire,
Breconshire,	Montgomeryshire,
Cardiganshire,	Pembrokeshire,
Carnarvonshire,	Radnorshire.
Flintshire.	

KNIGHTS OF THE SHIRE.

7thly. The Isle of Wight is hereafter to be, for the purposes of Elections, a County of itself, separate from Hampshire, and will return one Knight of the Shire to Parliament; the Right of Voting and the mode of Election will be in all respects the same for this New County as for any other County in England. *S.* 16.

Isle of Wight to be a County returning One Knight.

There are at present 19 Cities and Towns in England and Wales being Counties of themselves, which, although locally situate within Counties at large, were not, with the exception of Three of them (viz. Canterbury, Poole, and Southampton,) for the purposes of Parliamentary Representation, an integral part of the Counties at large;

Certain Counties of Cities and Towns incorporated with Counties at large.

Of these 19, the 13 enumerated in Schedule (G.) annexed to the Act will in future, for the purposes of County Elections, be included in the Counties at large with which they are locally connected;

The remaining 6, viz. Bristol, Exeter, Haverfordwest, Lichfield, Norwich, Nottingham, in which alone Freeholders have had the Right of Voting for the Cities or Towns themselves, will not share in the Representation of the Counties at large with which they are respectively connected; But, as an equivalent for the County Franchise, the Right of Voting, as will be afterwards explained, is to be continued in perpetuity to the Freeholders of those places by the 31st Section of the Act.

MEMBERS FOR BOROUGHS.

CHAPTER II.

NUMBER OF MEMBERS TO SERVE FOR CITIES AND BOROUGHS IN ENGLAND AND WALES.

MANY Boroughs, which used heretofore to Return Members to Parliament, being wholly Disfranchised by the Act on the grounds stated in the Preamble, it seems unnecessary to make any further observation with regard to them than, that they are Fifty-six in Number, and that they are enumerated in the First Section, and more particularly described in the Schedule (A.) annexed to the Act.

Number of members for Cities and Boroughs in England and Wales.

There will in future be 341 Members to represent the different Cities and Boroughs in England and Wales.

These may be classed as follows:—
There will be

1	City returning 4 Members	4
135	Cities and Boroughs returning 2 each	270
67	————————————————— 1 each	67
		341

The City of London is the only place which will continue to return Four Members.

Weymouth to return Two Members only.

The Borough of Weymouth and Melcombe-Regis, which formerly returned Four Members, will in future return only Two. *See S.* 6.

MEMBERS FOR BOROUGHS.

The following Cities and Boroughs in England will return Two Members each: (1)

What Cities and Boroughs in England to return Two Members.

Albans, St.	Carlisle,
Andover,	Chester
Aylesbury,	Chichester,
Barnstaple,	Chippenham,
Bath,	Cirencester,
Bedford,	Cockermouth,
Berwick-upon-Tweed,	Colchester,
Beverley,	Coventry,
Birmingham,	Cricklade,
Blackburn,	Derby,
Bodmin,	Devizes,
Bolton,	*Devonport,*
Boston,	Dorchester,
Bradford,	Dover,
Bridgenorth,	Durham,
Bridgewater,	East Retford,
Bridport,	Evesham,
Brighton,	Exeter,
Bristol,	*Finsbury,*
Buckingham,	Gloucester,
Bury St. Edmunds,	Grantham,
Cambridge University,	*Greenwich,*
Cambridge, Borough,	Guildford,
Canterbury,	*Halifax,*

(1) The Boroughs printed in Italics have acquired the right of sending Members to Parliament by the Act. See S. 3, and Schedule (C.)

8   MEMBERS FOR BOROUGHS.

Harwich,	Newark-upon-Trent,
Hastings,	Newcastle-under-Lyne,
Hereford,	Newcastle-upon-Tyne,
Hertford,	Newport (**I.** of **Wight**),
Honiton,	Northampton,
Huntingdon,	Norwich,
Ipswich,	Nottingham,
King's Lynn,	*Oldham*,
Kingston-upon-Hull,	Oxford, University,
Knaresborough,	Oxford, City,
Lambeth,	Penryn,
Lancaster,	Peterborough,
Leeds,	Plymouth,
Leicester,	Pontefract,
Leominster,	Poole,
Lewes,	Portsmouth,
Lincoln,	Preston,
Lichfield,	Reading,
Liverpool,	Richmond,
Ludlow,	Ripon,
Lymington,	Rochester,
Macclesfield,	Salisbury,
Maidstone,	Sandwich,
Maldon,	Scarborough,
Malton,	*Sheffield*,
Manchester,	Shoreham,
Marlborough,	Shrewsbury,
Marlow, Great,	Southampton,
Mary-le-bone,	Southwark,

MEMBERS FOR BOROUGHS.

9

Stafford,
Stamford,
Stockport,
Stoke-upon-Trent,
Stroud,
Sudbury,
Sunderland,
Tamworth,
Tavistock,
Taunton,
Tewkesbury,
Thetford,
Tiverton,
Totness,
Tower Hamlets,

Truro,
Warwick,
Wells,
Wenlock,
Westminster,
Weymouth,
Wigan,
Winchester,
Windsor,
Wolverhampton,
Worcester,
Wycombe,
Yarmouth,
York.

The following Cities and Boroughs will return One Member each : (1)

What Cities and Boroughs in England and Wales to return One Member each.

Abingdon,
* Arundel,
* Ashburton,
Ashton-under-Lyne,
Banbury,
Beaumaris,
Bewdley,

Brecon,
Bury,
* Calne,
Cardiff,
Cardigan,
Carmarthen,
Carnarvon,

(1) The Boroughs printed in Italics have acquired the Right of Sending a Member to Parliament by the Act. See S. 4, and Sched. (D.) Those marked with an asterisk have been deprived of One Member by the Act. See S. 2, and Sched. (B.)

B 5

MEMBERS FOR BOROUGHS.

Chatham,
Cheltenham,
* Christchurch,
* Clithero,
* Dartmouth,
Denbigh,
* Droitwich,
Dudley,
* Eye,
Flint,
Frome,
Gateshead,
* Great Grimsby,
Haverfordwest,
* Helston,
* Horsham,
Huddersfield,
* Hythe,
* Ives, St.
Kendal,
Kidderminster,
* Launceston,
* Liskeard,
* Lyme Regis,
Merthyr Tydvil,
* Malmesbury,
* Midhurst,

Monmouth,
Montgomery,
* Morpeth,
* Northallerton,
Pembroke,
* Petersfield,
Radnor,
Rochdale,
* Rye,
* Ryegate,
Salford,
* Shaftesbury,
South Shields,
Swansea,
* Thirsk,
Tynemouth,
Wakefield,
* Wallingford,
Walsall,
* Wareham,
Warrington,
* Westbury,
Whitby,
Whitehaven,
* Wilton,
* Woodstock.

Shoreham, With respect to the Boroughs of New Shoreham,

MEMBERS FOR BOROUGHS.

11

Cricklade, Aylesbury and East Retford, it is to be observed that those Hundreds and Divisions, the Freeholders in which have by previous Statutes (*see* 11 *Geo.* 3, *c.* 55 ; 22 *Geo.* 3, *c.* 31 ; 44 *Geo.* 3, *c.* 60, *and* 1 *Will.* 4, *c.* 74,) the Right of Voting for those respective Boroughs, are by the 5th Section of the Act, for the purposes of Elections, included in those several Boroughs. But as to Shoreham, for which all the Freeholders throughout the whole of the Rape of Bramber have hitherto had the Right of Voting, that part of the Rape, which, under the Act for Settling the Boundaries of Boroughs, will be included in the Borough of Horsham, will confer no Right of Voting for Shoreham. And as to Cricklade, for which all the Freeholders throughout the Hundred of Malmesbury have heretofore had the Right of Voting, so much of that Hundred as will, under the Boundary Act, be included in the Borough of Malmesbury, will confer no Right of Voting for Cricklade. *S.* 5.

Cricklade,
Aylesbury,
and East
Retford to
include cer-
tain adjacent
districts.

The Borough of Penryn is, for the purposes of Elections, to include the Town of Falmouth, and the Borough of Sandwich the Parishes of Deal and Walmer. *S.* 6.

Penryn to
include Fal-
mouth;
Sandwich to
include Deal
and Walmer.

In the Election for several of the Shire Towns in Wales certain other Towns have hitherto shared,

Welsh Con-
tributory Bo-
roughs.

MEMBERS FOR BOROUGHS.

and have been called Contributory Boroughs. The Constitution of these Welsh Boroughs mainly depends upon Two Statutes of Henry VIII. (viz. 27 *Hen.* 8, *c.* 26, *s.* 28 *and* 29, *and* 35 *Hen.* 8, *c.* 11.) The Act creates several new Contributory Boroughs;

The following Places will hereafter be the Contributory Boroughs sharing in the Election with the Shire Towns or Principal Boroughs: (1)

Amlwch . . . . . .
Holyhead, and . .   sharing with **Beaumaris.**
Llangefni . . . . .

Aberystwith . . .
Lampeter, and . .   sharing with **Cardigan.**
Adpar . . . . . .

Llanelly . . . . . . sharing with **Caermarthen.**

Pwllheli . . . . . .
Nevin . . . .
Conway . . . . . .   sharing with **Caernarvon.**
Bangor . . . . . .
Criccieth . . . . .

Ruthin . . . . . .
Holt . . . .   sharing with **Denbigh.**
Town of Wrexham.

(1) The places printed in Italics are made **Contributory** Boroughs by the Act. See S. 8, and Sched. (E.)

MEMBERS FOR BOROUGHS. 13

Rhyddlan . . . . .
Overton . . . . . .
Caerwis . . . . . .
Caergwrley . . . . } sharing with Flint.
St. Asaph . . . . .
Holywell . . . . .
Mold . . . .

Cowbridge . . . . } sharing with Cardiff.
Llantrissent . . . .

Llanidloes . . . . .
Welsh Pool . . . .
Machynlleth . . . } sharing with Montgomery.
Llanfyllin . . . . .
Newtown . . . . .

Narberth . . . . . } sharing with Haverfordwest.
Fishguard . . . . .

Tenby . . . . . .
Wiston . . . . . . } sharing with Pembroke.
Town of Milford .

Knighton . . . . .
Rhayder . . . . .
Kevinleece . . . . } sharing with Radnor.
Knucklas . . . . .
Town of Presteigne

The Towns of Swansea, Loughor, Neath, Aberavon, and Kenfig, which have heretofore shared in

MEMBERS FOR BOROUGHS.

the Election of a Member for Cardiff, will no longer do so, but will together constitute One Borough. *S.* 10.

Boundaries of all Cities, Boroughs, &c. settled by Boundary Act. The Boundaries of all the Cities, Boroughs, and Contributory Boroughs in England and Wales, are for the purposes of Elections to be settled by a separate Act, which has been already alluded to as settling the Division of Counties. *See sections* 3, 4, 7, 9, *and* 10.

CHAPTER III.

ELECTORS FOR COUNTIES.

In considering who are the persons who will have a Right of Voting in the Election of Knights of the Shire to serve in future Parliaments, it may be proper to divide them into

Electors for Counties how divided.

1. Freeholders,
2. Copyholders,
3. Tenants in Ancient Demesne,
4. Leaseholders,
5. Occupying Tenants (without any reference to length of term).

1st. As to Freeholders.

No person will be hereafter entitled to vote in the Election for any County, or for any Riding, Parts, or Division of a County, in respect of his Estate or Interest as a Freeholder in any Lands or Tenements within such County, Riding, Parts, or Division, unless he shall have been duly Registered according to the provisions of the Act;

Freeholder's qualification defined.

Registration required.

In order to be so Registered, every such Freeholder must have been in the actual Possession, or

COUNTY ELECTORS.

Length of possession.

in the Receipt of the Rents and Profits of such Lands or Tenements for at least Six Calendar Months next previous to the Last day of July, in the year in which he is so Registered; (that day being, as will be afterwards explained, the day for making up the Lists of Persons Entitled to Vote.) *S*. 26.

Exception in case of property coming by descent, &c.

There is an Exception, however, as to the requisite time of Possession in the cases of Persons who shall have acquired qualifying property within the Six Months next previous to the Last day of July, by Descent, Succession, Marriage, Marriage Settlement, Devise, or Promotion to any Benefice or to any Office; In any such case, the Freeholder who has acquired such property, will not require any length of previous Possession or receipt to give him a title to be Registered. *S*. 26. This exception is taken from the Provisions of the 18 *Geo*. 2, *c*. 18, *s*. 5. (The word "Succession" is added to the cases provided for by that Act, and will meet the case of Leasehold property succeeded to upon Intestacy.)

Assessment to land tax no longer required.

It will no longer be necessary, in order to confer a Right of Voting, that the qualifying Property, (whether Freehold or otherwise) should be assessed to the Land Tax. *S*. 22. It may be proper to notice that the Act does not repeal or alter the provisions of 3 *Geo*. 3, *c*. 24, by which Annuities and Rent-Charges issuing out of Freehold Lands or Tene-

COUNTY ELECTORS.

17

ments are required to be Registered with the Clerk of the Peace, in order to confer a Qualification.

The foregoing observations are applicable to all Freeholders whether of Inheritance or for Life; but there is an Enactment with respect to the amount of the Qualification of Freeholders for Life, which does not extend to Freeholders of Inheritance, nor to such Freeholders for Life as shall be in actual and *bond fide* occupation; nor to such Freeholders for Life as shall have acquired their Freeholds by Marriage, Marriage Settlement, Devise, or Promotion to any Benefice or to any Office; as to no one of which Three classes, is the value of the Qualifying Freehold in any way varied from that required by the Law as it stood before the passing of the Act, that is to say, " 40 shillings by the year at the least above all Charges." (8 *Hen.* 6, *c.* 7; 18 *Geo.* 2, *c.* 18, *s.* 1.); The purport of this Enactment is, that, in future, no Freehold Lands or Tenements of which any Person may be seised for his own Life, or for the Life of another, or for any joint Lives, will, (except where he is in actual and *bond fide* occupation, or where the Lands or Tenements shall have come to him by Marriage, Marriage Settlement, Devise, or Promotion to any Benefice or office,) confer any Right of Voting for a County unless they shall actually be worth to the Person seised of such Lands or Tenements, 10*l. per annum* at the least, free from all Rents and Charges. *S.* 18.

Value of qualifying freehold in what cases not varied from old law.

Freeholders for life must in future have freehold worth 10l. yearly.

Exceptions.

COUNTY ELECTORS.

Meaning of word "Charges."

(The word " Charges," it is to be observed, is not intended, in this or any other instance where it is used in the Act, to include any Public or Parliamentary Tax, or any Church Rate, County Rate, or Parochial Rate. *S*. 21 ; *see also* 18 *Geo.* 2, *c*. 18, *s*. 6.)

Rights of existing freeholders for life reserved. No new condition as to value imposed.

There is an Exception, however, to this requisition as to the value of the qualifying Freehold, in favour of all those existing Freeholders for Life, who, as the Law stood before the passing of the Act, might vote, (or, if Minors, acquire upon coming of age a right to vote,) in respect of any Freeholds, of whatever value they may be: The Rights of those Individuals, so long as they may be seised of the same Freeholds as at the time of the passing of the Act are reserved, subject, however, to the condition of Registration.

There remains to be noted an important Restriction on the Right of Voting for Counties in respect of Freeholds ; but it extends merely to Freeholders in Occupation of their own Freehold property in a Borough, and not to Freehold Landlords. The Restriction is this ;

No person to vote for a county in respect of any freehold property occupied by himself in a Borough which would confer vote for Borough under S. 27.

No Freeholder in the actual occupation of Freehold property in a Borough of such nature and value as would, under those provisions of the Act which regulate the New Qualification of Voters for Boroughs (see *S*. 27.) entitle him to vote in the Election for the Borough, will be entitled to vote in

COUNTY ELECTORS.

19

respect of that property for the County; the nature and value of such property will alone, even without the accompaniment of the other qualifying requisites for a Borough Voter, be sufficient to disqualify the Freeholder in occupation from voting in respect of it for the County; so that, although the Freeholder may not in any respect have matured or completed his title as a Voter for the Borough, he will, if in the actual occupation of Freehold property of such nature and value as might confer a right of voting for the Borough, be disabled from voting in Respect of such property for the County:

To illustrate this by example; A Freeholder is Example. in the occupation of his own house and warehouse within a Borough, each being worth 10*l.* a year, and therefore, according to the 27th Section of the Act, as will be afterwards explained, of sufficient value to give a Right of Voting for the Borough: In consequence of having been omitted in some Rate for the Relief of the Poor, or of not having paid up his Assessed Taxes, or of having occupied for less than Twelve Months, he is not able to establish a perfect Right of Voting for the Borough in respect of either the House or Warehouse; He will also be excluded from voting for the County in respect of either, because each is of such a nature and value as *might* confer a Right for the Borough.

But in those Boroughs where the Right of voting In Boroughs is, according to the existing Law, in Freeholders, Freehold

COUNTY ELECTORS.

Right of Voting, Voters for Borough may also Vote for County if property not such as would confer a Borough Right under S. 27. or in Inhabitants paying Scot and Lot, in every case where the Freehold property owned or inhabited, (as the case may be,) is of such nature and value, that it would not, under the 27th Section of the Act, confer a Qualification for the Borough, the Freeholder will not be incapacitated by the operation of the 24th Section from voting for the County, although he may also have the Right of voting for the Borough as a Freeholder, or as an Inhabitant paying Scot and Lot:

But, as will hereafter be explained, such Freehold and Scot and Lot Rights of voting for Boroughs are reserved for a limited period only. *(Vid. post, Ch. IV.)*

2dly. As to Copyholders.

According to the Law as it stood before the passing of this Act, Copyholders had no Right of Voting for Counties ; indeed they were expressly **County Right of Voting extended to Copyholders.** excluded by the 31 *Geo. 2, c.* 14; but that right is extended to them for the future by the 19th Section of the Act ; according to the operation of which Section, coupled with the 26th Section, the right of voting in Copyholders may be thus defined ;

Right defined Every person, not labouring under any legal disability, who has, either at Law or in Equity an Estate of Inheritance, or for his own Life, or for the Life of another, or for any joint Lives, in any Lands or Tenements of Copyhold Tenure, of the clear

COUNTY ELECTORS. 21

yearly value of £10, over and above all Rents and Charges, and who shall have been in the actual Possession, or in the receipt of the Rents and Profits, of such Lands or Tenements for at least Six Calendar Months next previous to the Last day of July in the year in which he is Registered (Registration being essential to enable him to vote,) will, if duly Registered according to the provisions of the Act, be entitled to vote for the County, or the Riding, Parts, or Division, in which such Lands or Tenements may be situated. *Required Value.* *Length of Possession.*

But, as is the case with respect to Freeholders Voting for Counties, the Requisition as to length of Possession, or Receipt of Rent, is dispensed with, wherever the qualifying property shall have come to the person by Descent, Succession, Marriage, Marriage Settlement, Devise, or Promotion to any Benefice or Office, at any time within Six months next previous to the Last day of July in the year in which he is to be Registered; the necessity of Registration is of course in all cases to be enforced. *See Sections* 19 & 26. *No previous possession required in case of property coming by descent &c. within 6 months.*

The Restriction, which as to Freeholders extends merely to such of them as are in the occupation of their own freehold property, as to Copyholders, affects the whole class, (the words " by himself," which, in *S.* 24, characterize the Freeholder's occupation, being wholly omitted in *S.* 25, which relates to Copyholders). No person there-

COUNTY ELECTORS.

Where property will confer Right of Voting for a Borough it cannot also for a County.

fore, having any Estate or Interest as a Copyholder in any such property in a Borough (whether he be in the Occupation thereof or not), as would under the 27th Section of the Act entitle him to Vote in the election for the Borough, will be entitled to vote in respect of such property for the County; and, as has been already explained with regard to Freeholders, even although he may not have perfected his right of Voting for the Borough, yet if the property in which his Estate or Interest lies be of such nature and value as might confer a right of Voting for the Borough, he will be incapacitated from Voting in respect of such property for the County. *S.* 25.

Assessment to the Land Tax not necessary.

The necessity of Assessment to the Land-Tax is expressly removed. *S.* 22.

3dly. Tenants in Ancient Demesne.

Previous state of the law as to tenants in Ancient Demesne.

Before entering into any consideration of the manner in which the terms of the Act affect this class of persons, it seems to be important to advert to the previous state of the Law with regard to them, so far as it can be considered as having been clearly settled or understood.

There has been great difference of opinion as to the Right of Tenants in Ancient Demesne to vote in County Elections, and this difference has arisen from the disputed nature of their tenure, that is to say, as to whether it was or was not freehold;

COUNTY ELECTORS. 23

Although the authorities have been somewhat divided upon this point, it may be stated, as a conclusion which may fairly be come to on the subject, that while those Tenants in Ancient Demesne who hold by Copy of Court Roll, and who are therefore strictly Copyholders, have been expressly excluded from the Right of voting for Counties by the 31 *Geo.* 2, *c.* 14, such Tenants as hold by the Custom of the Manor and not by Copy of Court Roll, have been considered entitled to vote in the character of Customary Freeholders. *(See Gloucestershire Case, Heywood on County Elections, p.* 41. *Simeon, p.* 95. *Male, pp.* 134 *and* 282, *et seq.)*

Tenants by Copy of Court Roll.

Tenants by custom of the Manor.

Supposing this conclusion to be a right one, One Class of Tenants in Ancient Demesne, viz., those not holding by Copy of Court Roll, will in future enjoy the Right of voting for Counties as Freeholders; and the other Class, viz., those who hold by Copy of Court Roll, will be qualified, according to the 19th Section of the Act, under the words, " holding Lands or Tenements of Copyhold, or any other Tenure whatever except Freehold." But supposing any difference of opinion still to exist as to the nature of their tenure, they will at all events enjoy the Right of voting under the Act; for their property must necessarily be Freehold, or Copyhold, or some Tenure " other than Freehold." The only difference in substance as to which class they belong to, will be in the amount of the Qualifying value. If they are to rank as Freeholders, their Qualification

COUNTY ELECTORS.

will in all respects, whether as to value or otherwise, be governed by the same rules as that of Freeholders; but if they are to be considered either as Copyholders, or as holding by some Tenure "other than Freehold," their rights will be regulated by the 19th Section of the Act, of which the provisions have been already explained in treating of the Rights of Copyholders;

Their Registration will in any case be governed by the 26th Section.

4thly. As to Leaseholders.

Leasehold Right.

By the 20th Section of the Act, the Right of Voting for any County, or for any Riding, Parts, or Division of a County, is conferred, subject to the condition of due Registration, (*See S.* 26,) on those persons who hold within such County, Riding, Parts, or Division, either as Lessees, or as Assignees, any Lands or Tenements, (whether Freehold, Copyhold, or in Ancient Demesne,) of the clear annual value of 10*l.* above Rents and Charges, of which the term, which they are in the enjoyment of, was originally created, (that is to say, first granted by the Ground Landlord) for a period of Sixty years at the least;

Value 10l. per annum if term originally created for 60 years.

In order to be Registered, they must have been in actual Possession, or in the receipt of the Rents and Profits, for Twelve Calendar Months next previous to the Last day of July in the year in which they are Registered : no length of previous posses-

COUNTY ELECTORS. 25

sion or receipt is, however, required, if the qualifying property has come to the party within such Twelve Months by Succession, Marriage, Marriage Settlement, Devise, or Promotion to any Benefice or Office.

But no Sub-Lessee, or Assignee of a Sub-Lessee, is to vote in respect of such Leasehold property unless he be in the actual occupation of it.

Thus the due operation of this Section would seem to prevent all persons from voting in respect of the same Lease excepting two, viz., the party first taking from the ground Landlord, and the occupying Under-Lessee. The policy of such a provision is obvious, as, but for some such check, the creation of long terms might be made the means of fraudulently multiplying votes, for a Lessee for 70 years might grant an Under-Lease for 69 years to another, and he again for 68 years to a third, and so on. *First Lessee and Under-Lessee in occupation only to vote.*

But when it is said that none are to vote in respect of the same Leasehold property but the First Lessee and the occupying Under-Lessee, it is not meant that where there are several persons holding as Joint Tenants or Tenants in Common, they shall not all vote; in such cases, if the interest of each be of the requisite value, they will, according to the principle acted on in the case of Freeholders being Joint-Tenants, or Tenants in common, be each entitled to vote. *Case of Tenants in Common,&c.*

The 20th Section also confers the right of voting

c

COUNTY ELECTORS.

Value of 50l. per annum required if term originally created for 20 years. (subject to Registration, *see S.* 26,) on Leaseholders whose Terms shall have been originally created for a period of Twenty Years at the least, in property (whether Freehold, Copyhold, or in Ancient Demesne) of the clear yearly value of 50l. at the least, over and above all Rents and Charges.

In order to be Registered, they must have been in actual Possession, or in the receipt of the Rents and Profits for Twelve Calendar Months next previous to the Last day of July in the year in which they are registered. But this length of previous Possession or Receipt is dispensed with, where the qualifying property has come to the party within such Twelve Calendar Months by Succession, Marriage, Marriage Settlement, Devise, or Promotion to any Benefice or Office.

First Lessee and Under-Lessee in occupation only to vote. As to these Terms of Twenty Years, it is also and for the same reason provided, that none but the party first taking from the Ground-Landlord and the Under-Lessee in occupation shall vote in respect of the same property. The observations also which have been made as to Joint Tenants and Tenants in Common will apply to the Leaseholders for Twenty Years as fully as to the Leaseholders for Sixty Years. *See S.* 20.

Leaseholders cannot vote for County in respect of property which might confer a vote for a Borough. But Leaseholders, whether for Twenty or for Sixty Years are incapacitated from voting for the County in respect of any property which is of such a nature and value as would, according to the 27th

COUNTY ELECTORS.

Section, give them a Right of voting for a Borough; and the disability will hold equally whether they have or have not made perfect, by length of possession, &c. their right for the Borough. *S. 25.*

／ As has been already observed with regard to Freeholders and Copyholders, in computing the value of the Qualifying property above Charges, no Public or Parliamentary Tax, nor any Church Rate, County Rate, or Parochial Rate, is to be deemed a Charge within the meaning of the Act. *S. 21.*

Leasehold property, as has been explained with regard to other Rights of voting for Counties, need not have been assessed to the Land Tax. *S. 22.* <small>Assessment to Land Tax not necessary.</small>

5thly. As to Occupying Tenants (without reference to Length of Term.)

Any Tenant in the Occupation of Lands or Tenements for which he shall be *bonâ fide* liable to a rent of 50*l.* per annum, will hereafter, if duly Registered, (*see S.* 26,) be entitled to vote in the Election of a Knight of the Shire for the County, Riding, Parts, or Division, in which such Lands or Tenements may be situated. *S.* 20. <small>Occupying Tenants at rent of 50l. to vote for County.</small>

In order to be so Registered, he must have been in Occupation for Twelve Calendar Months next previous to the Last day of July, in the year in which he is to be Registered. *S.* 26. <small>12 months Occupation.</small>

But this length of previous occupation is dispensed

c 2

COUNTY ELECTORS.

with in cases where the Qualifying property has come to the party within such Twelve Months by Succession, Marriage, Marriage Settlement, Devise, or Promotion to any Benefice or Office.

Exception.

This Right of Voting in Occupying Tenants is subject to the same restriction as has been stated to prevail in the case of Occupying Freeholders, and

No vote for County to be acquired in respect of property which would confer right for Borough.

of Copyholders, and of Leaseholders; If, therefore, the Qualifying property be of such a nature and value as would, under the 27th Section of the Act, confer a Right of Voting for a Borough, the Occupying Tenant will, whether such Right be or be not complete in other respects, be disabled from voting for the County in respect of such property. *S.* 25.

Assessment to Land Tax not necessary.

It will not in any case be necessary that the Qualifying property should have been assessed to the Land Tax. *S.* 22.

Having thus gone through the several classes of County Voters, there remains to be noticed an important general provision as to Equitable Estates.

Provision as to Equitable Estates.

By the 23rd Section of the Act it is enacted, " that no person shall be allowed to have any Vote " in the Election of a Knight or Knights of the " Shire for or by reason of any Trust Estate or " Mortgage, unless such Trustee or Mortgagee be " in actual possession or receipt of the rents and " profits of the same Estate, but that the Mortgagor " or *cestui que trust* in possession shall and may

COUNTY ELECTORS. 29

" vote for the same Estate, notwithstanding such
" Mortgage or Trust."

This Section is copied *verbatim* from the 7 and 8
W. 3, c. 25. s. 7, upon which Enactment the Right
of voting in respect of Equitable, as contradistin-
guished from Legal Estates, is founded. As the *Semble,* that
it applies to
decisions upon that Enactment as to the Right of Leasehold as
well as to
voting in respect of Equitable Freeholds appear in Freehold
Estates.
principle to apply equally to Equitable Leaseholds,
it should seem that in all cases where there is an
Equitable Estate in Leasehold property, of the requisite value, coupled with possession for the requisite period, (viz., Twelve Calendar Months next
previous to the Last day of July in the year in
which the party is to be Registered,) the party
having such Equitable Estate, will be entitled to be
Registered as a Voter.

Equitable Estates in Copyhold property are
expressly provided for by the terms of the 19th
Section.

BOROUGH ELECTORS.

CHAPTER IV.

ELECTORS FOR CITIES AND BOROUGHS.

Division of Rights of Voting in Cities and Boroughs.

THE Rights of Voting in the choice of Members to serve in future Parliaments for Cities and Boroughs may be divided into three classes:

1st. New Rights.

2dly. Old Rights Reserved (under certain conditions) in Perpetuity.

3dly. Old Rights Reserved (under certain conditions) for a Time.

1st. New Rights.

New Rights for Cities and Boroughs.

The New Qualification for Boroughs is mainly defined by the 27th Section of the Act:—That Section requires that a party, in order to gain a Qualification, shall occupy as Owner or Tenant, in a Borough or Contributory Borough, a House, Warehouse, Countinghouse, Shop, or other Building, which, either of itself or jointly with any land in the Borough (or, if his Qualification arise in a Contributory Borough, in such Contributory Borough,) occupied therewith by him as Owner, or occupied therewith by

Qualifying Property.

BOROUGH ELECTORS.

31

him as Tenant under the same Landlord, shall be of the clear annual value of £10 at the least : But he cannot vote unless Registered, and in order to be Registered he must have occupied the Qualifying Premises for Twelve Calendar Months next previous to the Last day of July in the year in which he is Registered, (that day being the day for making up the Electoral Lists,) and he must have been included in respect of those premises in every Poor-Rate that may have been made during those Twelve Months in the Parish or Township in which the premises are; and he must have paid up by the 20th of July in the year in which he is Registered, all the Poor-Rates and Assessed Taxes which shall have become payable from him in respect of the qualifying premises previously to the 6th day of April then next preceding; and he must have resided within the Borough, or within Seven Statute Miles of it, (or, if his Qualification arise in a Contributory Borough, within such Contributory Borough, or within Seven Miles of it,) for Six Months next previous to the Last day of July in the Year in which he is Registered. *S.* 27.

Required Value.

Registration essential.

Length of Occupation.

Rating to the Relief of the Poor.

Payment of Poor-Rate and Assessed Taxes.

Residence.

The Occupation of the Qualifying Premises required by the 27th Section is explained by the 28th Section to be not necessarily an Occupation of the *same* premises during the whole Twelve Months required. The Premises may be different, provided they be each of the required value, and be occupied

Qualifying premises may be different premises occupied in succession.

BOROUGH ELECTORS.

in immediate succession during the required period, and provided the person seeking to vote have paid up by the 20th of July all the Poor-Rates or Assessed Taxes which shall have become payable from him previously to the preceding 6th of April, in respect of *all* the premises from which he derives his claim. *S.* 28. But a change of premises after the Last day of July and before the Election will deprive the party of his Vote, as he will be unable to swear, as required by Section 58, (which will be afterwards explained,) that he has the *same* Qualification for which he was originally Registered.

Change of premises between last day of July and day of Election will disqualify from voting.

Some Question may arise as to the effect of the Words " which shall have become payable," used in the 27th Section with reference to the Poor-Rates and Assessed Taxes; It may possibly be suggested that the word " payable" involves the supposition of a demand for the amount due having been made upon the party rated; and it may be contended in support of this position, that upon the Cases with respect to persons voting as Inhabitants, paying Scot and Lot, it has been held that non-payment of Rates is no disqualification, except in cases where there has been a demand and refusal; *(see Cullen v. Morris, 2 Stark. N. P. Ca.* 577;) But the true construction of the Section would seem to be, that the Rates must have actually been paid, whether any demand has or has not been made. The words of the Section are, " unless such Person shall have paid

Rates must have been paid, whether demanded or not, in order to confer Qualification.

BOROUGH ELECTORS. 33

" on or before the 20th day of July in such year, all " the Poor's Rates and Assessed Taxes which shall " have become payable from him in respect of such " such Premises previously to the 6th day of April " then next preceding." Now it is clear that the assessments in a Rate become payable from the moment that it is allowed and published. (*See* 1 *Nolan's Poor Laws, p.* 258, 4*th edit.*) If it should be urged .that a demand of payment is necessary in order to authorize the Issuing of a Warrant of distress for levying a sum due for Rates, the Answer is, that, the distress being in the nature of an execution, no person can be subjected to such a process without first having the opportunity of showing cause why it should not issue : But the reason of this rule is wholly inapplicable to the case of a Right conferred upon parties subject to their fulfilment of certain conditions, by a certain time expressly pointed out; It is for the parties themselves by the voluntary performance of those conditions to entitle themselves to the advantage conferred upon them: And this construction of the Act is the only one that would be found uniform and impartial in practice; for, were it otherwise, the Overseers might exempt any party from the performance of the condition by forbearing to make the demand; and might on the other hand enforce the condition by making the demand; so that the application of this Provision of the Act would depend upon the caprice or partiality

c 5

BOROUGH ELECTORS.

of the Overseers, which is a policy that can hardly be attributed to the Legislature: And further, it is evident that any such construction as would encourage partial Overseers to forbear levying the Rate, would tend to disappoint rather than aid the due collection of it, which is not a Legislative intent that it would be reasonable to presume. Again, with respect to the word " payable" itself, it is clear that it involves nothing like a supposition of demand— on the contrary, being "payable" is a state of things prior to demand—a demand cannot be properly made of anything which is not payable, therefore it would be absurd to contend that the word " payable" by itself can signify something which is not merely payable, but has also been demanded. Nor can the analogy of the case of Scot and Lot Voting, so far as regards this point, be considered as applicable to this newly conferred Right; The decisions as to Scot and Lot were with reference to a particular class of persons, " persons paying Scot and Lot," that is to say, persons who were liable to pay, and in the habit of paying Poor Rates, and when it was attempted to bring disqualification home to any person seeking to vote in that character, the course was to show that the person was not fit to exercise the Right, because he was in fact insolvent, and not a person " paying Rates." To prove this it was reasonable to require evidence not merely of non-payment, which might be accidental, but of refusal to

BOROUGH ELECTORS.

pay when demanded, which would be the strongest proof of inability, and therefore good ground of disqualification: But upon this Statute quite a different question will arise—the question will be whether or no the party has brought himself within the words of the Statute, whether he has done that which the Act conferring this New Right has made a condition precedent to the enjoyment of it, that is to say, whether he has paid by a certain day the Rates which became payable before a certain other day; and it is to be observed, that the Legislature has allowed considerable latitude in point of time to the party rated; for he is allowed the whole interval between the 6th of April and the 20th of July to pay up his Rates. It is also to be remarked, that the Poor's Rates are placed on the same footing in this Section with the Assessed Taxes, as to which there can be no question whatever of a demand being necessary in order to establish non-payment, for the 43 Geo. 3, c. 161, s. 23, has specified the particular days on which they are payable, and the parties assessed are therefore bound to take notice of those days of payment.

With respect to the limit within which it will be necessary to have resided, doubts may be suggested as to the mode in which the Seven Miles are to be calculated, but the sound construction of the Act would seem to be, that the Seven Miles are to be calculated according to " the nearest way of access," Seven Miles how to be measured.

and not, to use a popular expression, " as the Crow " flies:" This is the construction which has been adopted by Courts of Law in explaining agreements between individuals where covenants were entered into not to carry on a particular Trade within a certain number of miles from a given point. (*See Woods v. Dennet, 2 Stark. N. P. Ca. 89. Leigh v. Hind, 9 Barn. & Cr. 774. See also Minze v. Earl, Cro. Eliz. 212 and 267.*) The Law laid down in the cases cited agrees with the construction put by Hawkins upon the Statutes as to Popish Recusants, (35 Eliz. c. 2, and 3 Jac. 1, c. 5, s. 6, 7,) which require " that every Popish Recusant shall repair to " his place of Dwelling, &c. and not remove above " Five Miles from thence;" He says, " It seems " that the Miles shall be reckoned not by straight " lines, as a Bird or Arrow may fly, but according " to the nearest and most usual way." *Hawk. P. C. Book I. cap.* 12, *s.* 15. And any other construction would be attended with considerable practical difficulty, for by nothing short of a Trigonometrical Survey, or some such process, could the distance, if measured according to " the Crow's flight," be precisely ascertained. Perhaps no better definition of " the nearest way of access" could readily be given than that laid down by Mr. Justice J. Parke, in the case of *Leigh v. Hind* already alluded to; He says, " That is to be considered the nearest way of access " which a person making the best of his way from

BOROUGH ELECTORS.

37

" house to house would be likely to take, that is,
" using the Footway where there was one, and
" where it was most convenient to use, and the Car-
" riageway, either where it could be most conveni-
" ently used, or where there was no Footpath."

There is in the 29th Section a further explanation
of the New Right of Voting for Boroughs as to
cases of Joint Occupation:

It is provided, that where there are several Joint *Joint Occu-piers.*
Occupiers, either as Owners or Tenants, and the
premises occupied are not in the whole of such value
as would, if equally divided among the Occupiers,
give £10 for each Occupier, no one of such Occupiers shall vote; but if the value be sufficient, upon
division, to give £10 to each, every Occupier, whether Owner or Tenant, will, if qualified in other
respects, be entitled to vote. *S. 29.*

Rating to the relief of the poor having been made
essential to the Right of voting, and the exercise of
the Franchise being consequently liable to be de-
feated by the accidental or wilful omission of names
from the Poor-Rate; in order to remedy this evil, *Occupiers*
all persons occupying any House, Warehouse, *may demand to be rated,*
Counting-house, &c. in a Borough are enabled to *in case of wilful or ac-*
claim to be put upon the Poor-Rate, and upon pay- *cidental omis-sion.*
ing the whole amount of the Rates (if any) then due
in respect of such premises, are entitled to be put *Claim and*
on the Rate; a tender of the sum due will be for *tender of sum due to be*
this purpose tantamount to payment, and the party *equivalent to payment.*

BOROUGH ELECTORS.

claiming and tendering will, notwithstanding the refusal or neglect of the Overseer, be considered, so far as regards his right of voting, to have been rated from the period at which the Rate shall have been made, in respect of which he shall have claimed to be rated. *S. 30.*

As to places where Landlords alone are liable and Occupiers are exempt.

The 30th Section applies also to those places where, by Local Acts, the Landlords alone are liable to the Poor Rates, and the Occupiers are exempt. There the Occupier may claim to be put upon the Rate, and upon claim and tender of the amount (if any) due, is to be considered, for the purposes of Election, to be upon the Rate, in respect of which he claims or tenders, although the Overseer may neglect or refuse to put him upon it.

Analogy of New Right of Voting to Scot and Lot.

Upon a consideration of these Sections it will appear that the New Qualification for Boroughs, is in substance a Scot and Lot Right of Voting, with the addition of Value, the payment of Assessed Taxes, and an occupation for Twelve Months instead of Six Months, the latter being the period required in the case of Scot and Lot Voters by the 26 Geo. 3, c. 100.

This analogy is strictly kept up in the provisions already noticed as to the occupation of different Qualifying premises in succession; for according to the present state of the Law as to Scot and Lot Voters, they are not required to continue in the same premises for Six Months, but may change

BOROUGH ELECTORS.

from house to house, provided they continue upon the Rate for the Six Months.

It is to be observed that the Universities are not affected by these newly conferred Rights in Boroughs; they are expressly exempted from the operation of the Act. *S.* 78.

Universities not affected by the Act.

But the New Rights of voting will be fully applicable to the Cities and Towns which are Counties of themselves. There, whatever reservation there may be of existing Rights, the new Qualifications will take effect as fully as in any other towns.

New Rights will apply to Counties of Cities and Towns.

2dly. *Old Rights Reserved in Perpetuity.*

It may be stated generally in the first instance that the Elective Rights of all Freeholders and Burgage Tenants in those Cities and Towns being Counties of themselves, where the Right is in both or either of those classes of Voters, are reserved in perpetuity subject always to the condition of Registration; and that the Rights of all Burgesses and Freemen, (with certain exceptions,) and of the Freemen and Liverymen of the City of London, are also reserved in perpetuity, subject likewise to the condition of Registration.

Certain Old Rights reserved in perpetuity.

To give a more particular definition of the Franchise as it is to be hereafter enjoyed by those Classes of Voters, the Right as determined by the Act is, with respect to them, as follows:—

BOROUGH ELECTORS.

40

Freeholders and Burgage Tenants in certain Counties of Cities and Towns.

1st. As to Freeholders and Burgage Tenants.

In every City or Town, being a County of itself, in the Election for which Freeholders or Burgage Tenants, either with or without any further Qualification (i.e. of value, &c.) have the Right of voting, every Freeholder or Burgage Tenant will, if duly Registered, be entitled to vote in the Election of a Member or Members (as the case may be) to serve in any future Parliament; But in order to be Registered, he must have been in Possession, or in the Receipt of the Rents and Profits of his Freehold or Burgage Tenement for Twelve Calendar Months next previous to the Last day of July in the year in which he is to be Registered, and he must have resided for Six Calendar Months next previous to that day within the City or Town, or within Seven Miles of it. *S.* 31.

Length of Possession.

Residence.

Exception in case of property coming by Descent, Marriage, &c. within 12 months.

No length of previous Possession or Receipt will, however, be requisite if the Qualifying Freehold or Burgage Tenement has come to the Party by Descent, Succession, Marriage, Marriage Settlement, Devise, or Promotion to any Benefice or Office, within Twelve Months before such Last day of July. *S.* 31.

Limits within which Freeholds, &c. will confer Rights settled by Boundary Act.

The Limits within which Freeholds or Burgage Tenements will confer a Right for any such City or Town, being a County of itself, are determined by the Boundary Act, so that all Freeholds or Burgage Tenements situate within the New Boundaries of any

BOROUGH ELECTORS.

41

such City or Town, although without its previous Limits, will confer Qualifications. *S.* 31.

The Places to which the 31st Section will apply are Bristol, Exeter, Haverfordwest, Lichfield, Norwich, and Nottingham. In Exeter, Haverfordwest, and Norwich, Freeholders in general, without any distinction of value, have a right to vote; in Bristol and Nottingham, Forty Shilling Freeholders only; in Lichfield, Forty Shilling Freeholders and Burgage Tenants. The value of the Qualifying Freeholds in these places will remain unaltered, except so far as relates to Freeholders for Life or Lives, as to whom the 18th Section, (referred to by a Proviso in the 31st Section,) contains the following provision:

Places to which 31st section applies.

No Person is to Vote in the Election for any such City or Town in respect of any Freehold Lands or Tenements of which he is seised for his own Life, or the Life of another, or for any Joint Lives, unless he satisfies one of Three conditions: He must be in the actual and *bonâ fide* Occupation of the Qualifying property;—*or* he must have acquired it by Marriage, Marriage Settlement, Devise, or Promotion to some Benefice or Office;—*or* the Property must be of the clear value of £10 a year above all Rents and Charges. *S.* 18.

Provision as to Freeholders for life or lives.

But those existing Freeholders for Life or Lives are excepted who, as the Law stood before the passing of the Act, might Vote (or if Minors, acquire, upon coming of age, a Right to Vote) in respect of

BOROUGH ELECTORS.

any Freeholds, of whatever value they may be. The Rights of these Individuals, so long as they may be seised of the same Freeholds as at the time of the passing of the Act, are Reserved, subject however to the condition of Registration.

By the 19th Geo. 2, c. 28, all Forty Shilling Freeholders in Counties of Cities and Towns are required to be assessed to the Land Tax, in order to enable them to vote;

Freeholders in Counties of Cities and Towns need not be assessed to the Land Tax.

The necessity for such assessment is expressly removed by the Act. *S. 22.*

Burgesses andFreemen, and Freemen and Liverymen.

2dly, As to Burgesses and Freemen, and as to the Freemen and Liverymen of the City of London.

The Elective Rights of all Burgesses or Freemen, (with certain exceptions which will be presently noticed,) and of the Freemen and Liverymen of London, are continued in perpetuity, subject however to the condition of Registration. *S. 32.*

Rights continued in perpetuity.

In order to Vote Qualification must, on Last day of July, be as complete as it was formerly required to be on day of Election.

Residence.

In order that a Burgess or Freeman, or Freeman and Liveryman may be registered, his Qualification as such must, on the Last day of July in the Year in which he is registered, be as complete and perfect as, according to the Old Law, it was required to be on the Day of Election itself; he must also have resided for Six Calendar Months next previous to such Last day of July within the City or Borough, or within Seven Statute Miles of what was the usual Polling Place before the passing of the Act. If he be a Burgess or Freeman of a Contributory Borough,

BOROUGH ELECTORS.

43

he must have resided for the required period within that Contributory Borough, or within Seven Miles of the place by which the measurement of distance as to that Contributory Borough is to be ascertained. In the Schedule (E. 2,) annexed to the Act, is a list of the places in the Contributory Boroughs from which the Seven Miles are to be calculated. *S.* 32. *Contributory Boroughs.*

The Exceptions to this reservation of Right are two :— *Exceptions.*

1st. No Burgess or Freeman, in respect of any other right than Birth or Servitude, who shall have become so subsequently to the 1st of March, 1831, will hereafter be entitled to vote as a Burgess or Freeman. This exception will exclude from the Reserved Right all honorary Freemen or Burgesses made after the 1st of March, 1831, and all persons become Burgesses or Freemen by Marriage subsequently to that day. *S.* 32.

2dly. No Person is to be entitled as a Burgess or Freeman in respect of Birth, unless the Person from or through whom his Right was originally derived, actually was a Burgess or Freeman before the 1st of March, 1831, or was entitled to be admitted as such before that day, or unless the Person from or through whom he so derives his right shall have become a Burgess or Freeman in respect of Servitude subsequently to that day. *S.* 32.

There is a particular Provision as to the Burgesses and Freemen of the Towns of Swansea, Loughor, *Burgesses and Freemen of Swansea, &c.*

BOROUGH ELECTORS.

Neath, Aberavon, and Ken-fig, which used to share in the Election for Cardiff; They will cease to vote for Cardiff, but their Reserved Right will apply to the Election of a Member for the Borough composed of the Towns of Swansea, Loughor, Neath, Aberavon, and Ken-fig, and will be subject to the provisions by which the Rights of Freemen and Burgesses in Contributory Boroughs are regulated. *S.* 32, *and see Sched.* (E. 2.)

With regard to these Rights Reserved in perpetuity, it may be useful to illustrate by example the meaning of the expressions " Qualified in such " Manner as would entitle him then to vote if such " Day were the Day of Election, and this Act had " not been passed." The effect of the Enactment is, that whatever defect of Qualification existing on the Day of Election itself would, according to the Old Law, deprive a Burgess or Freeman, or Freeman and Liveryman of London, of the Right of Voting, will, in future, if it exist on the Last day of July, have the effect of excluding the party from the Register;

Example showing effect of provisions as to Right Reserved in Perpetuity.

Thus, supposing the Right to be in Freemen resident in the Borough, and paying Scot and Lot— under the Old Law, if, on the day of Election, the fact of Non-Residence or of Non-Payment of Rates was established against a Freeman, he would have been disqualified from Voting; So, in future, if on the Last day of July he be not Resident, or have not

BOROUGH ELECTORS.

duly paid his Rates, he will not be entitled to be Registered as a Voter.

3d. *Old Rights Reserved for a Time.*

The 33d Section of the Act begins by summing up the Result of the previous Sections as to those Rights of Voting for Cities and Boroughs which are intended to be permanent. It declares that no person shall be entitled to Vote in the Election for any City or Borough (which words " City or Borough," by the Interpretation given in Section 79, clearly include Counties of Cities and Towns,) unless his Right be one conferred by this Act, (viz. under the 27th Section,) *or* unless he is a Burgess or Freeman, or in the City of London a Freeman and Liveryman, *or* unless he has a Qualifying Freehold or Burgage Tenement in some County of a City or Town where the Right of Voting has been heretofore in Freeholders or Burgage Tenants.

Section 33.

Summary of previous Sections as to Cities and Boroughs.

The Section then proceeds to make a Reservation in favour of all Persons who, at the time of the passing of the Act, (viz. on the 7th of June, 1832,) had a Right to Vote for any City or Borough, not disfranchised by the Act, in virtue of any Qualification not included among those which, by the previous Sections, have been declared to be permanent. It provides that every such Person shall retain, subject to the condition of Registration, the Right of Voting for the City or Borough so long as he shall

Old Right Reserved for a time.

BOROUGH ELECTORS.

be qualified as an Elector according to the usages and customs of that particular City or Borough, or any Law now in force. In order to be Registered as such Elector, his Qualification as such must, on the Last day of July in the year in which he is Registered, be as complete and perfect as before the passing of the Act it was required to be on the Day of Election itself; He must also have resided for Six Calendar Months next previous to such Last day of July within the City or Borough in which his Qualification is, or within Seven Statute Miles of what was the usual Polling Place for the City or Borough before the passing of the Act. If his Qualification be within a Contributory Borough, he must have resided for the required period within that Contributory Borough, or within Seven Miles of the Place named for that purpose in the Schedule (E. 2.) *S. 33.*

Example, showing effect of Provisions as to Right Reserved for a time.

With regard to the Rights thus reserved for a time by the 33d Section, an example may be given for the purpose of more fully showing the practical application of the words " Qualified as such Elector, " in such manner as would entitle him then to Vote " if such day were the day of Election and this Act " had not been passed ;"

Supposing the Right of Election to be in Inhabitants paying Scot and Lot—According to the Old Law, if on the Day of Election it was shown that the person tendering his Vote had not been *bonâ fide*

BOROUGH ELECTORS.

47

an inhabitant paying Scot and Lot within the Borough for Six Calendar Months previous to the Day of Election, his Vote would have been rejected: (*See* 26 *Geo.* 3, *c.* 100.) So, in future, if on the Last day of July he be not *bonâ fide* an Inhabitant paying Scot and Lot within the Borough for Six Calendar Months previous to such Last day of July, he will not be entitled to be Registered as a Voter;

To apply the same principle generally to all the Rights Reserved for a Time by the Act, it may be stated that, whatever defect of Qualification would, according to the Old Law, if it existed on the day of Election, disqualify a Party from Voting, will, in future, if it exist on the Last day of July, deprive him of the Right of being Registered as a Voter.

The persons whose Rights are Reserved by the 33d Section, comprising (amongst others) Inhabitants paying Scot and Lot, Pot-Wallopers, and Freeholders and Burgage Tenants in Cities and Boroughs (not being Counties of themselves in which Freeholders and Burgage Tenants have a Right to Vote,) may, by complying with the conditions of the Act, retain their Rights for Life:

It is to be observed also with respect to all these persons that they may have their Qualifications suspended for a time without wholly losing their right;

Qualification may be suspended for a time, and recovered.

For instance, if a Scot and Lot Voter ceases to reside, or is omitted from the Poor Rate, such absence or omission may for the time suspend his Right

BOROUGH ELECTORS.

of Voting; but on his resuming his residence and having been again Rated for the due period, he may recover his Qualification:

Right Forfeited by two years omission from Register.

Exceptions.

But if any Voter, whose Right is Reserved by this Section, be omitted for Two successive Years from the Register of Persons entitled to Vote in respect of Reserved Rights, (Except he be so omitted in consequence of his having received Parochial Relief within Twelve Calendar Months, or in consequence of absence on the Naval or Military Service of His Majesty,) he will for ever after be disqualified from Voting in respect of such Reserved Right. *S. 33.*

Certain Old Rights of Voting acquired since 1st of March, 1831, excluded from Reservations.

It is to be observed, that the operation of the 33d Section, so far as it includes Freeholders and Burgage Tenants in Cities and Towns, not being Counties of themselves, under the general words " every person now having a Right to Vote in virtue of any other Qualification than as, &c." is narrowed by the 35th Section: That Section enacts that no Person shall be entitled to Vote in the Election for any City or Borough, (except a City or Town being a County of itself in which Freeholders or Burgage Tenants have a Right to Vote,) in respect of any Freehold or Burgage Tenement which he shall have acquired

Exception.

subsequently to the 1st of March, 1831, unless it shall have come to him in the interval between that day and the passing of the Act (viz. the 7th of June, 1832,) by Descent, Succession, Marriage, Marriage

BOROUGH ELECTORS.   49

Settlement, Devise, or Promotion to any Benefice or Office. *S. 35.*

It would seem that the Rights Reserved under the 33d Section must be considered with reference to the Boundaries of Cities and Boroughs as they existed at the time of the passing of the Act. This would appear to be so, as well from the reason of the thing itself, as from the wording of the Section:

Semble.
Rights re-served under Section 33 apply to Old Boundaries only.

The words are, "That every person now having "a right to vote in the Election for any City or "Borough (except those enumerated in the said "Schedule (A.)) in virtue of any other qualification "than, &c. shall retain such Right so long as he "shall be qualified as an Elector according to the "usages and customs of such City or Borough, or "any Law now in force, and such Person shall be "entitled to vote in the Election, &c. if duly regis-"tered, but that no such Person shall be so regis-"tered in any Year unless he shall, on the Last "day of July in such Year, be qualified as such "Elector in such manner as would entitle him then "to vote, if such Day were the Day of Election, "and this Act had not been passed;"

The Reservation then is in favour of those who had *the Right of voting at the time of the passing of the Act,* and they are required, in order to Registration, to be qualified on the Last day of July *in such manner as if the Act had not been passed;"*

D

50   BOROUGH ELECTORS.

Now an Elector could only be qualified at the time
of the passing of the Act in reference to the Old
Boundary, because the New Boundary did not then
exist; and he would not be qualified " in such man-
" ner as if the Act had not been passed," if his
Qualification were acquired out of the Old and
within the New Boundaries. This construction is
not repugnant to the 7th Section, which provides
that the different Boroughs shall " for the purposes
" of this Act" have their Boundaries settled and
described; for that Section must be taken to con-
template the New Boundaries as parts of the respective Boroughs for all the purposes of the Elective
Rights *created by the Act*, whereas the 33d Section
refers to Rights which *existed before the Act*, and the
continuance of which is to be governed by the same
rules as if the Act had not been passed. More-
over the special Provision at the end of the 31st Section, extending the Old Rights thereby reserved to
property within the New Boundaries, strongly forti-
fies the construction now put on the 33d Section, in
which no provision of that kind occurs.

Provision as to Freeholds in New Shoreham, &c. By the 34th Section all persons having, at the
time of the passing of the Act, a right to Vote for
New Shoreham, Cricklade, Aylesbury, or East Retford, in respect of Freeholds in the adjacent Hundreds, have that Right Reserved to them, subject to
the conditions contained in the 33d Section, except

BOROUGH ELECTORS.

that the Residence may be either within the particular Borough as defined by the 5th Section of the Act, or within Seven Statute Miles of any part of the Borough as so defined.

The 36th Section of the Act states one ground of Temporary Disqualification which applies equally to all Voters for Cities and Boroughs ; viz. that no Person shall be entitled to be Registered in any year as a Voter for any City or Borough, who shall, within Twelve Calendar Months next previous to the Last day of July in such year, have received Parochial Relief, or other Alms, which by the Law of Parliament disqualify from Voting. Where according to any Local Act or Custom, or any Determination of the House of Commons, the non-receipt of Alms within a longer period is an essential ingredient in the Right of Voting for any City or Borough, the 36th Section of this Act will not vary the Right in that respect; as every Elector, whose Right is reserved either permanently or for a time by the Act, must, in order to be Registered, be qualified on the Last day of July " in such manner as would en-" title him then to Vote if such day were the day " of Election, *and this Act had not been passed.*"

Disqualification by Receipt of Alms

A Six Months' Residence having been made an indispensable condition to every Borough Right of Voting, whether Reserved or Conferred by the Act, the Question of Residence or Non-Residence

BOROUGH ELECTORS.

Construction of the term "Residence." will of course perpetually arise: It seems hardly possible to define what will be a " Residence" within the meaning of the Act. The cases upon the subject which have been decided by Committees of the House of Commons have turned upon the Interpretation of the Term Residence, as with reference to the usage of each Borough, or to the last determination affecting that Borough, rather than upon any general principle of construction that would be applicable to all Boroughs. It may, however, be safely laid down, that the Residing must be *bona fide*, and substantially permanent, and not colourable or merely occasional; and that the best criterion of its being *bona fide* will be the fact of the Party's having during the whole Six Months a fixed (1) Domicile within the Borough, or within the required distance from it: Too strict a construction of this Rule should not be enforced with regard to absence; for instance, if a Party absent himself from the Place in which he is usually domiciled, and his absence be merely temporary and with the intention of returning, it would be unreasonable to impute to him a discontinuance of Residence. *See Rex* v.

(1) In the case of *Rex* v. *Adlard,* 4 *B. & Cres.* 772, the authorities on the subject of Residence, as distinguished from Occupation and Inhabitancy, are fully referred to. It was there held, that a Party is to be considered as Resident in that Parish in which he has his Sleeping Place.

BOROUGH ELECTORS.

Sargent, 5 Term Rep. 466 ; *and Rex* v. *the Duke of Richmond,* 6 *T. R.* 560. This view of the question of Residence is analogous to that which has always been acted upon in criminal cases, in determining, with reference to the question of Burglary, whether the particular premises were at the time of the offence the Dwelling-house of the party; There it has been held, that notwithstanding a temporary absence, wherever there is an *animus revertendi,* the party is to be considered as dwelling upon the premises. *See* 1 *Hale,* 566. *Foster, Cr. L.* 76.

CHAPTER V.

PROCEEDINGS WITH REGARD TO THE REGISTRATION OF VOTERS FOR COUNTIES.

It has been already stated that no Person will be entitled to Vote for any County, Riding, Parts, or Division of a County, unless he has been duly Registered as a Voter for such County, Riding, Parts, or Division.

Before explaining more in detail the process by which the Registration for Counties is to be effected, it may be stated generally, That,

General outline of Process of Registration for Counties. For the purpose of making the Registers of Voters for Counties, the Overseers of every Parish are annually to make out a List of all the Persons entitled in respect of property situated within their Parish, to Vote for the County in which it is;

In order to obtain the means of making out this List correctly, they are at a stated time in each Year to give a Public Notice, requiring all persons claiming to be entitled as Voters for the County in which their parish is, to notify their Claims to them by a certain Day:

The Claims made in pursuance of this Requisition, (together with, in all future years, the names

COUNTY REGISTRATION. 55

of Persons on the Register for the time being; for a Person once on the County Register need not make a fresh claim,) will furnish the materials for the List; and from these materials it is to be made out by the Overseers within a given period, and to be published in such a manner as will afford a sufficient opportunity for objections and appeals, which are not to be decided by the Overseers, but are afterwards to be disposed of by a Barrister especially appointed to Revise the List.

The Overseers after the publication of the List are to transmit it by a fixed day to the Clerk of the Peace, in whose custody it is to remain till the time arrives for its being laid before the Barrister appointed to Revise it.

The Barrister is to hold an open Court for the purpose once in every year at some convenient time within a stated period; He is then to Revise and finally settle the List of Voters, and this List, when so settled, will, together with all the other Lists of Voters for the same County, Riding, Parts, or Division, be copied into a Book, which Book will then become the Register of Voters entitled to vote in any Election that may take place before the corresponding period in the next Year, when a New Register will be made in a similar manner.

To give a more accurate account of the process of making up the Register of Voters for Counties, it will be necessary to go step by step into the details which are provided for *seriatim* in the 37th,

COUNTY REGISTRATION.

38th, 39th, 40th, 41st, 42d, and 43d Sections, and in the Schedule (H.) annexed to the Act.

Overseers to give Notice to Persons Claiming to Vote.

In the first instance, the 37th Section requires the Overseers of the Poor of every Parish and Township to have fixed on the (1) 20th of June in every year on the doors of all Churches and Chapels (or, if there be no Church or Chapel, in some other conspicuous situation,) in their respective Parish or Township, a Printed Notice, of which a Form is given (No. 1) in the Schedule (H.) requiring all Persons entitled to vote for the County, Riding, Parts, or Division, in respect of any Property situate wholly or in part in that Parish or Township, to deliver or transmit to them by (2) the 20th of July a Notice of Claim, according to a Form also given (No. 2) in Schedule (H.) *S.* 37.

Claimant to transmit Notice of Claim.

Shilling to be paid with Notice of Claim.

With that Notice a Shilling is to be paid to the Overseers by the party claiming; and till it has been paid, the Notice of Claim will not be valid. *S.* 56.

Persons on Register need not make fresh Claim.

It may be here observed that, when a Voter is once upon the County Register he is not required to make a fresh Claim in any future year, so long as he continues to have the same Residence and Qualification as described in the Register. *S.* 37.

Alphabetical List of Persons entitled.

The Overseers in every Parish and Township must, by (3) the Last day of July in every year, have

(1) In the year 1832, the 25th of July.
(2) In the year 1832, the 20th of August.
(3) In the year 1832, the Last day of August.

COUNTY REGISTRATION.

57

completed an Alphabetical List (according to the Form (No. 3) in Schedule (H.)) of all Persons who shall have sent in claim to be therein inserted as Voters for the County, Riding, Parts, or Division, in respect of any Lands or Tenements situate wholly or in part within that Parish or Township. *S*. 38.

In the year 1832 this List will only include the Names of Persons who have sent in their Claims to Vote, but in every succeeding year, the List to be made out by the Last day of July, must *also* contain the Names of such Persons as shall already be upon the Register for the time being: *S*. 38.

The List must state the Christian Name and Surname of every Person at full length, together with the Place of his Abode, the Nature of his Qualification, and the Local or other Description of the Qualifying Lands or Tenements as each of such particulars is expressed in his Notice of Claim; with the Name of the Occupying Tenant, if it is stated in the Notice of Claim; *S*. 38.

List must contain description of Voter's Name, Abode, &c.

The Overseers are to insert in the List the Name of every one who claims a Right to Vote, and, also, in future years, of every one whose name is on the Register for the time being of Voters in respect of Property situate wholly or in Part in that Parish or Township; for they will not be at liberty to exercise any discretion as to whether they shall insert the Name of a claimant or reject it, their duty in this respect being purely ministerial; So also, in future

Overseers bound to insert in List Names of all Claimants.

D 5

COUNTY REGISTRATION.

years, they will be bound to insert in the List every Name that they find upon the Register for the time being of Voters in respect of property within their Parish or Township, the words of the Act being, " the Names of *all* Persons who shall be upon the " Register," &c. *S.* 38.

But by way of a partial restraint upon the facility of advancing fictitious claims, and in order to remove from the List in a later stage of the Proceeding, those whose Qualifications shall have been changed or wholly lost since they were put upon the Register, it is provided, that where the Overseers shall have reasonable cause to believe that any Person is not entitled to Vote in the Election for the County, Riding, Parts, or Division in which their Parish or Township is, they shall have power to put the words " objected to" in the margin of the List, opposite to his Name; This will entail upon the party against whose Name the mark appears upon the List, Proof of his Qualification before the Barrister who is finally to Revise the List, as will be afterwards explained; *S.* 38.

Overseer's Mark of objection in cases of doubtful Qualification.

Overseers must sign List.

Publication of List.

Overseers to keep Copy of List.

The List must be signed by the Overseers, and a sufficient number of Copies written or printed, and fixed upon the Doors of all the Churches and Chapels (or, if there be no Church or Chapel, in some other conspicuous situation,) within the Parish or Township, on the Two Sundays next after the completion of the List; The Overseers are to keep a True Copy of the List, for the Perusal of any Per-

COUNTY REGISTRATION.

son, free of payment, at all reasonable hours, during the Two first Weeks after it shall have been made. *S. 38.*

There is also a Provision made for such Precincts or Places (whether Extra-parochial or not,) as have no Overseers of the Poor; For the purposes of making the List of Voters any such Precinct or Place is to be considered within the adjoining Parish or Township in the same County, Riding, Division, or Parts, and if it adjoins Two or more Parishes or Townships in the same County, Riding, &c. it is to be deemed to be within the least populous of such Parishes or Townships, (according to the last Census for the time being,) and the Overseers of that Parish or Township are required to insert in their List of Voters, the Names of all Persons claiming a Right to Vote in respect of Property situated wholly or in part within that Precinct or Place. *S.* 38. *Provision for Places having no Overseers of the Poor.*

In addition to the Overseers' mark of objection already mentioned, all Persons who shall be upon the Register for the time being, or who shall have claimed to be inserted in any List for the current year of Voters for any County, Riding, Parts, or Division, are entitled to object to any other Person who has had his Name inserted in any List for the same County, Riding, Parts, or Division, as not being duly Qualified. The mode of objecting must be by giving or sending before the (1) 25th of August, a Notice according to the Form (No. 4) in Sched. *Who may object to Persons being retained on the List.*

Mode of Objection.

(1) In the year 1832, the 25th of September.

COUNTY REGISTRATION.

Notice to Parties objected to.

(H.) to the Overseers who have made the List in which the Name of the Person objected to appears, and by also giving a Notice in writing, according to the Form (No. 5) in Sched. (H.) to the Person objected to, or sending it to him at his place of Abode as described in the List, or delivering it to his Tenant in Occupation of the Premises described in the List; This Notice also must be sent or delivered on or before the (1) 25th of August. *S.* 39.

Overseers to Publish List of Persons objected to by Third Parties.

The Overseers are then to make out a List, (according to the Form No. 6 in Sched. (H.) of all the Persons who have been thus objected to by other Persons, and they are required to fix Copies of it on the Doors of all the Churches and Chapels (or if there is no Church or Chapel, in some other conspicuous situation,) within their Parish or Township, on the Two Sundays next preceding (2) the 15th of September; and they must also keep a true copy of this List of Persons objected to for the Perusal (without payment of fee) of all Persons at all reasonable hours during the Ten Days next before the (2) 15th of September. *S.* 39.

Overseers to deliver List of Voters and Statement of the Number of Persons objected to to High Constable.

The Overseers having made out the List of Voters in their Parish or Township, are to deliver it on the (3) 29th of August, together with a written Statement of the Number (not the Names) of Persons objected to (either by the Overseer's mark of

(1) In the year 1832, the 25th of September.
(2) In the year 1832, the 15th of October.
(3) In the year 1832, the 29th of September.

COUNTY REGISTRATION.

61

objection against their Names in the List, or by the formal objection of other Parties,) to the High Constable, or High Constables of the Hundred or other such District in which their Parish or Township is, by whom the List and the Statement are to be immediately delivered to the Clerk of the Peace of the County, Riding, Parts, or Division to which the Parish or Township belongs ; *S.* 40.

The Clerk of the Peace on receiving the List and Statement is required to make without delay an Abstract of the whole number of Persons objected to in each Parish or township; This Abstract he is to transmit immediately to the Barrister or Barristers appointed to Revise the Lists for the County, Riding, Parts, or Division to which it refers: The List of Voters will remain in the Custody of the Clerk of the Peace. *Clerk of the Peace to transmit to the Revising Barrister an Abstract of whole number of Persons objected to in each Parish, &c.*

The Barrister will thus be apprized of the number of disputed Votes in each Parish or Township which are to come under his consideration, and will be enabled to judge what will be the most proper Times and Places for holding the Courts for a Revision of the Lists. *S.* 40.

The Barristers by whom the final Revision of the Lists of County Voters is to be made, are to be annually appointed for the purpose. *Barristers to be appointed to Revise the Lists of County Voters.*

The Nomination of the Barrister or Barristers to Revise the Lists of Voters for the County of Middlesex is to rest with the Chief Justice of the Court of King's Bench, and is to be made in the Month of

COUNTY REGISTRATION.

July or August. For every other County the appointment will be made by the Senior Judge in the Commission of Assize for that County, when travelling the Summer Circuit.

No Member of Parliament eligible.

No Member of Parliament, nor any person holding any Office or Place of Profit under the Crown, will be eligible; and the appointment will have the effect of disqualifying a Barrister for the next Eighteen Months from serving in Parliament for the County, Riding, Parts, or Division for which he shall have been appointed. If, in consequence of the collocation of the words in which the Provision upon this point is expressed, it should be suggested that they are open to a construction giving them a larger operation, and that they may possibly imply a general disqualification from serving in Parliament during those Eighteen Months, it must be observed, that had any such effect been intended, the wording of the Clause would probably have been " from the Time of such his appointment for " *any* County, Riding, Parts, or Division." The insertion of a comma after the word "appointment" in the Proviso as it now stands, would have the effect of making clear that which, without doubt, must have been the intention of the Legislature, viz. that the disqualification was merely to apply to the particular County, Riding, Parts, or Division for which the Barrister may have been appointed.

Number of Barristers in discretion of

The Judge making the appointment is to decide what number of Barristers it will be necessary to

COUNTY REGISTRATION.

appoint for any County, Riding, Parts, or Division, *Judge making the Appointment.* and there will be no objection to his naming, if he think fit, the same Barrister for several Counties, &c. *S.* 41.

The Barristers appointed to Revise the Lists *Barristers to make a Circuit.* will make a Circuit of the County, Riding, Parts, or Division, for which they are respectively appointed, at some time in the interval between the (1) 15th of September and the 25th of October in each year: Having ascertained from the Abstract of the number of objected Votes transmitted to them by the Clerk of the Peace what will be the probable duration of their Sittings at each place within their Jurisdiction, they are to determine accordingly when and where they are to hold their Courts;

They are then to give Notice of the appointed *To give Three Days' Notice of the Times of holding their Courts.* Times and Places by an Advertisement in some Newspaper circulating in the respective County, Riding, Parts, or Division for which they are appointed, and also by a Notice to be fixed (Three Days before the commencement of their Circuit) in some public and conspicuous situation, at the principal Place of Election for the County, Riding, Parts, or Division. *S.* 41.

Having thus gone through all the preliminary *Proceedings before Barrister.* steps directed to be taken in order to bring under the consideration of the Barrister the Lists made out by the Overseers, and the Claims and Objec-

(1) In the year 1832, between the 15th of October and the 25th of November.

COUNTY REGISTRATION.

tions of the various parties as connected with those Lists, the Proceedings before the Barrister by which the Lists are to be corrected and made perfect remain to be explained.

It has already been stated that the Barrister's Court is to be an open Court: The Act also directs that the Barrister is to Sit singly; that is to say, where more Barristers than one are appointed for the same County, Riding, Parts, or Division, although they are to attend together at the same Places, their Courts are to be held separately; By this arrangement it is evident that the Business in each Place will be more speedily dispatched, the attendance of Overseers and other parties will be shortened, and their expenses of course diminished;

Barristers to hold separate Courts.

The Act invests the Barristers with the power of Adjournment from Time to Time, and from one Place to any other Place in the same County, Riding, Parts, or Division; they will also have the Power of administering Oaths, (or in the case of Quakers or Moravians, Affirmations,) to Persons objecting to others as not qualified, to Persons who are themselves objected to, to Persons who having given due Notice of Claim have been omitted from the Lists, and to all Witnesses who may be examined before them; Wilfully False Swearing or Affirming before them is to be punishable as Perjury: and it is directed that their mode of Proceeding for the purpose of finally determining the Validity of Claims and Objections, shall (except

Barrister to have powers of Adjournment and of administering Oaths, &c.

COUNTY REGISTRATION.

where otherwise provided) be similar to that us\
pursued before the Returning Officer, according\
the previous practice at Elections. So that it wou.... |
seem to be intended that the Barrister is not to require more strict evidence than has hitherto been
necessary before the Assessor. *S*. 52.

It is expressly provided that the Barrister is not
to be attended by Counsel. *S*. 52.

If it should, from the Death, Illness, or Absence
of any of the Barristers, or from any other cause,
appear probable in the Judgment of the Chief Justice or Judge by whom the appointment for any
County, Riding, Parts, or Division was made, that
the Lists for that County, or Riding, &c. will not
be gone through within the required period, the Act
authorizes and indeed requires the appointment of
an additional Barrister or Barristers, who will be
clothed with the same Powers and Authorities as
the Barristers originally nominated. *S*. 53.

At the first Court to be holden by the Barrister
the Clerk of the Peace is to produce before him the
several Lists of Voters for the County, Riding,
Parts, or Division for which he is appointed; and
the Overseers who have made out each List will
attend at the Court held by the Barrister for Revising the Lists relating to their particular Parish
or Township, and will deliver to the Barrister a
Copy of the List of the Persons objected to in that
Parish or Township; and they are to furnish on

Clerk of the Peace to pro-
duce Lists of Voters before Barrister.

Overseers will be in at-
tendance and Deliver Lists of Objected Voters;

and give all necessary information on oath.

COUNTY REGISTRATION.

oath to the Barrister all the information in their power for the purpose of enabling him to Revise the List, and for the same purpose all Assessors, Collectors of Taxes, and other Officers having the Custody of Tax Assessments or Rate Books, are required to produce them before the Barrister upon his requiring them to do so. *S.* 51.

The Barrister will then go through each List, and will retain upon it the Names of all those to whom no objection has been made either by the Overseers or by any other person; he will also retain the Names of those Persons who have been objected to (not by the Overseers, but by other parties,) in cases where the Party Objecting does not appear in person, or by some one in his behalf, in support of his objection; He will also retain the Name of every Person objected to by other Parties than the Overseers, where the Objecting Party fails to prove the due service of the required Notice of Objection on the Overseers, or the due service of the required Notice on the Person objected to. *S.* 52.

In what cases Barristers will retain Names on the List.

Such will be the grounds upon which the Barrister will retain Names upon the List. The cases in which he will expunge Names will be as follows:

In what cases Barrister will expunge Names.

Wherever the Name of any Person has the Overseer's mark " Objected to" against it in the Margin of the List, or has been objected to in due form by some other Party, who appears in Person or by some one in his behalf to support the objection, the

COUNTY REGISTRATION. 67

Barrister will expunge the Name of the Person objected to, unless it be proved to his satisfaction that that Person was entitled on the preceding Last day of July, to have his name Inserted in the List of Voters, in respect of the *same* Qualification as described in that List:

He will also expunge the Name of any Person so objected to, as to whom any Incapacity by Law or Statute to Vote in the Election of Members to serve in Parliament shall be shown to have existed on that Last day of July:

He will also expunge the Name of every Person who shall be proved to him to be dead;

The Barrister will have power to rectify Mistakes in the List; that is to say, if it shall be proved to him that any Error has been made as to any of the particulars directed by the Act to be inserted in the List, he may correct it. *Power for Barrister to rectify Mistakes,*

He is also authorized to supply omissions; and the exercise of this power will arise where any one particular required by the Act to be Inserted in the List, as the Christian Name of a Person, or his Place of Abode, or the Nature of his Qualification, has been wholly omitted from the List; In such case, if the omitted matter be supplied to the satisfaction of the Barrister at any time before the very last moment when he finally completes the Revision of the List by Signing it, it may be inserted in the List, and the Name of the Party of course retained *and supply Omissions.*

COUNTY REGISTRATION.

upon it: But if it be not so supplied, the Barrister will treat the entire entry as void, and expunge the Name of the Party from the List.

With respect to these cases of Omission of some one particular, (as for instance the absence of the Christian Name from the First Column of the List,) although it is by no means required of the Barrister to give any Notice to the Party affected by such omission, (and indeed the necessity of such Notice is expressly dispensed with in the Proviso at the end of the 42d Section;) it will probably appear reasonable, wherever it can be effected without difficulty, to give some intimation to the Person with respect to whose Name, or Qualification, &c. there is any such omission in the List, in order that he may have an opportunity of supplying the defect before the Barrister's Sitting is closed. *S*. 42.

This power of supplying Omissions is a great indulgence to the Parties; inasmuch as ample time having been allowed to enable them to send in a full description of their Names, Places of Abode, and the other particulars of their Qualification, they have, in strict justice, no right to complain of being excluded from the List on account of an omission arising from the want of proper vigilance on their own part: Should the omission not have been made by the party in the first instance, but have originated with the Overseer who made out the List, this mode of remedying the defect will have equal operation; and in such case should the omission be *wilful* on

COUNTY REGISTRATION.

69

the part of the Overseers, they will be liable to penalties under the 76th Section, for wilful contravention of the Provisions of the Act.

In addition to all these Rules for the conduct of the Barrister in Settling the Lists of Voters, a further Provision is made for those cases in which the Overseers shall have omitted (whether wilfully or accidentally) to insert in any List of Voters the Name of any Person who has given due Notice of his Claim to be put upon it: In any such case, the Barrister, upon satisfactory proof that the Party omitted was actually entitled on the preceding Last day of July to be inserted in the List upon which he claimed to be inserted, *and* that he gave due Notice of his Claim to the Overseers, is empowered to insert his Name in that List at the time of his Revising it. *S. 43.*

When Barrister may insert Names of Persons who have been wholly omitted from List.

This Provision will operate as a protection to parties against fraud or negligence on the part of Overseers, who might otherwise wilfully or through carelessness exclude from the List Persons well entitled to be upon it, at the same time that it is so limited as not to be any encouragement to parties to be negligent in attending to their rights at the proper season, due Notice of Claim to the Overseers being made a necessary condition to the Insertion of the Party's Name in the List by the Barrister.

It is to be observed, that in every instance the Proof of Qualification before the Barrister is to

Proof of Qualification to refer back

COUNTY REGISTRATION.

to Last day of July.

have reference back to the Last day of July;(1) no party therefore can establish a Title to be inserted in the List by proving before the Barrister a Right which has accrued or been matured subsequently to the preceding Last day of July, when the Lists under the Barrister's consideration were completed by the Overseers; or by proving a Qualification in any way varying from that in respect of which he gave in his Claim to the Overseers; and this would seem to be reasonably so provided, for the Barrister's Court being in the Nature of a Court of Appeal from the Overseers, it would clearly be improper that the Barrister should take cognizance of facts which were not cognizable by the Overseers.

The Barrister, having finally determined upon the validity of the various Claims and Objections submitted to him, is in open Court to write his Initials against all the Names which he has struck out or inserted, and against every Insertion or Alteration **Barrister having finally settled Lists to sign them.** which he may have made; and having so settled the several Lists of Voters, he is to sign his Name to every Page of them. *S.* 52.

Lists when settled to be transmitted to Clerk of the Peace. The Lists, when settled by the Barrister, are to be forthwith transmitted by him to the Clerk of the Peace for the County, Riding, Parts, or Division to **Originals to be arranged and kept** which they refer; The Originals are to be kept by that Officer among the Records of the Sessions,

(1) And in the year 1832, notwithstanding the alteration of dates, the Last day of July will still be the Day by which the Qualification is to be regulated. *See Proviso at the end of Sect.* 80.

COUNTY REGISTRATION.

arranged in Alphabetical order according to Hun- *amongst Re-cords of the Sessions.* dreds; the Lists for each Hundred being also sub-divided into an Alphabetical arrangement according to Parishes and Townships;

The Clerk of the Peace is also to provide a Book *Lists to be copied into a Book.* into which he is to have all the Lists for the County, Riding, Parts, or Division to which they relate, fairly and truly copied, according to the same plan of Alphabetical arrangement as to the Hundreds, and as to the Parishes and Townships within the Hundreds: and Numbers are to be prefixed to the Names, so as to follow in a regular series from the first Name to the last.

The Book is to be delivered by the Clerk of the *Book to be in the Custody of the Sheriff.* Peace in a complete state on or before the Last day of October, to the Sheriff or Under-Sheriff for the County to which it relates; in whose Custody it will remain till the expiration of his Office, when it will be delivered over to his Successor.

The Book thus completed will be the Register of *The Book to be the Register of Electors;* Electors entitled to Vote at any Election for the County, Riding, Parts, or Division to which it re-lates, which may take place between(1) the Last day *How long to be in force.* of October (exclusive) on which it was delivered to the Sheriff or Under-Sheriff, and the First day of November in the following year. *S. 54.*

The mode of remunerating the Barrister and de- *Remunera-tion of Barristers.* fraying his travelling and other expenses is provided for by the 57th Section.

(1) In the year 1832, the First day of December.

CHAPTER VI.

PROCEEDINGS WITH REGARD TO THE REGISTRATION OF VOTERS FOR CITIES AND BOROUGHS.

ACCORDING to the plan which has been adopted in explaining the process by which the Registers of County Voters are to be made out, it may be useful, before entering into the more minute details, to give some general Outline of the mode of effecting the Borough Registration; and the more so that there are several leading points of difference between the System in Counties and that in Boroughs.

General Outline of Borough Registration.

It has already been observed with respect to Cities and Boroughs, that Registration is essential to the Right of Voting. The making out the List, which is to be the first step towards the formation of the Register, will be for the most part the business of the Overseers of the Poor: The Overseers of the Poor in every Parish are to make out annually an Alphabetical List of All the Persons entitled to Vote for the City or Borough, in which their Parish is, in respect of the New £10 Qualification conferred by the Act; and, if there be any Reserved Right of Voting, another List of Persons entitled in

BOROUGH REGISTRATION.

73

respect of such Reserved Right; (If the Reserved Right however be in *Freemen*, the Town Clerk will make out that List, instead of the Overseers;) No Public Notice, however, is required to be given by the Overseers preparatory to making out the Borough Lists, as it has been shown to be in the case of County Lists; Nor are the Voters required to give to the Overseers any Notice of Claim in the first instance, as in the case of County Voters. The Lists of Voters when made are to be published in a conspicuous part of the Borough on two successive Sundays; and any Persons who suppose themselves aggrieved by being omitted from either of the Lists are to give within a certain time to the Overseers Notice of their Claim to be inserted in it; So also those who object to the Qualification of others whose Names appear on the Published Lists, may object, within a prescribed period, to their being retained on the Lists;

The Overseers will make Lists of these Two Classes of Persons, that is to say, a List of Claimants, and a List of Parties objected to, and publish them openly within the Borough for Two consecutive Sundays.

The Lists of Voters will afterwards be revised and corrected by a Barrister specially appointed for the purpose, who will hold an open Court at a fixed time of the year; The Overseers will produce the Lists for each Parish and Township before him, and

E

BOROUGH REGISTRATION.

after hearing the various Claims and Objections discussed, the Barrister will finally settle the Lists:

All the Lists for the different Parishes and Townships in each City and Borough being thus revised and signed by the Barrister, will be copied into a Book which will become the Register' of Electors for that City or Borough, and be in force till the corresponding period in the following Year, when a New Registration will again begin.

Details of Borough Registration. The different successive proceedings by which the Register of Electors for Cities and Boroughs is to be made up, are contained in the 44th, 45th, 46th, 47th, 48th, 49th, and 50th Sections of the Act.

Overseers, however, are not in Boroughs as in Counties the only persons charged with the making out the Lists; In Places where Freemen Vote, the Town Clerks are entrusted with the performance of this duty, so far as the Freemen are concerned, and in the City of London the Clerks of the different Livery Companies will make out the Lists of Freemen and Liverymen. There will, however, be no Place in which Lists will not be made out by Overseers, for the New £10 Qualification, under the 27th Section of the Act, will prevail in every City, Borough, or Contributory Borough in England or Wales, and the Lists of all Voters in respect of that Qualification will be made out by the Overseers: Wherever also there is any Right Reserved by the Act, (except that of Freemen, · or in the City of

BOROUGH REGISTRATION.

London, of Freemen and Liverymen,) the Overseers will make out the Lists of Voters in respect of such Reserved Right.

By the 44th Section the Overseers of the Poor of every Parish or Township situated wholly or in part within any City or Borough, or within any Place sharing in the Election for any City or Borough, are required to make out in each year an Alphabetical List of All the Persons entitled under those Provisions of the Act which have been already explained, (see Chapter IV.) to Vote for the City or Borough in respect of the Occupation of Premises of the clear Yearly Value of Ten Pounds at the least, situated wholly or in part in their Parish or Township: This List must be completed by the (1) Last day of July. The Overseers are also to make out, wherever there is any Reserved Right, a List of all the Persons entitled to Vote in respect of such Reserved Right. This List must also be made out by the (1) Last day of July. Each List must contain at full length the Christian Name and Surname of every Person, and the Nature of his Qualification must be stated; and where the Qualification is in respect of Property, the Overseers must insert a sufficient description of the Place where the Property is situate; where however it is

Overseers to make out Alphabetical List of £10 Voters.

List to be completed by Last day of July.

List of Voters in respect of Reserved Rights to be also made out by Overseers before Last day of July. What the List must contain.

(1) In the year 1832, *the Last day of August*, according to the substitution of dates made by the Order in Council, in pursuance of the 80th Section of the Act. *Vide post, Chapter XII.*

E 2

BOROUGH REGISTRATION.

List how published.

not in respect of Property, there must be a specific description of the Person's Place of Abode. Each of these Lists is to be signed by the Overseers, and they are then to give Publicity to them by having a sufficient Number of Copies printed, which are to be fixed on or near the Doors of all the Churches and Chapels (or, if there be no Church or Chapel, in some public and conspicuous situation) in their Parish or Township on the Two Sundays next after the time appointed for the completion of the Lists.

Overseers to keep Copies for perusal.

The Overseers are also to keep True Copies of these Lists, to which all Persons are to have access without paying any fee at all reasonable Hours during the first Fortnight after the completion of the Lists. *S.* 44.

As there are within some Boroughs certain Precincts and Places which have no Overseers of their own, an express Provision was necessary to secure the Registration of Persons entitled to Vote in respect of Property situated in such Places. The

Provision as to Precincts or Places without Overseers of their own.

Act therefore provides, that as to any such Precinct or Place the Overseers of the adjoining Parish or Township, situate wholly or in part within the same Borough, shall consider it as part of their own Parish or Township, and include in their List the Names of the Persons entitled in respect of Property in the Precinct or Place to Vote for the Borough; If there should happen to be in the same Borough several Parishes or Townships adjoining to such a Precinct or Place, the Overseers of the least popu-

BOROUGH REGISTRATION.

lous (according to the latest Census at the time) of such adjoining Parishes or Townships, will consider it as within their Parish or Township. *S. 45.*

With respect to the Lists of Freemen in places where they have a Right to Vote, the Town Clerk of the particular Borough, or Place sharing in the Election with it, is to make out by the (1) Last day of July a List of the Freemen entitled under the 32d Section to Vote for the Borough; This List must contain the Christian Name and Surname of each Freeman at full length, and also the Place of his Abode; and a Copy of the List must be fixed on or near the Door of the Town-Hall, or in some public and conspicuous situation in the Borough, or Place sharing with it, as the case may be, on the Two Sundays next after the completion of the List: And the Town Clerk is to keep an exact copy of the List, to which all Persons are to be allowed gratuitously free-access for the purpose of perusal during the first Fortnight after its completion. *S. 46.*

List of Freemen to be made out and Published by Town Clerk.

The Lists made out by the Overseers and Town Clerks being thus open to the inspection of all, the opportunity will be given for those Persons who have been improperly omitted in any of the Lists to have timely Notice of their Omission, and if there should be any Persons inserted in the Lists, who to the knowledge of any one are not qualified to be so, a facility of objection will be given which will lead to the ultimate removal from the List of parties really

(1) In the year 1832, *the Last day of August.*

BOROUGH REGISTRATION.

Parties may Claim to be inserted in List; or may object to the insertion of others.

disqualified. A particular course is pointed out by the Act, according to which both the parties objecting to their own omission from any of the Lists, and persons objecting to the Names of others as being improperly introduced in the Lists, are to proceed.

Notice of Claim.

With respect to those Persons who being omitted claim to be Inserted in any List, they must give a Notice, according to a form prescribed by the Act (Schedule (I.) No. 4,) to the Overseers who shall have made out the particular List in which they claim a Right to be; If it should be a person claiming to Vote as a Freeman of any City, or Borough, or any Place sharing in the Election with it, he must transmit his Notice of Claim not to the Overseers but to the Town Clerk of the particular City, Borough, or Place. The Notice of Claim whether to the Overseers or to the Town Clerk must be in Writing, and must be given on or before the (1) 25th of August. *S.* 46.

Notice of Objection.

The Persons who object to others as having been inserted in the List, although not duly qualified on the preceding Last day of July, are also to pursue the course of giving a Notice to the Overseers who have made out the List in which the Name of the Person objected to is. The Notice will contain the Name of the Party objected to, with an intimation of the Objector's intention to bring forward his objection at the time when the List is Revised. This

(1) In the year 1832, *the 25th of September.*

BOROUGH REGISTRATION.

Notice must be delivered to the Overseers on or before the (1) 25th of August. A form for it is given in the Act, Schedule (I.) No. 5. *S.* 46.

If the Party objected to be in the List of Freemen, the Notice of Objection must of course be delivered to the Town Clerk. It is to be observed, that any Person on any List of Voters for a City or Borough, may object to any other person upon *any* List for the same City or Borough, although it be not the same List as that upon which he himself is.

No Notice, however, is required to be given to the Party objected to, as in the case of a County Voter, (see Chapter V. p. 60,) because, as Residence is required in the case of a Borough Voter, the Publication, as will be presently mentioned, of the Names of the Persons objected to will supersede the necessity of personal notice.

The Overseers are immediately to make out two Lists of these different sets of parties, one of Claimants, and the other of Persons objected to, according to the Forms No. 6 and 7 in the Schedule (I.) and they are to have Copies of them both fixed up on or near the Doors of all the Churches and Chapels in their Parish or Township, on the Two Sundays next before the (2) 15th of September. If there should be no Church or Chapel in the parti-

Overseers to make out List of Claimants and List of Parties Objected to;

These Lists to be published.

(1) In the year 1832, *the* 25*th of September.*
(2) In the year 1832, *the* 15*th of October.*

BOROUGH REGISTRATION.

cular Parish or Township, they must have them fixed up in some public and conspicuous situation. *S.* 46.

Copies to be kept for perusal and for sale.

And they must keep copies of these Lists for public inspection, to which all persons are to be allowed free access, without payment of any Fee, at all reasonable hours during the Ten days next before the (1) 15th of September; and they are also bound to have Copies of them ready for delivery at a Shilling for each Copy. These directions to Overseers as to making these Two Lists of Claimants and Parties Objected to, and as to keeping and delivering Copies, are extended to Town Clerks with regard to Freemen. *S.* 46, *and Schedule (I.) Nos. 8 and 9.*

As to the mode of making out the Lists of the Liverymen of London.

The mode of proceeding with regard to the making out the Lists of the Freemen and Liverymen entitled under S. 32, to vote for the City of London, differs from that prescribed by the Act with regard to the Lists of Freemen in Boroughs in general.

The Returning Officers of the City of London are required on or before the (2) Last day of July in each year, to issue their Precepts to the Clerks of the several Livery Companies, requiring them forthwith to have an Alphabetical List made out of the Liverymen of their respective Companies entitled to vote in the Election for the City; These

(1) In the year 1832, *the 15th of October.*
(2) In the year 1832, *the Last day of August.*

BOROUGH REGISTRATION.

Lists are to be made out at the expense of the several Companies, and the Clerk of each Company is to sign his List and to transmit it with Two Printed Copies to the Returning Officers, who are immediately to fix one Copy in the Guildhall, and the other in the Royal Exchange, there to remain for Fourteen days; each Clerk is also to have a sufficient number of copies of his List printed at the expense of his Company, and to keep a Copy for the inspection of any person, without fee, at all reasonable hours during the Two first weeks after it has been printed. *S.* 48.

Publication of these Lists.

Any person who considers himself improperly omitted out of any Livery List, may bring his Claim for admission under the consideration of the Barrister who is to Revise the List, upon giving a Notice according to Form numbered 1 in Schedule K, by the (1) 25th of August to the Returning Officers, and also to the Clerk in whose List he shall claim to have his Name inserted. The Returning Officers are to make out a List of all these Claimants according to the Form numbered 2 in Schedule K, and to publish it by fixing it in the Guildhall and Royal Exchange on the Two Mondays next before the (2) 15th of September; and they are also to keep a Copy of this List of Claimants to which they are to permit any Person to have gratuitous access

Claims and Objections in respect of the Lists of Liverymen.

(1) In the year 1832, *the 25th of September.*
(2) In the year 1832, *the 15th of October.*

E 5

BOROUGH REGISTRATION.

during the Ten days next before the (1) 15th of September; The Clerk of each Livery Company must also keep a Copy of the Names of the Claimants in respect of his List, which he must allow any Person to inspect gratuitously during the same period. *S.* 48.

Every Person who objects to any one whose Name appears in any List of Liverymen, must proceed by a Notice, according to the Form numbered 3 in the Schedule K, which must either be personally served upon the Party objected to, or left at his usual Place of Abode, by the(2) 25th of August. *S.* 48.

This Section does not state *who* are entitled to object to Persons inserted in the Lists of Liverymen, but merely that every one who does object must proceed in a given manner; perhaps, however, this right of objecting must be understood to be limited as in other Cities and Boroughs, viz. that in order to object, the Person objecting must himself be upon some List of Voters for the City of London. *Vide S.* 47.

Appointment of Barristers to Revise Lists of Borough Voters. All Lists of Borough Voters are to be Revised by Barristers annually appointed for that purpose.

The nomination of the Barristers for revising the Lists of Voters for London and for Westminster, and for the different Boroughs in Middlesex, is to

(1) In the year 1832, *the 15th of October.*
(2) In the year 1832, *the 25th of September.·*

BOROUGH REGISTRATION.

rest with the Chief Justice of the Court of King's Bench, and is to be made in July or August. The Barristers for revising the Lists of Voters for the Boroughs in any other County are to be appointed by the Senior Judge in the Commission of Assize for that County, while travelling the Summer Circuit; in order to prevent any doubt as to those Counties of Cities or Towns which are situated on the confines of Two Counties, it is expressly provided, that for the purpose of these appointments Kingston-upon-Hull is to be considered as next adjoining to the County of York, Newcastle-upon-Tyne as next adjoining to the County of Northumberland, and Bristol as next adjoining to the County of Somerset. *S.* 49.

A Member of Parliament, or any Person holding any Office or Place of profit under the Crown, is disqualified from being appointed to Revise the Lists for a Borough; and every Barrister appointed for any Borough is disqualified for the next Eighteen Months from serving in Parliament for that Borough, and for that Borough alone. *S.* 49, *and see ante, p.* 62.

Who disqualified.

The same Barrister may be appointed for several Boroughs, or for a County and one or more Boroughs in the County, according to the discretion of the appointing Judge. *S.* 49. The Remuneration of the Barrister is provided for by the 57th Section.

The period appointed for the Revision of Borough *Period for*

BOROUGH REGISTRATION.

the Revision of Borough Lists. Lists is from the (1) 15th of September to the 25th of October; the Revising Barrister is to hold his Court at some time during that period in each Borough for which he is appointed, (and if there be any Contributory Borough or Boroughs connected with it, then in the Contributory Borough or Boroughs also;) Of the time and place for holding his Court, he must first give Three clear days Notice, the Notice to be fixed on the Doors of the Churches and Chapels in the Borough, (and in the Contributory Borough also, if there be one,) and if there should happen to be no Church or Chapel, then the Notice must be fixed in some public and conspicuous situation. *S.* 50.

Proceedings before Barrister, The Proceedings at the Barrister's Court will vary according as the Borough is a New one created by the Act, or an Old Borough for which none but Freemen used to Vote, or an Old Borough where there were Elective rights in others exclusive of Freemen, or in others together with Freemen.

will vary in different Boroughs, and how. In the case of a New Borough, the only Lists to be produced before the Barrister will be those made out by the Overseers, viz. of Persons having the £10 Qualification.

In the case of every Old Borough, where none but Freemen used to Vote, the Lists of the Freemen made out by the Town Clerks, and in London

(1) In the year 1832, *from the 15th of October to the 25th of November.*

BOROUGH REGISTRATION.

the Lists of Freemen and Liverymen, must be produced before the Barrister, as well as the Overseer's Lists of the Persons having the £10 Qualification.

In every Old Borough where there were Elective Rights in others exclusive of Freemen, or in others together with Freemen, the Overseers must in either case produce their Lists of Persons having the £10 Qualification, and also their Lists of Persons entitled in respect of Rights reserved under Section 31 or 33, as the case may be; and in addition to these Two sets of Lists, in the case of every Old Borough where the Right of Voting has hitherto been enjoyed by Freemen as well as by others, the Town Clerk must also produce his List of the Freemen. *S. 50.*

At the opening of the first Court which the Barrister holds for any Borough, or Contributory Borough, the Overseers, or the Overseers and Town Clerk, as the case may be, must produce their respective Lists before him, and deliver to him a Copy of the List of Persons objected to, and in London the Returning Officers must produce the Lists of Liverymen. It will be the duty of the Overseers and Town Clerk, and of the Clerks of the Livery Companies in London, to attend the Court during the time that their respective Lists are under the Revision of the Barrister, and to answer upon Oath any Questions which he may put to them, for the purpose of enabling him to Revise

Overseers and Town Clerk to produce their Lists before Barrister,

to attend during Revision and give necessary Information on Oath.

BOROUGH REGISTRATION.

the Lists; *S.* 50. And for the same purpose, the Overseers will be bound to produce the Rate Book, if required by the Barrister to do so; and all Officers having the custody of any Tax Assessments must produce them before him upon his requisition. *S.* 51.

The Barrister will then go through the several Lists for the Borough, with a view to dispose of the Claims and Objections made in respect of those Lists.

Proceedings as to Decision on Claims.

Before he enters upon the hearing of a Claim, he will require proof of due Notice of Claim having been given to the Overseers, and, that condition being satisfied, he will hear the evidence offered on behalf of the Claimant in support of the Qualification stated by him in his Notice of Claim.

It should seem from the wording of the Notice of Claim, (see Form 4, Schedule I.) that Proof cannot be admitted of any other Qualification than that stated in the Notice of Claim, and it must be proved that that Qualification was perfect on the preceding Last day of July: On such a Qualification being proved, the Barrister must insert the Name of the Claimant in the List in respect of which he advanced his Claim. *S.* 50.

Although the Act is silent on the subject, it should seem that any person competent to object to a party inserted in any Borough List, would, if present at the hearing of a Claim, be at liberty to

BOROUGH REGISTRATION.

87

disprove or invalidate the case made out by the Claimant; if this were not so, a Person, who could only make out a mere *primâ facie* claim, would, by being omitted from the List in the first instance, be in a better condition than if he had been originally inserted in it; because, if he had been originally inserted in it, he would clearly have been liable to be objected to, and to have his *primâ facic* case disproved by the objector.

The Barrister will retain on the Lists the Name of every Person to whom no objection has been made; he will also retain the Name of every Person who has been objected to, if the party objecting does not appear in person, or by some one on his behalf, in support of his objection, or if he fails to prove due service of the required Notice of Objection on the Overseers. *S.* 50.

What Names to be retained on Lists.

But where the Name of any Person on a List has been objected to in due form by some other party, who appears in person or by some one on his behalf in support of the objection, the Barrister will expunge the Name of the Person objected to, unless it be proved to his satisfaction that that Person was entitled on the preceding Last day of July to have his Name inserted in the List of Voters in respect of the *same* Qualification as described in that List. *S.* 50.

What Names to be expunged.

He will also expunge the Name of any Person so objected to, as to whom any Incapacity by Common

BOROUGH REGISTRATION.

Law or Statute to Vote in the Election of Members of Parliament shall be proved to have existed on that Last day of July: He will also expunge the Name of every Person who shall be proved to him to be dead. *S*. 50.

Power for Barrister to correct mistakes and supply omissions.

The Barrister appointed to Revise any Borough Lists is by the 50th Section invested with the same power of correcting Mistakes and supplying Omissions in those Lists, as has been already fully explained in relation to County Lists; and to that explanation the Reader is now referred. *See* pp. 67 and 68.

Power to adjourn, to administer Oaths, &c.

The Barrister may adjourn his Court from time to time, and from one Place to any other Place in the same Borough or Contributory Borough; he is not to be attended by Counsel. *S*. 52.

His power of administering Oaths and Affirmations, and his mode of proceeding for the purpose of finally determining the validity of Claims and Objections, with regard to Borough Lists, is in all respects the same as has been explained with regard to County Lists; *See* p. 64. So also the power of appointing additional Barristers where it may be necessary, applies equally to Boroughs and to Counties. *S*. 53, *and see* p. 65.

Barrister having settled Lists to sign them.

The Barrister is in open Court to write his Initials against all the Names which he has struck out or inserted, and against every part of the Lists in which he may have made any insertion or correction, and

BOROUGH REGISTRATION.

89

having so settled the several Lists, he is to sign his Name to every Page of them. *S.* 52.

All the Lists for any Borough or Contributory Borough when settled by the Barrister are to be immediately delivered by him to the Returning Officer for the Borough, who is to keep the Originals in safe custody, and to provide a Book into which he is to have all these Lists fairly and truly copied, and Numbers are to be prefixed to all the Names, so as to follow in a regular series from the first Name to the last. It seems almost unnecessary to remark, that this Book will not be a List of all the Voters for the Borough arranged in Alphabetical order, but merely a collection of the Lists for the several Parishes and Townships in the Borough and of the Freemen's List, each of such Lists being Alphabetical. This Book is to be completed by the Returning Officer on or before the(1) Last day of October, and is to remain in his custody till the expiration of his Office, when he will deliver it over, together with the Original Lists, to his Successor.

To deliver them to Returning Officer for the Borough.

Who is to have them copied into a Book.

The Book thus completed will be the Register of Electors entitled to Vote at any Election for the Borough to which it relates, which may take place between the (1) Last day of October (exclusive) in the year in which it was completed, and the 1st day of November in the following year. *S.* 54.

This Book to be the Register of Electors.

How long to be in force.

(1) In the year 1832, *the 1st of December.*

CHAPTER VII.

PROCEEDINGS PREPARATORY TO AND DURING COUNTY ELECTIONS.

***

All Election Laws to remain in force, except where superseded by the Reform Act.

By the 75th Section of the Act, it is provided that all Laws, Statutes, and Usages heretofore in force, respecting the Election of Members to serve in Parliament for England and Wales, shall still remain in force, and shall apply (except where they are altered or repealed by the Act, or are inconsistent with any of its Provisions,) to the Election of Members to serve in Parliament for all the Counties, Ridings, Parts and Divisions of Counties, and all the Cities and Boroughs, which by the Act are empowered to return Members ; and by the 77th Section it is provided, that all Writs for the Election of Members, and all Mandates, Precepts, Instruments, Proceedings, and Notices, are to be framed and expressed in such manner as may be necessary for carrying the Provisions of the Act into effect.

Duty of Returning Officer.

In order to ascertain what will be the Duties of the Returning Officers under the Act, with regard to County Elections, we must refer to those parts of

AND DURING COUNTY ELECTIONS.

91

the old Statutes which are virtually adopted by the Act, as well as to the provisions of the Act itself.

By 25 Geo. 3, c. 84, s. 4, the Sheriff of a County, within two days after the Receipt of the Writ, must cause Proclamation to be made, at the Place where the Election is to be holden, that a County Court will be holden there for the purpose of Election, on some day, not later than the 16th, nor sooner than the 10th, from the day of making such Proclamation : *Notice of the Day of Election.*

To apply this Provision, as directed by the 61st Section of the Act, to the Divided Counties, it will be necessary for the Sheriff of each of those Counties, to make Proclamation of the day of Election for each Division of his County, at the Place which is fixed by the Boundary Act as the Principal Place of Election for that Division, and for the Sheriff of Yorkshire to make a similar Proclamation of the day of Election for the North Riding of Yorkshire at the City of York, for the West Riding at Wakefield, and for the East Riding at Beverley ; and for the Sheriff of Lincolnshire, to make a similar Proclamation of the day of Election for the Parts of Lindsey at the City of Lincoln, and for the Parts of Kesteven and Holland at Sleaford.

In all the undivided Counties in England and Wales, and in all the Divisions of Counties, and in the Ridings of Yorkshire, and in the Parts in Lincolnshire, certain Places are appointed by the Boundary *Polling to be conducted in Districts.*

PROCEEDINGS PREPARATORY TO

Act at which the Polls are to be taken ; and Districts are to be assigned to each of these Polling Places, in the mode pointed out by that Act. *See S. 63 of the Reform Act.*

A Deputy to preside at each Polling Place. Before the day fixed for the Election, the Sheriff, if a contest be expected, will probably find it convenient to appoint a Deputy to preside at each of the Polling places. It is presumed that the Sheriff will preside, either in person or by his Under-Sheriff, at the Principal Place of Election, though he may appoint a Deputy to preside there as well as at any other Polling place. *S. 65.*

In all matters relating to County Elections, the Sheriff, his Under-Sheriff, or any Deputy of the Sheriff, may act in places of exclusive Jurisdiction. *S. 66.*

Provision as to Booths. The day fixed for the Election being arrived, the Sheriff, his Under-Sheriff, or Deputy, is bound, on a Demand being then made by any Candidate or by any one on his behalf, and in the absence of such demand is authorized, if he shall think it expedient, to order a reasonable number of Booths to be erected, both at the Principal Place of Election and at the other Polling Places, *S. 64 ;* or instead of ordering Booths, he may hire any Houses or Buildings to be used for the purpose of Polling in.

Booths to be marked with the Names of the Parishes. *S. 71.* In either case, he must take care that the Names of the Parishes and Townships, for the use

AND DURING COUNTY ELECTIONS.

of which each Booth or Building is intended, are fixed on a conspicuous part of the Booth or Building. *S.* 64.

The Polling is to commence on the day next but two after the day fixed for the Election, unless such next day but two shall be Saturday or Sunday, and then it is to commence on the Monday following. *S.* 62. Before the commencement of the Poll, the Sheriff must provide, for the use of every Booth, a Copy of the Register of Voters, certified under his hand as a true Copy, *S.* 72, and he must also appoint Poll Clerks for each Booth. *S.* 65. A Cheque Clerk for every Poll Clerk will also be appointed as usual.

Polling when to commence.

Copy of Register for each Booth.

Appointment of Poll Clerks and Cheque Clerks.

The Expense of Booths at County Elections is limited, so that no greater cost than £40 can be incurred for Booths at any one Polling Place, whether it be the principal Place of Election, or any other Polling Place. The candidates may contract for the Booths, if they think proper : if they do not, the Sheriff must make the contract subject to the limitation of expense just mentioned. *S.* 71.

Expenses of Booths, Deputies, and Poll Clerks.

The Deputies appointed to preside at the several Polling Places are each to be paid two guineas *per diem;* and the Poll Clerks are each to have one guinea *per diem. S.* 71. All the foregoing expenses of Booths, Deputies, and Poll Clerks, are to be borne by each of the Candidates, in equal portions ; if any person proposes a Candidate without his consent,

By whom defrayed.

PROCEEDINGS PREPARATORY TO

such person will be liable to a share of these expenses, as if he were himself a Candidate. *S*. 71.

Duration of Poll. The polling is to commence and be carried on simultaneously at the Principal Place of Election, and at all the other Polling places; it is to continue for two days only, such days being successive days, and it is to commence on the first day at nine o'clock in the Morning and to continue for seven hours, and on the second day it is to continue for eight hours, and to close not later than Four in the Afternoon of that day. *S*. 62.

No Person to Poll out of the District where his Qualifying Property is. No Person is to be admitted to Vote except at the Booth appropriated to the Parish or Township in which his Qualifying Property is situated; but if there be no Booth appropriated to his Parish or Township, then he may Vote at any of the Booths for the same District. In case any Parish or Township shall happen not to be included in any of the Polling Districts, Persons whose Qualifying Property is situated in any Parish or Township so omitted must Vote at the principal Place of Election. *S*. 64.

Duties of Poll Clerks. It should seem that the duties of the Poll Clerks will not be varied by the Act, but that they will still be required to set down the Name of each Voter, the situation of his Qualifying Property, and the Place of his Abode, (all of which particulars, it should be observed, will be found in the Register,) and the Name of the Candidate for whom he polls. *See 7 & 8 Wm. 3. c. 25, s. 3, and 10 Anne, c. 23, s. 5.*

AND DURING COUNTY ELECTIONS.

For although these Acts apply in terms to *Freeholders* only, it is reasonable to presume that the effect of the 75th Section of the Reform Act is to extend their operation to all those Persons who will in future have a Right of Voting for Counties, the term *Freeholders* having evidently been used in those Acts as a designation of County Voters in general. The same reasoning will probably be held to apply as to the Oath to be administered under the 7 & 8 *Wm. 3*, to Poll Clerks; and there will be little practical difficulty as to this, as no precise form of Oath is prescribed by that Act; It will merely be necessary in Swearing the Poll Clerks to substitute the word " *Voter*" for " *Freeholder.*"

The Questions which may arise at the Poll respecting the Right of any Party to Vote, and the mode of disposing of such Questions, will be explained hereafter.

The Poll Clerks at the close of each day's Poll are publicly to deliver their Poll Books enclosed and sealed to the Person presiding at the particular Polling Place; at the final Close of the Poll all the Poll Books received by any presiding Deputy are to be immediately delivered or transmitted by him to the Sheriff or Under-Sheriff, who is to keep them unopened until the next day but one after the Close of the Poll, (unless such next day but one happens to be Sunday, and then till the Monday following,) when he is to open the Books publicly,

Custody of Poll Books and final Declaration of the Poll.

and to declare the State of the **Poll, and** to make Proclamation of the Member or Members chosen not later than Two o'Clock on that day.   *S.* 65.

There are some points common to all proceedings at Elections, whether for **Counties** or **Boroughs,** which will be adverted to after the points peculiar to Borough Elections have been explained.

BOROUGH ELECTIONS IN ENGLAND.

CHAPTER VIII.

PROCEEDINGS PREPARATORY TO AND DURING BOROUGH ELECTIONS IN ENGLAND.

It may be proper to observe, that under the former Statutes regulating the practice at Elections, there is a difference as to the Notice of Election between Cities and Towns being Counties of themselves and Boroughs in general, and this difference is not varied by the Reform Act. The Sheriff of every City and Town being a County of itself is required by 19 Geo. 2, c. 28, s. 7, immediately upon the Receipt of the Writ, to give Public Notice of the Time and Place of Election, which must be proceeded upon not later than eight days and not sooner than three days after the day of the Receipt of the Writ. In all other Boroughs, the Returning Officer of the Borough, upon the Receipt of the Precept from the Sheriff, must immediately cause Public Notice to be given of the Time and Place of Election; this Notice must be given four days at least before the day appointed for the Election, and the Election must be proceeded upon within eight

Notice of Election in Cities and Towns being Counties of themselves.

Notice of Election in other Boroughs.

F

PROCEEDINGS PREPARATORY TO

days next after the Receipt of the Precept. *See 7 & 8 Wm. 3, c. 25, s.* 1.

Provision as to Booths.

To proceed to the Provisions of the Reform Act— the day fixed for the Election being arrived, the Returning Officer of every Borough in England, (except Monmouth,) will be bound, if then required by any Candidate or by any one on his behalf, or if not so required, is authorized, if he shall think it expedient, to order Booths to be erected, (*S.* 68,) or Houses or Buildings to be hired for the purpose

Polling to be according to Districts.

of Polling in. *S.* 71. In order to facilitate the Polling he must have a sufficient number of Booths provided for the use of different Districts, (1) and

(1) The words of the Act are, " different Booths for different Parishes, Districts, or Parts of such City or Borough;" Now there is nothing in these words to show expressly whether, by " Districts or Parts," it is intended to describe acknowledged and existing Districts or Parts, or to refer to Districts or Parts to be created for the occasion by the Returning Officer: But it is apprehended that the latter is the true construction ; and this will be apparent upon considering this (the 68th) Section in conjunction with the 71st Section : It is there provided that £25 shall be the limit of expense incurred for Booths erected for any one Parish, District, or Part; And in the 68th Section it is required that not more than 600 Persons shall be required to Poll in any one Compartment of a Booth ; Now it would in general be difficult, and in some cases impossible, to carry these Provisions into effect, unless a power were assumed to be vested in the Returning Officer to make such a Division and Subdivision of the Borough into Districts or Parts, (in case there were no such existing Division or Subdivision,) as would enable him to furnish the necessary accommodation to the Persons Polling

AND DURING BOROUGH ELECTIONS IN ENGLAND. 99

on a conspicuous part of each Booth must be fixed the Name of the District for which it is intended.

(With regard to the Four Boroughs of Shoreham, Cricklade, Aylesbury, and East Retford, it is expressly provided by the 69th Section, that the Polling Districts for those Boroughs are to be settled by the Boundary Act.) *Polling Districts for Shoreham, &c.*

It is in the discretion of the Returning Officer, whether the Booths for each District shall be placed within that District, or whether there shall be one common situation for all the Booths belonging to all the Districts; if the Booths are placed in the different Districts, he must appoint a Deputy to preside at each Polling Place. The Division of the Booths into Compartments is left to the discretion of the Returning Officer, but with the restriction that not more than 600 Persons shall be required to Poll at any one Compartment, and a Poll Clerk must be appointed for each Compartment.

S. 68. Whatever Regulations the Returning Officer may make respecting the situation, division, and allotment of the Booths, he is to give Public Notice of them two days before the commencement *Notice of the Booths for each District.*

---

without exceeding the expense limited by the Act; And perhaps the language of the 68th Section may be taken as favouring this construction, the words being " for different Parishes, Districts, &c." and not for " *the* different Parishes, Districts, &c." which would seem to be the appropriate wording to express acknowledged and existing Districts and Parts.

F 2

PROCEEDINGS PREPARATORY TO

Copy of the Register for each Booth. of the Poll; (*S.* 68.) and he must provide for the use of each Booth a Copy of the Register of Voters for the Borough, certified under his hand as a true Copy. *S.* 72.

Expenses of Booths, Deputies, and Poll Clerks. The expense of Booths at Borough Elections is limited, so that where Booths are provided for the use of the different Polling Districts into which the Borough may be divided, no larger sum than £25 can be legally incurred for any one such District. The Candidates may contract for the Booths if they think fit; if they do not, the Returning Officer must make the contract, subject to the limitation of expense just mentioned. *S.* 71.

Where Deputies are appointed to preside at the Polling Places, they are each to receive Two Guineas *per diem;* and the Poll Clerks are each to re-
By whom to be paid. ceive One Guinea *per diem.* All the foregoing expenses of Booths, Deputies, and Poll Clerks, are to be borne by each of the Candidates in equal portions; and if any person proposes a Candidate without his consent, such person will be liable to a share of the expenses, as if he were himself a Candidate. *S.* 71.

Commencement and duration of Poll. The Polling for every Borough in England (except Monmouth) is to commence on the day fixed for the Election, or on the following day, or at the latest on the third day, (unless any of these days shall be Saturday or Sunday, and then it is to commence on the Monday following,) the particular day

AND DURING BOROUGH ELECTIONS IN ENGLAND.

for the commencement to be fixed by the Returning Officer. The Polling is to continue for two days only, such days being successive days; it is to be kept open for seven hours on the first day, and for eight hours on the second day, and must be finally closed not later than Four o'clock in the Afternoon of that day. *S.* 67.

No Person is to be allowed to Vote except at the Booth appropriated to the Parish or District in which his Qualifying Property is situated; or, in case he does not claim to Vote in respect of Property, at the Booth for the Parish or District in which his Place of Abode, as described in the Register, may be; but in case there happens to be no Booth provided for any particular Parish or District, Persons, whose Qualifying Property is situated in any Parish or District so omitted, may Vote at any of the Booths within the Borough; and Freemen residing out of the limits of the Borough may Vote at any of the Booths. *S.* 68.

Each Person to Poll at the Booth appointed for his District.

In the City of London no Booths are to be provided for the Reception of the Votes of Liverymen, but all the Liverymen are to poll in the Guildhall. *S.* 48.

Liverymen of London where to Poll.

It should seem that the directions in the 25 Geo. 3, c. 84, s. 7, with regard to the Duties of Poll Clerks at Borough Elections will not be varied in consequence of the Reform Act, but that they will still be sworn to set down the Name of each

Duties of Poll Clerks.

102   PROCEEDINGS PREPARATORY TO

Voter, his Addition, Profession, or Trade, and the Place of his Abode, and for whom he Votes.

What Questions may arise at the time of Polling as to the Right of any Party to Vote, and how those Questions are to be disposed of, will be explained hereafter. *Vide post, Chapter X.*

Custody of Poll Books and final Declaration of Poll. The Poll Clerks at the close of each day's Poll are publicly to deliver their Poll Books enclosed and sealed to the Returning Officer or Deputy presiding; at the final close of the Poll, all the Poll Books received by any Deputy are to be immediately delivered by him to the Returning Officer, who is to keep all the Poll Books unopened until the following day, (unless it happens to be Sunday, and then till the Monday following,) when he is to open the Books publickly and to declare the State of the Poll, and to make Proclamation of the Member or Members chosen, not later than Two o'clock on that day. A discretionary power, however, is given to the Returning Officer to declare the State of the Poll, and to make the Return *immediately* after the close of the Poll, if he thinks fit so to do. *S.* 68.

Who are to be the Returning Officers for those New Boroughs for which none are named in the Act. The Persons who are to act as Returning Officers for several of the New Boroughs are named in the Schedules C and D annexed to the Act; *S.* 11; and as to every New Borough for which no Person is named in either of those Schedules as Returning Officer, the Sheriff of the County in which such

AND DURING BOROUGH ELECTIONS IN ENGLAND. 103

Borough is situated is annually to appoint some Person to be the Returning Officer for that Borough. The first Appointment must be made within Two Months after the passing of the Act, and every succeeding Appointment must be made in the month of March in each year; the Appointment must be in Writing under the hand of the Sheriff, and must be delivered to the Clerk of the Peace within a week after it is made, who is to file it among the Records of his Office. The Person appointed is to act until the nomination of his Successor in the month of March following, but in the event of his Death, or of his becoming incapable to act by reason of Sickness or any other sufficient impediment, the Sheriff on Notice thereof must immediately appoint another person in his stead to act as Returning Officer for the remainder of the current year. *S.* 11. *How they are to be appointed.*

No Person can be appointed Returning Officer for any New Borough, unless he is resident in it at the time of the Appointment; Persons in Holy Orders, and Churchwardens and Overseers within the Borough are disqualified from being appointed; Any Person who has once served the office of Returning Officer under such an Appointment, is exempt for life from serving again for the same Borough. Every Person who possesses the Qualification of a Member of Parliament, may, if appointed by the Sheriff as Returning Officer for any New Borough, exempt himself from serving, *Who are disqualified.*

Who exempt.

if within a week after he shall have received Notice of his Appointment, he shall make Oath of his being so Qualified before a Magistrate, and immediately notify the same to the Sheriff. *S*. 11.

It must be observed that the 11th Section is so framed as to make it compulsory on the Sheriff to appoint, and on the party appointed to act, unless he can bring himself within some one of the exemptions specified; and it is apprehended that a refusal to perform the duty cast upon him by the Statute would subject him to an Indictment.

It is provided by the 11th Section, that in the event of the Crown granting a Charter of Incorporation to any of the New Boroughs not already incorporated, the Mayor or other Chief Municipal Officer named in the Charter, shall thenceforth be the Returning Officer for the Borough.

ELECTIONS FOR BOROUGHS IN WALES. 105

CHAPTER IX.

PROCEEDINGS PREPARATORY TO AND DURING ELEC-TIONS FOR BOROUGHS IN WALES.

According to the Law as it stood before the passing of the Reform Act, all the Voters of the Contributory Boroughs in Wales were obliged to give their Votes at the Principal Boroughs; and the Voters of Newport and Usk, which are the Contributory Boroughs connected with Monmouth, were obliged to give their Votes at Monmouth. The object of the 74th Section of the Act is to establish Regulations for the purpose of enabling and requiring every Person who may be entitled to Vote for the Borough of Monmouth, or for any Principal Borough in Wales, either in respect of a Right accruing in the Borough or in any Contributory Borough, to give his Vote at the Borough or Contributory Borough where his Right accrues. In order to accomplish this object, the Returning Officer of Monmouth, and of each of the Principal Boroughs in Wales, is to appoint a Deputy for the purpose of taking the Poll at each of the Contributory Boroughs, and is to give Notice of the

Regulations for Polling for Monmouth, and for the Welsh Boroughs.

F 5

PROCEEDINGS PREPARATORY TO

day fixed for the Election to every such Deputy, and to deliver to him before the Election a certified Copy of the Register of Voters for the Principal Borough. Where there is a Mayor, Portreeve, or Chief Municipal Officer in a Contributory Borough, the Returning Officer is bound to appoint him as the Deputy. *S.* 74.

At every contested Election for Monmouth, or for any Borough in Wales, the Polling is to commence on the day next after the day fixed for the Election, unless such next day happens to be Saturday or Sunday, and then it is to commence on the Monday following; the Polling is to commence and be carried on simultaneously at the Principal Borough and at all the Contributory Boroughs connected with it, and it is to continue for two days only, such days being successive days, and the Poll is to be kept open for seven hours on the first day, and for eight hours on the second day, and is to be finally closed not later than Four o'clock in the Afternoon of that day. Every Person entitled to Vote in respect of a Right accruing in any Principal Borough must give his Vote at that Borough, and every Person entitled to Vote in respect of a Right accruing in any Contributory Borough must give his Vote at such Contributory Borough before the Deputy appointed to take the Poll there. The Deputies are to take and conduct the Poll, and to deliver or transmit the Poll Books

AND DURING ELECTIONS FOR BOROUGHS IN WALES. 107

to the Returning Officer of the Principal Borough, in the same manner as the Deputies of the Returning Officers for English Boroughs are required to do by the Provisions of the Act, and are to execute the same powers and duties as such Deputies in England.

Loughor, Neath, Aberavon and Kenfig, which by the 10th Section of the Act have, together with Swansea, been formed into one Borough, are for the purposes of Polling treated by the 74th Section as if they were Contributory Boroughs to Swansea; and the Portreeve of Swansea is by the 10th Section declared to be the Returning Officer. *Borough of Swansea.*

The Reform Act has expressly abstained from extending to Monmouth, or to any Boroughs in Wales, the Provisions respecting Booths; but it should seem that the 9 Geo. 4, c. 59, will still apply to every Principal Borough in Wales where the number of Electors shall exceed 600.

With regard to the Borough of Brecon, which has no Contributory Boroughs, it is provided, that the commencement and duration of the Poll are to be the same as in the other Welsh Boroughs. *S.* 74. *Brecon.*

CHAPTER X.

POINTS COMMON TO ALL ELECTIONS, WHETHER FOR COUNTIES OR BOROUGHS.

Certain Points common to Elections for Counties and Boroughs.

THE Proceedings peculiar to Borough Elections in England and Wales having been explained, it will now be necessary to advert to certain points which are common to all Elections, whether for Counties or Boroughs, in England and Wales.

The first of these points relates to the Questions which may arise at the time of Polling as to the Right of any Party to Vote.

Register how far conclusive.

As all the Questions relating to Qualification which used to be disputed before the Assessor at the Poll, may in future be submitted to the Barrister at the time of his Revising the Lists, it seems reasonable that the Register should be regarded as conclusive evidence that every Person, whose Name appears upon it, had, at the time of making up the Lists from which the Register is formed, the Qualification for which he is Registered. On the other hand, it seems equally reasonable that the Register should not be conclusive as to the fact of a Person still *continuing* to have, at the time of Election, the

COUNTY AND BOROUGH ELECTIONS. 109

same Qualification for which he was *originally Registered*. In accordance with this principle, the Act allows that the continuance of the Qualification at the time of Polling may be a subject of inquiry; but in order to give due effect to the Register, and to shorten the duration and diminish the expense of Elections, it only allows two other Questions, besides that of the continuance of the Qualification, to be raised at the time of Polling; so that when a Party tenders his Vote at the Poll, the *only* objections that can be made to his Right to Vote are the three following:—1st. That he is not the same Person whose Name appears on the Register; 2ndly. That he has already voted at the same Election; 3dly. That he does not still retain the *same* Qualification for which his Name was originally inserted in the Register. *S. 58.* The mode of deciding these points is by means of Three Questions, the Forms of which are given in the 58th Section, and a Form of Oath is also given embracing the two first points; the third point, which would be in many cases a Question rather of Law than of Fact, is not included in the Oath; and all former Qualification Oaths, whether under General or Local Acts, are abolished. *S. 58.* These Questions are to be put by the Returning Officer or his Deputy, if required on behalf of any Candidate, to the Voter at the time of his tendering his Vote, and not afterwards; the Oath is to be put to the Voter on the

Three subjects of Inquiry only at the time of Polling.

Mode of Inquiry.

Former Qualification Oaths abolished.

POINTS COMMON TO

same requisition and at the same time, by the Returning Officer or his Deputy, or by a Commissioner appointed by either of them for that purpose. *S.* 58. If the Voter answers the Questions, or such of them as are put to him, in the Affirmative, or takes the Oath when proposed to him, he must be admitted to Vote. Should his Answer to any of these Questions be *wilfully* false, he will be liable to be indicted and punished as for a Misdemeanor, viz. by Fine and Imprisonment, *S.* 58; should he wilfully take a False Oath, he may be punished as for Perjury. *See S.* 52. If he refuses to take the Oath, or if he does not answer such of the Questions as are put to him, to the satisfaction of the Returning Officer or his Deputy, then his Vote must be rejected. *S.* 58.

Certain Oaths, unconnected with Qualification, may be proposed to Voters as heretofore.

There are, however, certain Oaths, unconnected with the Qualification, which are recognized by the 58th Section of the Act as still being in force, and which an Elector may, on proper demand, still be required to take before he can be admitted to Poll; such are the Bribery Oath, the Oaths of Allegiance, Supremacy, and Abjuration, and the Oath prescribed for Roman Catholics by 10 Geo. 4, c. 7, ss. 2 and 5. Of these, however, the Oath against Bribery is the only one which must be taken at the Poll; *see* 2 *Geo.* 2, *c.* 24, *s.* 1, *and* 43 *Geo.* 3, *c.* 74; all the rest may be administered at a separate Place during the Election by Commissioners specially appointed for the purpose under the 34 Geo. 3, c. 73, and the 42

COUNTY AND BOROUGH ELECTIONS.

Geo. 3, c. 62, who are to deliver to each Elector a Certificate of his having taken the Oath or Oaths required, and upon the production of this Certificate at the Poll the Party is to be admitted to Vote.

By the 73d Section of the Reform Act, every Deputy of a Returning Officer is invested with the same power of appointing Commissioners to administer Oaths as the Returning Officer himself possesses under the two Statutes last referred to.

In order to prevent any objection that might perhaps be raised to the Right of any Person to Vote, on the ground that his real Name or Description is not accurately given in the Register, it is provided in the 79th Section of the Act, that no misnomer or inaccurate description of any Person or Place named in the Register shall in anywise prevent or abridge the operation of the Act with respect to such Person or Place, provided the Person or Place intended to be designated by the Register be actually designated so as to leave no doubt of the identity of the particular Person or Place in the minds of Persons in general. *Mere misnomer, &c. in Register not to affect Right of Voting.*

Although no Person can Vote unless his Name be on the Register, yet any Person, who has been excluded from the Register in consequence of the decision of the Barrister, may tender his Vote at any Election at which that Register shall be in force, and the Returning Officer or his Deputy is bound to enter the tender upon the Poll Book, distinguish- *Persons excluded from the Register may tender their Votes.* *Tender to be recorded by Returning Officer.*

112   POINTS COMMON TO

ing all Votes so tendered from Votes actually admitted; the object of this arrangement is, to furnish the means of adding to the Poll the Votes of Parties so circumstanced, in the event of a Petition to the House of Commons.   *S. 59.*

Scrutiny abolished. No Scrutiny is in future to be allowed before the Returning Officer as to any Votes tendered or admitted at any Election.   *S.* 58.

How far the Register may be questioned before a Committee of the House of Commons. Though the Register cannot be questioned at the time of the Election, it may be questioned to a certain extent, on Petition to the House of Commons, before a Select Committee appointed under 9 Geo. 4, c. 22.   As the Committee are meant to be a Court of Appeal from the decision of the Barrister, they can only take cognizance of those cases which have been actually decided by the Barrister; consequently, their inquiry is limited to the cases of those Persons who, after hearing, have been struck off, or retained, or inserted in the Lists by the Barrister; they have no jurisdiction over cases where the Parties have omitted to assert or defend their Claims as Voters in due time, or where the Parties have been allowed to remain on the List of Voters as not having been objected to before the Barrister.   The Committee are to alter the Poll according to their decision upon the different Votes, and the House is to order the Register to be corrected accordingly. *S.* 60.

Power to Although the Act has fixed a certain period for

COUNTY AND BOROUGH ELECTIONS. 113

the duration of the Poll, the Returning Officer or *close the Poll before the time fixed by the Act.* his Deputy will be justified in closing the Poll before the expiration of that period under any circumstances which would have justified him in so doing under the Law as it stood before the passing of the Act. *S.* 70.

The Act contains an entirely new Provision as to *Adjournment of Poll in case of Riot.* the course to be pursued by the Returning Officer in the event of the Proceedings at the Election being interrupted by Riots; in such case he is not finally to close the Poll, but is to adjourn the Poll at the particular Polling Place where the Riot has occurred; He is to adjourn it in the first instance till the next day only, and then, if necessary, for any further time until the disturbances shall have ceased, when he is again to proceed with the Polling at the Place where the interruption occurred. Wherever the Poll shall be adjourned by any Deputy of a Returning Officer on account of a Riot, he must immediately notify the Adjournment to the Returning Officer, who is not to declare the result of the Election until he has received the Poll Books from the Place at which the Polling shall have been adjourned. *S.* 70. Any day on which there shall be an Adjournment of the Poll on account of Riot, is not to be considered, as regards the particular Place at which there is such Adjournment, as one of the Two Polling Days prescribed by the Act. *S.* 70.

CHAPTER XI.

EXPENSES INCIDENT TO REGISTRATION IN COUNTIES
AND BOROUGHS, AND PENALTIES FOR NEGLECT OF
DUTIES UNDER THE ACT.

Remuneration of Barrister for Revising the Lists.

THE Remuneration of the Barristers appointed to Revise the Lists of Voters, both for Counties and Boroughs, is to be at the rate of Five Guineas *per diem*, in addition to their travelling and other expenses—viz. those incurred in the Publication of Notices and Advertisements as required by the Act; In some places also they will, perhaps, find it necessary to hire a Room in which to hold their Court. Each Barrister, after the termination of his Last Sitting, must lay an account before the Lords of the Treasury, stating the number of Days occupied by him in Revising the Lists, and the whole Expenses incurred by him in respect of his Employment; and the Lords of the Treasury will make an Order for the Payment of the Sum that may appear to be due to him. *S.* 57.

Copies of the Lists and Registers to be printed for Sale.

By the 55th Section of the Act, the Overseers of every Parish and Township are required to have

EXPENSES.

Copies written or printed of the Lists of Voters made out by them, and to sell these Copies to all persons applying for them, on payment of a reasonable price for each Copy; the proceeds of the Sale to be paid over to the Poor Rate. The Clerks of the Peace in Counties are also, by the same Section, required to have copies written or printed of the Registers of Voters for their respective Counties, or for the Ridings, Divisions, or Parts of their respective Counties, as the case may be; and the Returning Officers in Boroughs are to have Copies written or printed of the Registers of Voters for their Boroughs; and each Clerk of the Peace, and each Returning Officer, is to sell these Copies at a reasonable price to all persons applying for them, and to pay over the proceeds of the Sale to the County Treasurer.

For the purpose of defraying the Expenses attending the County Lists and Registers, and the Borough Lists and Registers, the following course is prescribed by the 56th Section of the Act: every County Voter, upon giving Notice of his Claim under the 37th Section, must pay one shilling to the Overseers, who are to add all sums so paid to the money applicable to the Relief of the Poor. Every Borough Voter named in the Register for the time being is made liable to the annual payment of a Shilling, which is to be collected from him in ad-

Mode of defraying expenses of Overseers, Clerks of Peace, &c. connected with Registration.

EXPENSES.

dition to and as part of his Poor Rate; and all sums so collected are to be applicable to the Relief of the Poor. These sums, from County and Borough Voters, having thus been thrown into the Poor Rate, the Poor Rate is charged with all the Expenses incurred by the Overseers in making out, printing, and publishing the County and Borough Lists, and in executing the various Duties imposed upon them by the Act; the Returning Officer's Expenses in making out the Borough Register, and in having Copies of it printed, are to be defrayed out of the Poor Rates of the several Parishes and Townships in the Borough, each Parish and Township contributing in proportion to the number of its Rate Payers placed on the Register. The effect of the foregoing arrangement is, that, if the Receipts exceed the Expenses of the Overseers and Returning Officers, the Poor Rate will have the benefit of the Surplus; but if the Expenses exceed the Receipts, the Poor Rate will be chargeable with the Difference. By blending these sums with the Poor Rate, the Overseers in passing their Parochial Accounts will be obliged to account for their Receipt and Expenditure under this Section, as well as for the proceeds of the Sales of Lists directed by the 55th Section. The Expenses incurred by the Clerk of the Peace in making up the County Register from the Lists, and in having Copies of it written or printed, and in

EXPENSES. 117

executing the various duties imposed upon him by the Act, are to be paid by the County Treasurer; but to warrant such payment the Account of these Expenses must have been audited and allowed at the first Quarter Sessions after they shall have been incurred. *S. 56.* The proceeds of the Sale of the Copies of the County Register are, by the 55th Section, o be paid to the County Treasurer. As the County Rate is payable out of the Poor Rate, this Provision as to the Expenses of the County Register is substantially uniform with the corresponding Provision as to Borough Registers, and enables the Clerk of the Peace to obtain payment from one specific fund, and from one person, (viz. the County Treasurer,) without the impracticable process of apportioning and collecting the Sum to be contributed by each particular Parish throughout the County.

With a view to enforce the fulfilment of their duties upon all the persons who are to be employed in executing the Provisions of the Act, the Legislature has provided, by the 76th Section, that any Sheriff, Returning Officer, Barrister, Overseer, or any person whatsoever, wilfully contravening or disobeying any of the Provisions of the Act, with respect to any matter which he is thereby required to do, shall be liable to a Penalty not exceeding £500, the amount to be assessed by the Jury before whom the Action shall be tried. This Action for

Penalties on Officers and others for neglect of Duties under the Act.

113 PENALTIES.

the Penalty can be brought only by a person being an Elector or claiming to be so, or by a Candidate or Member returned, or by some other Party aggrieved. It is expressly provided, however, that this penal Action, so far as regards the Returning Officer, shall not supersede any existing Remedy against him.

PROCEEDINGS UNDER THE ACT. 119

CHAPTER XII.

PROCEEDINGS UNDER THE ACT FOR THE YEAR 1832.

AT the time of the passing of the Reform Act it being uncertain whether the Boundary Act would pass within such time as to allow the proceedings preparatory to Registration to take place at the several times named for that purpose in the different Sections of the Reform Act, it was provided by the 80th Section that, in the event of the Boundary Act passing at any time in the year 1832 subsequently to the 20th of June, the various dates for all the proceedings connected with the first Registration under the Reform Act should be settled by an Order in Council, substituting other dates in lieu of the dates specified in the Act. It is, however, expressly provided in the latter part of the Section, that this substitution of dates shall not extend to vary the day with reference to which the Qualifications of Electors are throughout the Act directed to be measured and ascertained: So that the Last Day of July, although no longer the day for completing the Lists for the year 1832, will continue to be the day on which the Qualification of every Voter seeking to

Dates for first Registration in the year 1832 fixed by Order in Council.

Day by which Qualification is measured not varied.

120 PROCEEDINGS UNDER THE ACT

be registered in the year 1832 must be complete and perfect.

The Boundary Act having received the Royal Assent on the 11th of July, 1832, an Order in Council was made on the same day in pursuance of the power contained in the 80th Section of the Reform Act. A Copy of the Order in Council is subjoined to this Chapter.

Provision for the event of a Dissolution of Parliament before first Registration is completed. In the event of a Dissolution of Parliament taking place in the year 1832, before the day on which the first Register of Voters to be completed under the Act is to come into operation, (which day, according to the effect of the Order in Council, will be the 2d of December, 1832,) it is provided by the 81st Section, that all the Provisions of the Act, (except as to the Duration of Polls, which is to remain the same as it was under the Old Law) shall take effect without Registration; and at an Election under such circumstances the Returning Officer is to admit such Persons only to Vote as would on the Day of Election be entitled to be inserted in the Lists of Voters, if that Day of Election were the Day for making out those Lists.

Thus.—If an Election were to take place on the Last Day of September in the year 1832, the Returning Officer would, in every disputed case, be bound to measure the Qualification of the Voter as to length of Possession, Residence, &c. by the Last Day of September, and not by the Last Day of July.

FOR THE YEAR 1832.

By the operation of this Section, therefore, the Lists of Voters to be made out under the Act cannot possibly be used at any Election which may take place before the 2d of December, 1832, that being the day on which the First Register under the Act is to come into operation.

The last Section of the Act, and the Schedule (L.) Section 52. annexed to the Act, were framed with a view to the possibility of a Dissolution of Parliament taking place before the passing of the Boundary Act. That Act having passed, and the contingency provided for being therefore no longer possible, this Section and the Schedule have become inoperative.

ORDER IN COUNCIL.

At the Court at St. James's, the 11*th of July,* 1832,

   Present—

       The King's Most Excellent Majesty in Council.

WHEREAS by an Act passed in the Second Year 2 W. 4, c. 45. sect. 50. of His Majesty's Reign, intituled *An Act to Amend the Representation of the People in England and Wales,* it is, amongst other things, enacted, that if the Act or Acts for settling the Boundaries of Cities, Boroughs, and other Places, and the Divisions

G

ORDER IN COUNCIL

of Counties, as therein-before mentioned, shall be passed in the present Year subsequently to the Twentieth Day of June, then and in such case His Majesty shall, by an Order made with the advice of his most Honourable Privy Council, appoint, in lieu of the Day for the present Year therein-before specified in that behalf, a certain other Day before or upon which the respective Lists of Voters shall be made out, and shall also appoint, in lieu of the several Days and Times for the present Year therein-before specified or limited in that behalf, certain other Days and Times upon or within which all Notices, Claims, Objections, and other matters whatsoever by the said Act now in recital required to be given, delivered, transmitted, done, or performed in relation to such Lists, either before or after the making out of such Lists, shall be respectively given, delivered, transmitted, done, and performed; and His Majesty shall also by such Order appoint, in lieu of the Period for the present Year therein-before limited in that behalf, a certain other Period for the Revision of the respective Lists of Voters by the Barristers, and shall also appoint within what Time, in lieu of the Time for the present Year therein-before limited in that behalf, such respective Lists shall be copied out into Books, and, where necessary, delivered to the Sheriff or Under Sheriff, and from what Day, in lieu of the Day for the present Year therein-before specified in that behalf,

FOR THE YEAR 1832.

such respective Books shall begin to be in force as the Registers of Voters; and His Majesty may also by such Order in Council appoint any Days and Times for doing the several and other matters required or authorized by the said Act now in recital, in lieu of the several Days and Times for the present Year therein-before specified; and all Days and Times so appointed by His Majesty as aforesaid shall be deemed to be of the same force and effect as if they had in every instance been mentioned in the said Act now in recital, in lieu of the Days and Times for the present Year therein-before specified in that behalf: And whereas the Act for settling the Boundaries of Cities, Boroughs, and other Places, and the Divisions of Counties, was not passed before the Twentieth Day of June in the present Year, but the same hath been passed subsequently thereto in the present Year, that is to say, on this Eleventh Day of July, under the Title of, (1) *An Act to settle and describe the Divisions of Counties and the Limits of Cities and Boroughs in England and Wales, in so far as respects the Election of Members to serve in Parliament;* His Majesty is thereupon pleased, by and with the advice of his most Honourable Privy Council, in pursuance of the power vested in His Majesty by the said Act for amending the Representation of the People in England and Wales, to order and appoint, and it is

(1) 2 & 3 Will. 4, c. 64.

G 2

ORDER IN COUNCIL

hereby ordered and appointed, so far as relates to Counties, Ridings, Parts, and Divisions of Counties, as follows ; (that is to say,)

Sect. 37.

In lieu of the Twentieth Day of June in the present Year, being the Day on which the Overseers are directed by the said Act to give a Notice according to the Form numbered (1.) in the Schedule (H.) to the said Act annexed, His Majesty, by and with the advice aforesaid, doth appoint the Twenty-fifth Day of July in the present Year ; and in lieu of the Last Day of July mentioned in the said Notice, His Majesty, by and with the advice aforesaid, doth order the Last Day of August to be substituted therein ; and in lieu of the Twentieth Day of July mentioned in the said Notice, His Majesty, by and with the advice aforesaid, doth order the Twentieth of August to be substituted therein.

Sect. 37.

In lieu of the Twentieth Day of July in the present Year, being the Day on or before which Persons are by the said Act required to deliver or transmit a Notice according to the Form numbered (2.) in the said Schedule (H.), His Majesty, by and with the advice aforesaid, doth appoint the Twentieth Day of August in the present Year.

Sect. 38.

In lieu of the Last Day of July in the present Year, on or before which the Overseers are by the said Act required to make out a List according to the Form numbered (3.) in the said Schedule (H.), His Majesty, by and with the advice aforesaid, doth

FOR THE YEAR 1832.

appoint the Last Day of August in the present year.

And in lieu of the Twenty-fifth Day of August in the present year, being the Day on or before which every Person entitled to object is required by the said Act to give a Notice according to the Form numbered (4.) in the said Schedule (H.), and also a Notice according to the Form numbered (5.) in the said Schedule (H.), His Majesty, by and with the advice aforesaid, doth appoint the Twenty-fifth Day of September in the present Year. *Sect. 39.*

And in lieu of the Two Sundays next preceding the Fifteenth Day of September in the present year, being the Days on which the Overseers are required by the said Act to cause Copies of the List according to the Form numbered (6.) in the said Schedule (H.) to be fixed on or near the Doors of Churches and Chapels, His Majesty, by and with the advice aforesaid, doth appoint the Two Sundays next preceding the Fifteenth Day of October in the present year. *Sect. 39.*

And in lieu of the Ten Days next preceding the Fifteenth Day of September in the present Year, appointed by the said Act for the Perusal of a Copy of the Names objected to, His Majesty, by and with the advice aforesaid, doth appoint the Ten Days next preceding the Ffteenth Day of October in the present Year. *Sect. 39.*

ORDER IN COUNCIL

Sect. 40.

And in lieu of the Twenty-ninth Day of August in the present Year, being the Day on which the Overseers are required by the said Act to deliver to the High Constable the List of Voters and the Statement of the Number of Persons objected to, His Majesty, by and with the advice aforesaid, doth appoint the Twenty-ninth Day of September in the present year.

Sect. 41.

And in lieu of the Fifteenth Day of September inclusive, and the Twenty-fifth Day of October inclusive, in the present Year, being the Days between which the Barristers are by the said Act to hold their Courts for the revising of the Lists of Voters, His Majesty, by and with the advice aforesaid, doth appoint the Fifteenth Day of October inclusive, and the Twenty-fifth Day of November inclusive, in the present Year.

And His Majesty, by and with the advice aforesaid, in further pursuance of the power vested in His Majesty by the said Act, doth, so far as relates to Cities and Boroughs, and Places sharing in the Election therewith, order and appoint as follows; that is to say,

Sect. 14.

In lieu of the Last Day of July in the present Year, on or before which the Overseers are by the said Act required to make out Lists according to the Forms numbered respectively (1.) and (2.) in the Schedule (I.) to the said Act annexed, His Majesty,

FOR THE YEAR 1832.

by and with the Advice aforesaid, doth appoint the Last Day of August in the present Year.

And in lieu of the Last Day of July in the present Year, being the Day on or before which the Town Clerks are required by the said Act to make out a List of the Freemen, His Majesty, by and with the Advice aforesaid, doth appoint the Last Day of August in the present Year. *Sect. 46.*

And in lieu of the Twenty-fifth Day of August in the present Year, being the Day on or before which Persons Claiming to have their Names inserted in the List of Voters, or objecting to Persons whose Names have been inserted in such Lists, are by the said Act respectively required to give Notices according to the Forms respectively numbered (4.) and (5.) in the said Schedule (I.), His Majesty, by and with the Advice aforesaid, doth appoint the Twenty-fifth Day of September in the present Year. *Sect. 47.*

And in lieu of the Two Sundays next preceding the Fifteenth Day of September in the present Year, being the days on which the Overseers are required by the said Act to fix, in the manner therein mentioned, Copies of the Lists according to the Forms numbered (6.) and (7.) in the said Schedule (I.), and being the days on which the Town Clerks are also required by the said Act to fix, in the manner therein mentioned, Copies of the Lists according to the Forms numbered respectively (8.) and (9.) in the said Schedule (I.), His Majesty, by and with the *Sect. 47.*

128   ORDER IN COUNCIL

Advice aforesaid, doth appoint the Two Sundays next preceding the Fifteenth Day of October in the present Year.

Sect. 17.   And in lieu of the Ten Days next preceding the Fifteenth Day of September in the present Year, appointed by the said Act for the Perusal of the Copies of the Names of Persons Claiming and Objected to, His Majesty, by and with the Advice aforesaid, doth appoint the Ten Days next preceding the 15th Day of October in the present Year.

Sect. 48.   And in lieu of the Last Day of July in the present Year, being the Day on or before which the Returning Officers of the City of London are by the said Act required to issue Precepts to the Clerks of the Livery Companies for the making out the Lists of Freemen and Liverymen, His Majesty, by and with the Advice aforesaid, doth appoint the Last Day of August in the present Year.

Sect. 48.   And in lieu of the Twenty-fifth Day of August in the present Year, being the Day on or before which Persons Claiming to have their Names inserted in any List of Freemen and Liverymen in the City of London, or Objecting to any Persons as not being entitled to be inserted in any such List, are required by the said Act to give Notices according to the Forms respectively numbered (1.) and (3.) in the Schedule (K.) annexed to the said Act, His Majesty, by and with the Advice aforesaid, doth appoint the Twenty-fifth Day of September in the present Year.

FOR THE YEAR 1832.

And in lieu of the Two Mondays next preceding Sect. 18. the Fifteenth Day of September in the present Year, by the said Act appointed for fixing on the Guildhall and Royal Exchange of the City of London the List according to the Form numbered (2.) in the said Schedule (K.), His Majesty, by and with the Advice aforesaid, doth appoint the Two Mondays next preceding the Fifteenth Day of October in the present Year.

And in lieu of the Ten Days next preceding the Sect. 48. Fifteenth Day of September in the present Year, appointed by the said Act for the Perusal of the Copy of the Names of Persons Claiming as Freemen and Liverymen, His Majesty, by and with the Advice aforesaid, doth appoint the Ten Days next preceding the Fifteenth Day of October in the present Year.

And in lieu of the Fifteenth Day of September in- Sect. 50. clusive, and the Twenty-fifth Day of October inclusive, in the present Year, being the Days between which the Barristers are by the said Act to hold their Courts for revising the Lists of Voters for Cities and Boroughs, His Majesty, by and with the Advice aforesaid, doth appoint the Fifteenth Day of October inclusive, and the Twenty-fifth Day of November inclusive, in the present Year.

And His Majesty, by and with the Advice aforesaid, in further pursuance of the Power vested in His Majesty by the said Act, doth, both as to Counties, Ridings, Parts, and Divisions of Counties, and as to

G 5

ORDER IN COUNCIL

Cities and Boroughs, and Places sharing in the Election therewith, order and appoint as follows; (that is to say,)

Sect. 51.

In lieu of the First Day of June and the Last Day of July in the present Year, being the Days between which the Overseers are by the said Act empowered to Inspect or make Extracts from any Duplicate or Tax Assessment, His Majesty, by and with the Advice aforesaid, doth appoint the Twelfth Day of July and the Last Day of August in the present Year.

And in lieu of the Twenty-fifth Day of October in the present Year, being the Day after which no adjourned Court can be held by any Barrister under the said Act, His Majesty, by and with the Advice aforesaid, doth appoint the Twenty-fifth Day of November in the present Year.

Sect. 54.

And in lieu of the Last Day of October in the present Year, being the Day on or before which the Clerk of the Peace is by the said Act required to cause the Lists of Voters for his respective County, or for the Riding, Parts, or Division of his County, to be copied into a Book, and to complete and deliver such Book, as in the said Act is directed, and being also the Day on or before which the Returning Officer for every City or Borough is by the said Act required to cause the Lists of Voters for such City or Borough to be copied into a Book, and completed, as in the said Act is directed, His Majesty, by and with the Advice aforesaid, doth appoint the First Day of December in the present Year.

FOR THE YEAR 1832. 131

And in lieu of the Last Day of October in the Sect. 54.
present Year, being the Day from and after which
every Book so to be completed as aforesaid is by
the said Act directed to be in force as the Register
of Electors, His Majesty, by and with the Advice
aforesaid, doth appoint the First Day of December
in the present Year as the Day from and after which
every such Book so to be completed as aforesaid
shall be deemed the Register of the Electors to Vote,
after the End of the present Parliament, in the
Choice of a Member or Members to serve in Parliament at any Election which may take place after the
First Day of December in the present Year and before the First Day of November in the Year 1833.

Wm. L. BATHURST.

132   DUTY OF OVERSEERS WITH REGARD TO

CHAPTER XIII.

DUTY OF OVERSEERS WITH REGARD TO MAKING OUT THE LISTS OF COUNTY ELECTORS.

No Person can Vote in the Election for a County, or for any Riding, Parts, or Division of a County, unless his Name is on the Register of Voters for such County, Riding, Parts, or Division. *S.* 26.

Overseers to make out List of Voters;

With a view to the formation of the Register, the Overseers of every Parish and Township in each County, Riding, Parts, or Division, are to make out by *the* (1) *Last day of July* in each year, a List of all the Persons entitled, in respect of Property in their particular Parish or Township, to Vote for the County, Riding, Parts, or Division in which their Parish or Township is;

The first Proceeding to be taken by the Overseers is *upon* (2) *the 20th of June. S.* 37.

To give Notice to Persons Claiming to Vote;

Upon that day in every year they are to have fixed on or near the doors of all the Churches and Chapels (or, if there be no Church or Chapel, in some public

(1) For the year 1832, the day substituted by the Order in Council is *the Last day of August.*

(2) In the year 1832, *the 25th of July.*

LISTS OF COUNTY ELECTORS. 133

and conspicuous Place) within their respective Parish or Township, a Notice in the following Form : (*See Sched.* (*H.*), *No.* 1.)

We hereby give Notice, that we shall, on or before the (1) Last day of July in this year, make out a List of all Persons entitled to Vote in the Election of a Knight or Knights of the Shire for the County of   [*or* for the Riding, Parts, *or* Division of the County of   , *as the case may be*], in respect of Property situate wholly or in part within this Parish [*or* Township]; and all Persons so entitled are hereby required to deliver or transmit to us, on or before the (2) Twentieth day of July in this year, a Claim in Writing, containing their Christian Name and Surname, their Place of Abode, the Nature of their Qualification, and the Name of the Street, Lane, or other like Place wherein the Property in respect of which they Claim to Vote is situated; and if the Property be not situated in any Street, Lane, or other like Place, then such Claim must describe the Property by the Name by which it is usually known, or by the Name of the Tenant occupying the same ; and each of such Persons so Claiming must also at the same time pay to us the Sum of One Shilling.   Persons omitting to deliver or transmit such Claim, or to make such Payment, will be excluded from the Register of Voters for this County [*or* Riding, Parts, *or* Division, *as the case may be*].   [*In subsequent Years after One thousand eight hundred and thirty-two, add the following words*: "But Persons whose Names are now on the Register are not required to make a fresh

(1) In the year 1832, *the Last day of August.*
(2) In the year 1832, *the 20th of August.*

134   DUTY OF OVERSEERS WITH REGARD TO

Claim so long as they retain the same Qualification and continue in the same Place of Abode as described in the Register.]

(Signed)   A. B. ⎫ Overseers of the
             C. D. ⎬ Parish [*or* Town-
             E. F. ⎭ ship] of   .

Persons claiming must transmit or deliver Notice of Claim.   In consequence of this Requisition, all Persons Claiming to be Inserted in the List of County Voters in respect of Property situate wholly or in part in that Parish or Township, must deliver or transmit Notice of their Claim to the Overseers (1) *on or before the 20th of July. S. 37.*

The Notice of Claim will be in the following Form, or to the like effect. (*Sched.* (*H.*), *No. 2.*)

I hereby give you Notice, that I Claim to be inserted in the List of Voters for the County of   [*or* for the Riding, Parts, *or* Division of the County of   , *as the case may be*], and that the particulars of my Place of Abode and Qualification are stated below. Dated the day of   , in the year   .

(Signed)   John Adams.

Place of Abode, Cheapside, London.

Nature of Qualification, Freehold House, [*or* Warehouse, Stable, Land, Field, Annuity, Rent-charge, *&c. as the case may be, giving such a description of the Property as may serve to identify it.*]

Where situate in this Parish [*or* Township], King Street. [*If the Property be not situate in any Street, Lane, or*

(1) In the year 1832, *the 20th of August.*

LISTS OF COUNTY ELECTORS.

135

other like Place, then say, " Name of the Property, High-field Farm," *or,* " Name of the occupying Tenant, John Edwards."]

Each Person giving Notice of Claim, must pay, or cause to be paid, a Shilling to the Overseers; and his Notice will not be deemed valid until he shall have paid it. *See S.* 56.

One Shilling to be paid to Overseers by Persons Claiming.

The Overseers are to proceed to make out, or to cause to be made out, a List, in Alphabetical order, of all Persons entitled, in respect of Property situate wholly or in part in their particular Parish or Township, to Vote for the County, Riding, Parts, or Division in which the Parish or Township is;

Directions for making out List of Voters.

And if there be adjoining to their Parish or Township, in the same County, Riding, Parts, or Division, any Precinct or Place (whether Extra-parochial or otherwise) having no Overseers of the Poor of its own, they must include in the List the Names of all Persons entitled, in respect of Property situate wholly or in part in such Precinct or Place, to Vote for the County, Riding, Parts, or Division in which it is : If any such Precinct or Place adjoins two or more Parishes or Townships in the same County, Riding, Parts, or Division, the Overseers of the least populous (according to the Latest Census at the time) of such Parishes or Townships must include in their List all the Persons entitled in respect of Pro-perty situated wholly or in part within such Precinct or Place :

DUTY OF OVERSEERS WITH REGARD TO

In the year 1832 the List will only include those Persons who have sent in Notice of their Claim; but in every future year it will *also* include all those whose names are on the Register for the time being as County Voters in respect of Property situated in the respective Parish or Township to which the Overseers making out such List belong.

Description of Voter, Name, Property, &c.

In making out the List the Overseers must give the Christian Name and Surname of each Person at full length,—his Place of Abode,—the Nature of his Qualification (that is to say, Freehold House, Copyhold Field, &c., as the case may be),—the Local Description of his Property,—and the Name of the Occupying Tenant (if that be stated in the Person's Claim to Vote). All these particulars will be taken from the Register of the Previous year, if the Person's Name be on such Register; if not, they will be taken from his own Notice of Claim. *S. 38.*

Form of List.

The following is the Form prescribed by the Act, (*Sched.* (*H.*), *No.* 1,) according to which the List is to be made out :

LISTS OF COUNTY ELECTORS.

137

County of   to wit, [*or*   }THE List of Persons entitled to
Riding, Parts, *or* Division of the } Vote in the Election of a Knight
County of   *as the case may be.*] } [*or* Knights] of the Shire for the
County of   [*or* for the   Riding, Parts, *or* Division of the
County of   *as the case may be*], in respect of Property situate
within the Parish of   [*or* Township, *as the case may be*].

Christian Name and Surname of each Voter, at full Length.	Place of Abode.	Nature of Qualification.	Street, Lane, or other like Place in this Parish [orTownship] where the Property is situate, or Name of the Property, or Name of the Tenant.
Adams, John	Cheapside, London,	Freehold House,	King Street.
Alley, James	Long Lane, in this Parish,	Copyhold Field,	John Edwards, Tenant.
Ball, William	Market Street, Lancaster,	Lease of Warehouse for Years,	Duke Street.
Boyce, Henry	Church Street, in this Parish,	50 Acres of Land, as Occupier,	Highfield Farm.

(Signed)   A. B. ⎱ Overseers of the
             C. D. ⎬ said Parish [*or*
             E. F. ⎰ Township].

It must be observed that the Overseers have not
the option of Inserting in, or Rejecting from the List,
the name of any Person who shall have given due
Notice of Claim, or whose Name shall be on the Register of Voters for the time being; They are bound
to insert the name of *every* such person; but they are

138   DUTY OF OVERSEERS WITH REGARD TO

Overseers to put "objected to" opposite the Name of Persons whose Qualification is doubtful. authorized (*see S.* 38) to write on the margin the words " *objected to*" opposite to the Name of any Person on the List, whose Qualification they have reasonable cause to doubt; and this mark will compel the person objected to to prove his Qualification before the Barrister who will Revise the List, as will be presently explained. It may often happen that the Overseers may know of their own knowledge that a particular Person whose Name is on the Register is dead; they must, however, still put his Name on the List, setting the mark " *objected to*" opposite to his Name; and upon its being afterwards shown to the Barrister that the Person is dead, the Name will be expunged. So, although the Overseers have a full conviction that the Claim of any particular Person is entirely without foundation, they must insert his name on the List, writing, of course, " *objected to*" opposite to it.

List to be completed by Last day of July. The List is to be signed by the Overseers, and being thus completed by (1) *the Last day of July,* the Overseers are to have a sufficient number of Copies written or printed, and fixed on or near the Doors of all the Churches and Chapels (or if there be no Church or Chapel, in some public and conspi-

How to be Published. cuous place) in the Parish or Township, on the *two next Sundays after the completion of the List. S.* 38.

They are to keep a true Copy of the List, to which any Person is to have access, without paying any

(1) In the year 1832, *the Last day of August.*

LISTS OF COUNTY ELECTORS. 139

Fee, at all reasonable Hours during the *Two First Weeks after the completion of the List. S. 38.*

The Act has provided, that any Person on the Register of Voters for the time being, or who shall have Claimed to be inserted in any List of Voters for the current year, may Object to any other Person who may have been put on any List for the same County, Riding, Parts, or Division, (it need not be the same List as that on which the Person objecting is,) as not having been entitled on the preceding Last day of July to be put on such List; He must give Notice of his Objection to the Overseers who made out the List in which the name objected to is, in the following or some such Form: (*Sched. (H.), No. 4.*) *Who may Object to Persons on the List.*

To the Overseers of the Parish of [*or* Township, *as the case may be*]. *Form of Objection.*

I hereby give you Notice, That I object to the Name of William Ball being retained in the List of Voters for the County of [*or* for the Riding, Parts, *or* Division of the County of]. Dated the Day of in the Year .

(Signed) A. B. of [*Place of Abode*].

This Notice must be given to the Overseers by (1) *the 25th of August. S. 39.*

The Overseers are then to make out and Sign a List of all the Persons so Objected to in the following Form: (*Sched. (II.), No. 5.*) *Overseers to make out List of Persons objected to.*

(1) In the year 1832, *the 25th of September*.

140 DUTY OF OVERSEERS WITH REGARD TO

The following Persons have been objected to as not being entitled to have their Names retained in the List of Voters for the County of [*or* for the Riding, Parts, *or* Division of the County of].

Christian Name and Surname of each Person objected to.	Place of Abode.	Nature of the supposed Qualification.	Street, Lane, or other like Place in this Parish [or Township] where the Property is situate, or Name of the Property, or Name of the Tenant.
Alley, James,	Long Lane in this Parish,	Copyhold Field,	John Edwards, Tenant.
Ball, William,	Market Street, Lancaster,	Lease of Warehouse for Years,	Duke Street.

(Sighed) A. B.⎫ Overseers of the Parish
C. D.⎬ of [*or* Township,
E. F.⎭ *as the case may be*].

List must be published. This List they must publish by having Copies of it fixed on *the Two Sundays next before* (1) *the 15th of September*, upon or near the Doors of all the Churches and Chapels (or if there be no Church or Chapel, in some public and conspicuous Place,) in their Parish or Township; *S.* 39.

Overseers to keep a copy for general Inspection. They must keep a Copy also of the Names of all the Persons objected to, to which they must allow all Persons to have access at all reasonable Hours

(1) In the year 1832, *the 15th of October.*

LISTS OF COUNTY ELECTORS.

141

during the *Ten days next before* (1) *the 15th of September*, without paying any Fee. *S. 39.*

On (2) *the 29th of August* the Overseers are to deliver the List of County Voters which they have made out, together with a written statement of the Number (not the Names,) of all the Persons objected to (either by themselves or by other Persons) to the High Constable or High Constables of the Hundred or other like District (whatever it may be) to which their Parish or Township belongs. *S. 40.* *Overseers to deliver List of Voters, and Statement, to High Constable.*

The Overseers must have a sufficient number of written or printed Copies made of the List of Voters which they have made out, and they must furnish them at a reasonable price to all Persons applying for them; *S. 55.* *Overseers to have a supply of Copies for Sale at a reasonable price.*

The next Duty of the Overseers is their attendance at the Court to be held by the Barrister who is to Revise the List of County Voters for their Parish or Township: This will be at some time (3) *between the 15th of September (inclusive) and the 25th of October (also inclusive)*, when he will make a Circuit of the County, Riding, Parts, or Division to which their Parish or Township belongs. *Overseers to attend Revising Barrister's Court.*

The Barrister will give Notice of the Time and Place at which he will Revise the List for their Parish or Township by Advertisement in some *Barrister to give Three Days Notice before holding his Court.*

(1) In the year 1832, *the 15th of October.*
(2) In the year 1832, *the 29th of September.*
(3) In the year 1832, *between the 15th of October and the 25th of November.*

DUTY OF OVERSEERS WITH REGARD TO

Newspaper circulating in the County, Riding, Parts, or Division, and by a Notice fixed up *Three clear Days before his Circuit begins* in some conspicuous situation at the Principal Place of Election for the County, Riding, &c. *S.* 41.

Overseers to deliver to Barrister a Copy of List of Parties objected to;

On Attending the Barrister's Court the Overseers must deliver to the Barrister a Copy of the List which they have already made out of all the Persons objected to. *S.* 42.

and to give information on Oath.

They are to Answer, on Oath, all the Questions which the Barrister may think it necessary to put to them for the purpose of Revising their List of Voters. *S.* 42.

As soon as the Barrister has finally settled the List of Voters, the Overseers to whose Parish or Township that List relates have no further duties to perform with reference to the Register of which it is to become a part.

Overseers may inspect Tax Assessments, &c.

It is, however, important to observe that, in order to facilitate the proceedings of Overseers in making out the Lists, they are, upon making application at any reasonable time (1) *between the 1st of June and the Last day of July* to any Officer having the Custody of any Duplicate or Tax Assessment, to have free liberty to inspect it, and to extract any particulars they may think necessary. *S.* 51.

Expenses of Overseers.

For the purpose of defraying the expenses to which Overseers may be put in all these proceed-

(1) In the year 1832, *between the 12th of July and the Last day of August.*

LISTS OF COUNTY ELECTORS.

ings, the following Provisions are made by the Act. All the Shillings which have been received by Overseers on account of Notices of Claim are to be added to the money collected for the Relief of the Poor in their Parish or Township.

. The monies arising from the Sale of Copies of the Lists of Voters are also to be added to the Poor Rate. The Expenses incurred by the Overseers in making out, printing, and publishing the Lists, Notices, &c., and otherwise carrying into effect the Provisions of the Act, are then to be repaid to them out of the Poor Rate for their Parish or Township. *S.* 56. *See also pp.* 114, 15, 16.

The following observations are for the guidance of all Overseers generally, whether as to Counties or Boroughs:

According to the 79th Section of the Act, ex- Interpreta-plaining the interpretation of certain Phrases and tain Terms in Terms used throughout the Act, it is to be under- stood tion of cer-the Act.

That, The Words " Parish or Township" are to extend to every Parish, Township, Vill, Hamlet, District, or Place maintaining its own Poor. *S.* 79.

That, The Words (1) " Overseers of the Poor" are to

(1) The Term " Overseers of the Poor" will of course include the Churchwardens of the Parish, who by virtue of their office are Overseers of the Poor under the 43 Eliz. c. 2.

DUTY OF OVERSEERS WITH REGARD TO

extend to all Persons who by virtue of any office or appointment shall execute the Duties of Overseers of the Poor, by whatever name or title they may be called, and in whatever manner they may be appointed ; *S. 79.*

With respect however to Persons "executing the Duties of Overseers of the Poor," it should seem that the 79th Section, in so explaining the term " Overseers of the Poor," must be taken as referring to those Places in which there are no " Overseers of the Poor" appointed under the 43 Eliz. c. 2, or the 13 and 14 Car. 2, c. 12, or under any Local Act; and also to Places in which, although there are " Overseers of the Poor" so appointed, other Persons are legally charged with Duties coextensive with those of Overseers of the Poor. Wherever there are no Overseers of the Poor appointed under any Statute, then the Duties required by the Reform Act must be discharged by such Persons (whatever be their title or description) as, under any General or Local Act, execute the Duties of Overseers of the Poor.

That, All matters directed by the Act to be done by Overseers may be lawfully done by the major part of the Overseers of any Parish or Township; Where any Notice is by the Act required to be given to the Overseers, it will be sufficient if the

LISTS OF COUNTY ELECTORS.   145

notice be delivered to any one of them, or be left at his place of abode, or at his office or other place for transacting Parochial Business, or shall be sent by the Post, addressed by a sufficient direction to the Overseers of the Parish or Township, or to any one of them, either by their or his Christian name and Surname, or by their or his name of office ; *S.* 79.

It must be observed by Overseers that if they wilfully contravene or disobey any of the Provisions of the Act, with respect to anything it requires of them, they will be liable to be sued, in an Action of Debt, by any party aggrieved ; the Penalty, which Penalty in is to be determined by a Jury, and may be any sum default. not exceeding £500, is, upon conviction to be paid to the party suing, with full costs of suit. *S.* 76.

case of wilf

CHAPTER XIV.

DUTIES OF OVERSEERS WITH REGARD TO THE LISTS OF VOTERS FOR CITIES AND BOROUGHS.

Duties of Overseers different in different Boroughs.

THE Duties of Overseers, as to making out the Lists of Voters, will not be precisely the same in all Cities and Boroughs. The Right of Voting not being uniformly the same, the Task of the Overseers with reference to the Registration of the Persons entitled, will differ accordingly.

How they may be classed.

1stly. In those New Boroughs which will, under the Act, be represented for the first time, the only Right of Voting will be in respect of a £10 Qualification under the 27th Section of the Act, and the Duty of the Overseers will therefore be founded on the Nature of that Qualification.

And in all those Old Boroughs in which the Right has hitherto been in Freemen *only*, the Future Right of Voting will be in Persons who are either Freemen, or have the new £10 Qualification under the 27th Section; The proceedings preparatory to the Registration of Freemen are directed, by the Act, to be conducted by the Town Clerk; The

AS TO BOROUGH VOTERS. 147

Duty of the Overseers will therefore in all these places also be confined to £10 Voters.

2dly. In those Old Boroughs where the Old Right is not in Freemen, or where the Old Right is in other Parties together with Freemen, the Duty of Overseers will be with reference to the new £10 Qualification under the 27th Section, and *also* to the Old Right which, in some Boroughs, will be reserved under the 33d Section, in some under the 31st Section, and in others under both these Sections of the Act.

1. *Duty of Overseers in New Boroughs on which the Right of Representation is conferred by the Act; And in Boroughs where the Old Right of Voting is in Freemen only.*

In both these descriptions of Cities and Boroughs the Duty of Overseers will be only with reference to making out the Lists, &c., of £10 Voters under the 27th Section of the Act, (as the Town Clerk is charged with making out the Lists of the Freemen :)

Duty of Overseers in New Boroughs, and in Boroughs where Right used to be in Freemen only.

The Overseers of the Poor of any Parish or Township situate wholly, or in part, in any such City or Borough, or in any Place sharing in the Election with any such City or Borough, are *on or before the Last day of July* (1) to make out an Al-

(1) In the year 1832 the day substituted by the Order in Council will be *the Last day of August.*

H 2

148   DUTY OF OVERSEERS

To make out an Alphabetical List of 10l. Voters by Last day of July.

phabetical List of All Persons entitled under the 27th Section, (qualified and explained as it is by the 28th, 29th and 30th Sections of the Act,) to Vote for such City or Borough, in respect of the Occupation of Premises of the clear Yearly Value of £10, situate wholly or in part in their Parish or Township; *S. 44.*

If there should happen to be adjoining to their Parish or Township in the same City, Borough, or Place sharing in the Election with it, as the case may be, any Precinct or Place, (whether Extra-

Provision as to Places having no Overseers of their own.

Parochial or not,) without any Overseers of its own, they must consider such Precinct or Place as within their Parish or Township, and must accordingly include in their List the Names of all Persons entitled in respect of the occupation of Property situated wholly or in part within such Precinct or Place; But if such Precinct or Place adjoins any other Parish or Township besides their own in the same City or Borough, &c., they must not consider it as within their Parish or Township, unless theirs be the least populous Parish or Township so adjoining such Precinct or Place;—This they must ascertain from the Latest Census at the time. *S. 45.*

What the List of Voters must contain.

I. the List must be written at full length,

     1st. The Christian Name and Surname of the Voter;

     2dly. The Nature of his Qualification;

AS TO BOROUGH VOTERS.   149

3dly. The Name of the Street, Lane, or other Place in which the Qualifying Property is situated;

The List must be Signed by the Overseers. The following is the Form of List prescribed by the Act. *See S. 44, and Sched.* (I.) *No.* 1.

THE LIST of PERSONS entitled to Vote in the Election of a Member [*or* Members] for the City [*or* Borough] of in respect of Property occupied within the Parish [*or* Township] of by virtue of an Act passed in the Second Year of the Reign of King William the Fourth, intituled "An Act to amend the Representation of the People in England and Wales."

Form of List of Voters.

Christian Name and Surname of each Voter at full Length.	Nature of Qualification.	Street, Lane, or other Place in this Parish where the Property is situate.
Ashton, John . .	House.	Church Street.
Atkinson, William	Warehouse . .	Bolt Court, Fleet Street.
Bates, Thomas .	Shop	Castle Street.
Bull, Thomas . .	Counting-house	Lord Street.

(Signed)   A. B. ⎰Overseers of the
            C. D. ⎱ said Parish [*or*
            E. F. ⎰ Township].

As the Duty of the Overseers in making out this List imposes upon them in the first instance the task of deciding (subject to the Revision of the

150 · DUTY OF OVERSEERS

Barrister in a later stage), who is, and who is not, Qualified under the Act to Vote, some remarks for their assistance in this task will be added at the end of this chapter.

To pursue the order of Dates in which the Overseers are to proceed; The List having been completed *on or before the Last day of July*,(1) they must next have a sufficient number of Copies of the List

Copies of the Lists to be Printed and Fixed on Church Doors &c. printed, and fixed on or near the Doors of all the Churches and Chapels (or if there be no Church or Chapel, in some public and conspicuous situation), in their Parish or Township, *on the Two Sundays next after the Last day of July :* (1)   *S.* 44.

Overseers must keep copies for general inspection. And they must keep true copies of the List, and must allow all Persons without paying any Fee to have access to them, and to read them, at all reasonable hours, *during the Two first Weeks after the Last day of July.*(1)   *S.* 44.

Notice of Claim by Persons Omitted. The Act having provided that Persons Omitted in any List of Borough Voters, may, if they consider themselves entitled to be inserted in it, give Notice of their Claim,—and that any Person whose Name is upon any List of Voters for a City or

Notice by Persons objecting to others. Borough, may object to any other Person who is in any List for the same City or Borough as not being entitled to remain upon the List, It has directed the two following Forms of Notices, in

(1) In the year 1832, *the Last day of August.*

AS TO BOROUGH VOTERS.

Writing, to be given *on or before the* (1) *25th of August*, by such respective classes of Persons to the Overseers who have made out the Particular List with respect to which the Claim or Objection is made. *S.* 47.

1st. The Form of Notice (*Sched.* (I.) *No.* 4) by persons Claiming is as follows:

To the Overseers of the Parish [*or* Township] of

I hereby give you Notice, That I claim to have my Name inserted in the List made by you of Persons entitled to vote in the Election of a Member [*or* Members] for the City [*or* Borough] of , and that my Qualification consists of a House in Duke Street in your Parish, *or otherwise* [*as the case may be*]. Dated the   Day of One thousand eight hundred and thirty- .

(Signed)   John Allen of [*Place of Abode.*]

Form of Notice of Claim;

The Form of Notice (*Sched.* (I.) *No.* 5) to be given to Overseers by Persons Objecting to others is the following:

To the Overseers of the Parish [*or* Township] of [*or otherwise, as the case may be*].

I hereby give you Notice, That I object to the Name of Thomas Bates being retained in the List of Persons entitled to vote in the Election of a Member [*or* Members] for the City [*or* Borough] of , and that I shall bring forward such Objection at the Time of the revising of such List. Dated the   Day of   in the Year .

(Signed)   A. B. of [*Place of Abode.*]

Form of Notice by Objector;

(1) In the year 1832, *the 25th of September.*

DUTY OF OVERSEERS

With reference to these Claims and Objections, which, as has already been stated, are to be given in to the Overseers *on or before the* (1)*25th of August*, the Overseers are to make out Two Lists ;

Overseers to make out List of Claimants,

One List containing the Names of all the persons who have sent in due Notice of Claim on or before (1) the 25th of August ;—

And List of Persons Objected to;

And the other List, containing the Names of all those who have been Objected to, by due Notices of Objection sent in on or before (1) that day. *S.* 47.

The List of Persons Claiming will be in the following Form, (*Sched.* (I.) *No.* 6) :

Form of List of Claimants;

The following Persons claim to have their Names inserted in the List of Persons entitled to vote in the Election of a Member [*or* Members] for the City [*or* Borough] of   .

Christian Name and Surname of each Claimant at full Length.	Nature of Qualification.	Street, Lane, or other Place in this Parish where the Property is situate.
Allen, John.	House.	Duke Street.

(Signed)   A. B.
C. D. } Overseers of, *&c.*
E. F.

(1) In the year 1832, *the 25th of September.*

AS TO BOROUGH VOTERS.

153

The List of Persons Objected to will be in this Form, (*Sched.* (I.) *No.* 7) :

The following Persons have been objected to as not being entitled to have their Names retained in the List of Persons qualified to vote in the Election of a Member [*or* Members] for the City [*or* Borough] of   .

Form of List of Parties Objected to.

Christian Name and Surname of each Person objected to.	Nature of the supposed Qualification.	Street, Lane, or other Place in this Parish where the Property is situate.
Bates, Thomas.	Shop.	Castle Street.

(Signed) A. B.
C. D. } Overseers of, &c.
E. F.

The Overseers must have Copies of both these Two Lists Fixed on or near the Doors of all the Churches and Chapels (or if there be no Church or Chapel, in some public and conspicuous situation) in the Parish or Township *on the Two Sundays next before the* (1)15*th of September.* *S.* 47.

Copies of both such Lists to be Fixed by Overseers on Church Doors, &c.

They must also keep a Copy of the Names of all the Persons Claiming, and a Copy of the Names of all the Persons Objected to ; to each of which Copies

And Copies to be kept by Overseers for general inspection;

(1) In the year 1832, *the* 15*th of October.*

H 5

154 DUTY OF OVERSEERS

they are to allow all Persons, without paying any Fee, to have access at all reasonable hours *during the Ten Days next before the* (1) 15*th of September.* *S.* 47.

Copies to be sold at a Shilling per Copy;

They must have a sufficient Number of Copies made of each of such Lists, and have them ready to deliver to any Person who may apply for one, at the price of a Shilling for each Copy. *S.* 47.

Overseers to attend Revising Barrister's Court;

The next thing to be done by the Overseers is to attend at the Court to be held by the Barrister who is to Revise the Lists of Voters for the City or Borough to which their parish or Township belongs :

This will be at some time to be fixed by the Barrister *between the Fifteenth of September (inclusive),*

Barrister to give Three Days' Notice of Time of holding his Court;

and the 25th of October (inclusive.) (2) Three clear Days' Notice of the precise Time and Place will have been given by Notice fixed up on the Doors of all the Churches and Chapels (if there be any) in the City or Borough, or if there be none, in some public and conspicuous situation. *S.* 50.

Overseers to produce List of Voters at Barrister's First Court;

At the Opening of the Barrister's First Court, the Overseers of each Parish or Township must produce before him the List of Voters which they have made out for their Parish or Township.

They must also produce a Copy of the List of Persons Objected to, and they must be in attendance

(1) In the year 1832, *the* 15*th of October.*
(2) In the year 1832, *between the* 15*th of October and* 25*th of November.*

AS TO BOROUGH VOTERS. 155

during the whole of the Time that their List is under
Revision by the Barrister; and they must answer on
Oath all such Questions as the Barrister in Revising
the List may think it necessary to put to them.
S. 50.

And to give information on Oath.

*2dly. Duty of Overseers in those Old Boroughs where
the Reserved Right is not in Freemen, or if in Freemen, is also in other Parties as well as in Freemen.*

The Overseers of every Parish or Township
situated wholly or in part in any(1) such City or
Borough, or in any Place sharing in the Election
with any such City or Borough, (in addition to
making out the List of £10 Voters in the manner

Overseers to make out List of Voters in respect of Reserved Right.

(1) There is a special Provision with regard to the making
out of the Lists of those Persons who may be entitled to vote for
the Borough of *Shoreham* in respect of any Freeholds situate in
the Borough of *Horsham,* or for the Borough of *Cricklade,* in
respect of any Freeholds situate in the Borough of *Malmsbury.*
This Provision is, that the Overseers of that Parish or Township
in the Borough of *Shoreham* or *Cricklade* (as defined by the 5th
Section of the Act) which next adjoins the Parish or Township
of the Borough of *Horsham* or *Malmsbury* in which the Qualifying Freeholds are situated, shall make out the List of Persons
entitled to vote in respect of such Freeholds for *Shoreham* or
Cricklade. And if the Parish or Township in the Borough of
Horsham or *Malmsbury* happens to adjoin more than one Parish
in *Shoreham* or *Cricklade* as defined by the Act, then the Overseers of the least populous (according to the Latest Census at
the Time) of such adjoining Parishes in *Shoreham* or *Cricklade*
must make out the List of these Freeholders. *S.* 34.

DUTY OF OVERSEERS

directed in the former part of this Chapter,) are, *on or before* (1)*the Last Day of July,* to make out an Alphabetical List of All Persons (except Freemen) entitled to vote for the City or Borough in respect of any Reserved Right under the 31st or 33d Section, or under both these Sections, as the case may be.

Provision as to Places having no Overseers;

In making out this List they must note that, if there is adjoining to their Parish or Township, within the same Borough, (or Contributory Borough, if it be one,) any Precinct or Place without Overseers of its own, they are to consider it as within their Parish or Township, and are to include in their List the Names of all Persons entitled to vote in respect of the occupation of Property situated wholly or in part within that Precinct or Place. If, however, the Precinct or Place adjoins any other Parish or Parishes besides their own in the same Borough, (or Contributory Borough, if it be one,) they must ascertain, from the latest Population Census at the time, whether their Parish or Township is the least populous of the Parishes or Townships so adjoining the Precinct or Place; If it be so, but not otherwise, they must consider the Precinct or Place as within their Parish or Township. *S.* 45.

What the List must contain.

In making out their List the Overseers must take care to give at full length the Christian Name and Surname of each Voter; and, if the Reserved Right

(1) In the year 1832, *the Last Day of August.*

AS TO BOROUGH VOTERS. 157

be in respect of Property, they must give the Name of the Street or Lane, or other like place, in which the Voter's qualifying Property is; and where the Reserved Right is not in respect of Property, they must state the Place of his abode;

The List will be in the following Form.

The List of all Persons (not being Freemen) entitled to vote in the Election of a Member [or Members] for the City [or Borough] of   in respect of any Rights other than those conferred by an Act passed in the Second Year of the Reign of King William the Fourth, intituled, " An Act to amend the Representation of the People in England and Wales." *Form of List.*

Christian Name and Surname of each Voter at full Length.	Nature of Qualification.	Street, Lane, or other Place in this Parish where the Property is situate. *If the Right of Voting does not depend on Property, then state the Place of Abode.*
Atkins, John	Pot-Walloper	John Street.

(Signed)   A. B.   Overseers of the Parish
C. D.   of   [or Township] within the said
E. F.   City [or Borough].

See S. 44, and Form (No. 2) in Sched. (1.)

DUTY OF OVERSEERS

List to be Published.

This List is to be signed by the Overseers, and they are to have a sufficient Number of Copies of it printed and fixed on or near the Doors of all the Churches and Chapels (or, if there be no Church or Chapel, in some public and conspicuous situation) in their Parish or Township *on the Two Sundays next after the Day appointed for the Completion of the List.* S. 44.

Copies to be kept for inspection.

They must keep true Copies of the List, and must allow all Persons to inspect them, *Gratis*, at all reasonable hours *during the Two first weeks after the time appointed for the Completion of the List.* S. 44.

The Overseers will receive, *on or before* (1)*the 25th of August,* Notices in writing from Persons who, being omitted in their List of Voters in respect of the Reserved Right, claim to be entitled to have their Name inserted in it; S. 47. These Notices will be in the Form, (Sched. (I.) No. 4), which has been given in the preceding part of this Chapter, of Notices of Persons claiming as £10 Voters, p. 151.

Notices by Parties Claiming.

Notices by Parties Objecting to others.

They will also receive, *on or before* (1)*the 25th of August,* Notices in writing from Persons who, being themselves on some List of Voters for the City or Borough, object to other Persons whom the Overseers have inserted in their List of Voters in respect of the Reserved Right, as not being entitled to have their Names retained upon that List. *S.* 47.

(1) In the year 1832, *the 25th of September.*

AS TO BOROUGH VOTERS. 159

These Notices will be in the same form as that already given, in the former part of this Chapter, of Notices by Persons objecting to others as not being entitled to have their Names retained upon the List of £10 Voters, p. 151.

It will be the duty of the Overseers to include all the Names of these Two Classes of Persons in the Two Respective Lists which in the former part of this Chapter they have been directed. to make out and to publish on *the Two Sundays next before* (1)*the 15th of September,*—viz. of Parties Claiming and of Parties objected to. *See pages,* 152, 153. But they must observe, as to both these Lists of Claimants and Parties Objected to, that, where the Reserved Right is not in Respect of Property, they are to state in the third Column of the List the Place of abode of the Party.

(marginal note: Duty of Overseers as to these Claims and Objections.)

As there will be no distinct List of Parties claiming in respect of the Reserved Right as apart from those claiming as £10 Voters ; nor any distinct List of Parties objected to as not entitled in respect of the Reserved Right as apart from those objected to as not being entitled as £10 Voters, but there will be only one List for each Parish or Township of Parties Claiming, and one List of Parties Objected to, it would be a needless repetition to give any further details as to the mode in which the Overseers

(1) In the year 1832, *the 15th of October.*

160

DUTY OF OVERSEERS

are to proceed with regard to these Lists, as it has been fully explained in the earlier part of this Chapter.

Having thus gone through, in their order of date, the different Proceedings to be carried into effect by the Overseers in Cities and Boroughs, those Points upon which it would seem that they may possibly require observations somewhat more specific by way of direction, remain to be noticed.

In order to assist Overseers in Cities and Boroughs in ascertaining the Rights of Parties to be inserted in their List, it may be useful to consider what are the several Points constituting a Qualification under the 27th Section. That Section requires that a Party, in order to be qualified, must—

Examination of the 27th Section, with a view to assist Overseers in Acting under it.

1st. Be the Occupier of a House, Warehouse, Counting House, Shop, or other Building, situated wholly or in part within the City, or Borough, or Place sharing in the Election with it;

2dly. He must be Rated to the Poor Rate in respect of such House, Warehouse, &c.;

3dly. He must have occupied *and* he must have been rated for Twelve Months next previous to the *Last day of July;*

4thly. He must have paid by *the 20th of July*, all the Poor Rates and Assessed Taxes which shall have become payable from him in respect of the House, Warehouse, &c. previously to *the 6th day of April* then next preceding;

AS TO BOROUGH VOTERS.

161

5thly. The House, Warehouse, &c. must either of itself, or together with any Land in the City, Borough, or Place, occupied therewith by him as Owner, or occupied therewith by him as Tenant under the same Landlord, be of the clear yearly Value of £10;

Lastly. The Party must have resided within the City, Borough, or Place, or within Seven Miles of it, for Six Months next previous to *the Last day of July.*

As to the 1st and 2d Points, the Overseers by going through the Rate Book will readily see what Persons are Rated as Occupiers of Houses, Warehouses, &c. and they will by the same means ascertain the Local description of each such House, Warehouse, &c.

How they are to ascertain who are Rated Occupiers.

As to the 3d Point, viz. the *Rating and Occupation for Twelve Months,* they will probably be obliged to refer to the preceding Rate; they must observe that the Act does not require the Premises to be *the same* Premises during the whole Time of Rating and Occupation; the Premises may be *different,* provided they are each of the proper Description and Value, *and* have been occupied in immediate Succession, *and* provided all the Poor Rates and Assessed Taxes which shall have become payable in respect of each of such Premises before the preceding 6th of April from the Party who is to gain the Qualification, shall have been paid by him by

As to Time of Rating and Occupation.

DUTY OF OVERSEERS

the 20th of July in the same year. *S. 28.* It should seem that the several Premises so occupied in Succession, may be of a different kind, provided each be of a Description specified in the Act; for instance, the same person may, during the course of the Twelve Months next before the Last Day of July, have occupied a £10 House for Three Months, —then a £10 Warehouse for Six Months,—and then a Shop being, together with some Land in the Borough occupied under the same Landlord, worth £10 for the remaining Three Months; If he has been rated in respect of each of such Premises, to every Poor Rate made during his Occupation of them, and has paid by the 20th of July whatever was due from him before the 6th of April, in respect of the Rates upon Each, the Overseers must insert him in the List: Any Assessed Taxes that may have become due from him before the 6th of April, in respect of the House, must also have been paid by him by the 20th of July. (1)

(1) But it would not seem to be sufficient, in order to give a Qualification, that the Required Value of £10 should be made up of more than one description of Premises; that is to say, a House of the Value of £7, together with a Warehouse of the Value of £3, would not make up a Qualification; It must be *a* House worth £10, or *a* Warehouse worth £10, or some one of the different kinds of Premises specified in the Act of the Value of £10: except that of course in any case the Value may be made up by Land jointly occupied with the House, Warehouse, &c.

AS TO BOROUGH VOTERS.

As to the 4th Point, *i. e.* the *Payment of the Rates and Taxes*, that fact will in general be noted in the Rate Book, or may be ascertained through the Parish Collector, from whom may be obtained the precise Date of the Payment; In the same way the Government Collector will be able to supply the Information required as to the Payment of the Assessed Taxes. In those Places where the Assessed Taxes and the Poor Rates are collected by the same Individuals, the Overseers will have much less trouble as to this Point. (1)

As to the 5th Point, viz. *Value;* the Scale on which the Rate has been made is well known to the Overseers, that is, whether it is an Assessment on the Full Value, or on Two-Thirds, or on Three-Fourths, or any other Proportion of the Full Value of the Property. The Overseers, being bound to regard the *Actual Value* of the Property, and not the Value assumed in the Rate Book, will include in their List the Occupiers of every House, Ware-house, &c. of such a Value, that its assessed Value in the Rate Book amounts to Two-Thirds or Three-Fourths (or whatever the Scale of the Assessment

---

(1) If a Party has failed to pay by the 20th of July, all the Poor Rates and Assessed Taxes which shall have become pay-able from him in respect of the Qualifying Premises, before the preceding 6th of April, it should seem that the Overseers must exclude him from their List, even although his Rates or Taxes have never been formally demanded. *See Chap. IV*. p. 32.

DUTY OF OVERSEERS

may be) of £10; Thus, if the Premises be assessed at £8, where the Rate has been made on an Assessment of Four-Fifths of the Full Value, the Overseers will include the Occupier of such Premises, because the Actual Value is to be taken at £10. Of course if the Assessed Value of the Premises be £10, there can be no question but that the Occupier is to be included in the List.

As to Joint Occupiers.

With regard to Premises jointly occupied by several Persons as Partners or otherwise, the Act has laid down a Rule for ascertaining the Value of each Occupier's Share; That Rule is, that the *total* Value of the Property is to be divided by the Number of Joint Occupiers, and if it gives £10 for each Occupier, then each will be qualified to vote; but if it give less than £10 for each, then no one of them will have a right to vote; so that whatever the disproportion of Shares as between the Occupiers themselves may be, all will be equally disqualified: Thus, where Three Persons, A., B., and C., jointly occupy Premises worth only £28 a year, although the Share of A. may be worth £12, and that of B. worth £10, no one of the Three will vote, because the entire Value, viz. £28, divided by Three, will not give £10 for each.

As to Residence.

As to the 6th Point, *Residence*, the Overseers and Parish Collectors have generally an opportunity of knowing whether the Persons included in the Rate

AS TO BOROUGH VOTERS.

165

reside within the requisite distance : It has already been stated, that the Seven Miles within which the Residence is to be measured, are to be taken as Seven Miles *according to the nearest way of access :* which may be defined as that which a Person making the best of his way from Point to Point would be likely to take ; that is, using the Footway where there is one, and where it is most convenient to use, and the Carriage Way where it can be most conveniently used, or where there is no Footpath. *See Chap. IV.* p. 35.

The Residence must be an actual and habitual, and not occasional or fictitious Residing; and where the Residing is interrupted by Absence, such Absence must be merely temporary, and consistent with a real intention to come back and reside in the particular City, Borough or Place, or within the Seven Miles appointed for the Limit of Residence. See p. 52.

Having thus shortly considered how the Overseers are to act with reference to Voters under the 27th Section, it may be useful to examine the nature of their Duties under the Act as to a Reserved Right of Voting : as for instance, where there is a Reserved Right in Inhabitants paying Scot and Lot. According to the Old Law, a Person Voting in respect of that right, must have been rated as an Inhabitant of the Borough for Six Calendar

How the Overseers are to ascertain who have the Reserved Right.

DUTY OF OVERSEERS

Months previous *to the day of Election,* (1) and he must have paid his Rates before Voting, (if demanded.) Those persons, therefore, who had not been Rated as Inhabitants, (unless it could be shown that they were Rateable, and had been fraudulently omitted from the Rate,) or, who having been so Rated, had failed to pay their Rates when demanded, had no right to Vote *on the Day of Election.* The Overseers, then, in making out the List of these persons up to the *Last day of July,* must act upon the same rule as if that day were the Day of Election ; and if a person has not been Rated as Inhabitant within the Borough for Six Calendar Months previous *to the Last day of July,* or if, although a Rated Inhabitant for that time, he has not paid by the *Last day of July* the Rates demanded of him, the Overseers are not to insert him in the List of Persons whose Rights are Reserved under the Act. And this Rule they must adhere to in the year 1832 as well as in succeeding years ; for although for the year 1832 the day for making up the Lists is not the Last day of July, but the Last day of August, it is expressly directed, as has already been observed, by the 80th Section of the Act, that the day by which the Qualification is to be measured is still to be the same in the year 1832 as in succeeding years.

(1) 26 Geo. 3, c. 100.

AS TO BOROUGH VOTERS. 167

It must be remembered, however, that as to all Reserved Rights the Act requires a Residence for Six Months next before the *Last day of July* within Seven Miles of that which used to be the Polling Place for the particular Borough, (and, in the case of any Contributory Borough, within Seven Miles of the place specified for the purpose in Sched. (E. 2.).

In addition to these suggestions for the use of (1)Overseers as to Borough Lists, there are some general observations applicable to all Overseers, whether as to Counties or as to Boroughs, which have been made in a preceding Chapter, to which it will be expedient for them to advert. *See Chapter XIII. pp.* 143, 144, 145.

(1) It must be observed, that as to the *City of Oxford*, and the *Town of Cambridge*, no person will be entitled to be inserted in the List of Voters for either of those places in respect of any Chambers or Premises in any of the Colleges or Halls of either University. *S.* 78.

163   DUTY OF TOWN CLERKS.

CHAPTER XV.

DUTY OF TOWN CLERKS IN PLACES WHERE FREEMEN HAVE A RIGHT TO VOTE.

Town Clerk to make out List of Freemen.

THE Town Clerk (1) of every City or Borough sending a Member or Members to Parliament is, *on or before the Last day of July* (2) in each year, to have an Alphabetical List made out of all the Freemen of the City or Borough entitled to vote in the Election for it. The List must contain the Place of Abode of each Freeman.   *S.* 46.

Town Clerk of Contributory Borough to make out a like List.

The Town Clerk of every place sharing in the Election for any City or Borough must have made

(1) The Act directs that when there is no Town Clerk in any Borough or Contributory Borough, in which Freemen have a Right to Vote, the matters required to be done by and with regard to the Town Clerk, are to be done by and with regard to the Person executing Duties similar to those of the Town Clerk; or if there be no such Person, then by and with regard to the Chief Civil Officer of that Borough or Contributory Borough. *S.* 46.

There is also a Provision specially applicable to the Freemen of *Swansea, Loughor, Neath, Aberavon, and Ken-fig.* The Right which a Freeman of any of those places would, but for the passing of the Act, have had to vote for *Cardiff*, is transferred to the New Borough composed of those Five Towns, so that he will be entitled to Vote, not for *Cardiff*, but for that New Borough, if he satisfy all the requisitions of the Act as to Freemen in Contributory Boroughs. *S.* 32.

(2) In the year 1832, *the Last day of August.*

DUTY OF TOWN CLERKS.

169

out, on or before the same day, a like List of all the Freemen of that Place who may be entitled to vote in the Election for the City or Borough with which it shares. *S.* 46.

The List must be in the following Form :—

The LIST of the FREEMEN of the City [*or* Borough] of [*or* of   being a Place sharing in the Election with the City [*or* Borough] of   ] entitled to vote in the Election of a Member [*or* Members] for the said City [*or* Borough].

Form of List.

Christian Name and Surname of each Freeman, at full Length.	Place of his Abode.
Aston, William,	Market Street, Lancaster.

(Signed)   A. B.   { Town Clerk of the said City [*or* Borough, *or* Place.]

The List when made must be fixed on or near the Door of the Town Hall, or in some public and conspicuous situation within the particular City, Borough, or Place *on the Two Sundays next after the List shall have been made.* *S.* 46.

List to be Published, how.

The Town Clerk must keep a true Copy of the List, which he must allow all Persons to peruse, **gratis**, at all reasonable hours during *the Two First Weeks after the List shall have been made.* *S.* 46.

Copy to be kept for Inspection.

I

170 DUTY OF TOWN CLERKS.

Notice of Claims by Persons omitted.

The Act having provided that any Person claiming to be entitled to Vote as a Freeman may, if omitted from any List, give Notice of his Claim, has directed every such Person to send in a Notice of his Claim, *on or before the 25th of August,* (1) to the Town Clerk of the particular City, Borough, or Place of which he is a Freeman, in the following Form :—

Form of Notice of Claim.

To the Town Clerk of the City [*or* Borough] of
[*or otherwise, as the Case may be.*]

I hereby give you Notice, That I claim to have my Name inserted in the List made by you of Persons entitled to vote in the Election of a Member [*or* Members] for the City [*or* Borough] of   and that my Qualification is as a Freeman of   and that I reside in Lord Street in this City [*or* Borough].   Dated the   day of   one thousand eight hundred and thirty-
(Signed)   John Allen of [*Place of Abode.*]

Notice of Objection.

The Act has also empowered any Person, who is himself upon *any* List of Voters for any City or Borough, to object to any Person whose name is upon any List of Freemen of that City or Borough, or of any Place sharing in the Election with it, by sending, *on or before* (1) *the 25th of August,* to the Town Clerk of the particular City, Borough, or Place, a Notice in the following Form :—

(1) In the year 1832, *the 25th of September.*

DUTY OF TOWN CLERKS.   171

To the Town Clerk of the City [or Borough] of   Form of No-
    [or otherwise, as the Case may be.]   tice of Ob-
                                                jection.

I hereby give you Notice, That I object to the Name of
Thomas Bates being retained in the List of Persons entitled to vote in the Election of a Member [or Members]
for the City [or Borough] of   and that I shall
bring forward such Objection at the Time of the revising
of such List. Dated the   day of   in
the year
             (Signed)   A. B. of [Place of Abode].

The Town Clerk must make a List of all the Town Clerk
Persons who have sent in their Claims, which List to make Lists
of Claimants.
will be in the following Form :—

The following Persons claim to have their Names inserted Form of List.
    in the List of the Freemen of the City [or Borough] of
         [or of   being a Place sharing in the
Election with the City [or Borough] of   ], entitled
to vote in the Election of a Member [or Members] for
the said City [or Borough].

Christian Name and Surname of each Claimant at full Length.	Place of his Abode.
Bell, William.	High Street, Bedford.

                               ⎧ Town Clerk of the
     (Signed)   A. B. ⎨ said City [or Bo-
                               ⎩ rough or Place].

I 2

172   DUTY OF TOWN CLERKS.

Town Clerk to make List of Persons objected to.   The Town Clerk must also make a List of the Persons who have been objected to by others, which will be in this Form.

Form of List.   The following Persons have been objected to as having no Right to be retained on the List of the Freemen of the City [*or* Borough] of   [*or* of   being a Place sharing in the Election with the City [*or* Borough] of   ], entitled to Vote in the Election of a Member [*or* Members] for the said City [*or* Borough].

Christian and Surname of each Person objected to.	Place of his Abode.
Andrews, Robert.	Market Street, Lancaster.

(Signed)   A. B. } Town Clerk of the said City [*or* Borough *or* Place].

These Lists to be published.   Copies of each of these last mentioned Lists must be fixed on or near the Door of the Town Hall, or in some public and conspicuous situation within the particular City, Borough, or Place, *on the Two Sundays next before*(1) *the 15th of September. S.* 47.

Copies to be kept for Inspection.   The Town Clerk must keep a Copy of the Names of all the Persons who have sent in Claims, and a Copy of the Names of all the Persons objected to, which he must allow any one to peruse *gratis* at

(1) In the year 1832, *the 15th of October.*

DUTY OF TOWN CLERKS.

all reasonable hours *during the Ten Days next before the 15th of September.*(1)

The Town Clerk must also have a sufficient number of Copies of each of these last mentioned Lists written or printed, as may be most convenient, in order that he may deliver them to any Persons demanding them, at the price of a Shilling for each Copy. *S.* 47. *Copies to be made for Sale.*

The next duty of the Town Clerk will be at the Barrister's Court holden for the Revision of Lists of Voters for the particular City or Borough. This will be at some time *between* (2) *the 15th of September (inclusive) and the 25th of October (inclusive).* Three clear days' Notice will have been given of the holding of the Court on the Doors of all Churches and Chapels or in some public and conspicuous situation. The Town Clerk is to attend at the opening of the Court, and produce his List of Freemen before the Barrister. He must also deliver to the Barrister a Copy of the List which he has made out of Persons objected to—it will be his duty to be in attendance whilst his own List is under Revision, and he is to Answer upon Oath all Questions which the Barrister may put to him in Revising his List. *S.* 50. *Town Clerk to attend Barrister's Court.*

Although the Office of Town Clerk is generally filled by Persons whose professional habits will ren-

(1) In the year 1832, *the 15th of October.*

(2) In the year 1832, between *the 15th of October and the 25th of November.*

174   DUTY OF TOWN CLERKS.

der it comparatively easy for them to apply the Law so as to ascertain who are to be inserted in their List of Persons entitled as Freemen to Vote for their particular Borough, yet it may not be altogether unnecessary to offer a few observations for their guidance in this duty.

Observations on Duty of Town Clerk. The Town Clerk of every Borough, or Contributory Borough, must take Notice that no Person will be entitled to be inserted in his List of Freemen, unless his Qualification as a Freeman shall, on *the*(1) *Last day of July* in the year in which the list is made out, be as complete and perfect as, according to the Old Law, it was required to be *on the day of Election* itself; and in addition to this, he must have resided for Six Calendar Months next previous to such Last day of July within the Borough, or within Seven Statute Miles of what used to be the Polling Place for the Borough before the passing of the Act: If the Person be a Freeman of a Contributory Borough, he must have resided for the Six Months within that Contributory Borough, or within Seven Miles of the place named with reference to that Borough in the second column of the Schedule (E. 2).

How Seven Miles by which Residence is limited, to be measured. The Seven Miles by which the Limit of Residence

(1) Although the Last day of August has, for the year 1832, been for some purposes substituted by the Order in Council for the Last day of July, yet it will still be the day by which the Voter's Qualification in the year 1832 will be measured, as well as in succeeding years. *See Proviso at the end of Section* 80.

DUTY OF TOWN CLERKS.

is fixed are to be measured *according to the nearest way of access;* that is to say, the way which a Person would take in making the best of his way from one point to another, using the Foot-way where there is one, and where it is most convenient to use; and the Carriage-way where it can most conveniently be used, or where there is no Foot-way. *See this rule of measurement more fully explained in Chap. IV. pp. 35 and 36.*

The Residence must be a *bonâ fide* and permanent residing, and not fictitious or occasional: if it be interrupted by any temporary absence of the Party, that absence must be accompanied by an intention to return within a reasonable period to his domicile within the Borough, or Contributory Borough, of which he is a Freeman, or within the Seven Miles by which the Limit of Residence is fixed. *See Chap. IV. p. 52.* *Residence must be bonâ fide and permanent.*

All Burgesses or Freemen, whether Honorary, or in respect of Birth, Servitude, or Marriage, who were so *on or previous to the First of March,* 1831, are to be included in the List, if they satisfy the Provisions of the Act in other respects, viz. as to Residence, &c. But the Town Clerk must take notice, that no Person who has been elected or admitted, *subsequently to the First of March,* 1831, an *Honorary* Freeman, or a Freeman in respect of *Marriage,* is to be included in the List of Freemen entitled to Vote; So also, no Person who shall hereafter become *What Freemen will be entitled.*

176   DUTY OF TOWN CLERKS.

a Freeman in respect of *Birth*, will be entitled to be
inserted in the List, unless the Person from or
through whom he derives his right was a Burgess or
Freeman *before the First of March*, 1831, or was entitled to be admitted as such before that day; or
unless the Person from or through whom he derives
his Right shall have become a Burgess or Freeman
in respect of *Servitude* since that day.

Penalty for Wilful Default.

Wilful contravention or disobedience by Town
Clerks of any of the Provisions of the Act, with respect to anything it requires of them, will subject
them to an Action of Debt at the suit of any Party
aggrieved; the Penalty, to be assessed by a Jury, is
not to exceed £500, and is to be paid, upon conviction, to the Party suing, with full Costs of Suit.
S. 76.

2 WILLIAM IV.

CHAP. XLV.

An Act to amend the Representation of the People in *England* and *Wales*. [7th June, 1832.]

WHEREAS it is expedient to take effectual measures for correcting divers abuses that have long prevailed in the choice of members to serve in the Commons House of Parliament, to deprive many inconsiderable places of the right of returning members, to grant such privilege to large, populous, and wealthy towns, to increase the number of knights of the shire, to extend the elective franchise to many of His Majesty's subjects who have not heretofore enjoyed the same, and to diminish the expense of elections; be it therefore enacted by the King's most Excellent Majesty, by and with the advice and consent of the Lords Spiritual and Temporal, and Commons, in this present Parliament assembled, and by the authority of the same, That each of the boroughs enumerated in the Schedule marked (A.) to this Act annexed, (that is to say,) *Old Sarum, Newtown, St.* *Michael's* or *Midshall, Gatton, Bramber, Bossiney, Dunwich, Ludgershall, St. Mawe's, Beeralston, West Looe, St. Germain's, Newport, Blechingley, Aldborough, Camelford, Hindon, East Looe, Corfe Castle, Great Bedwin, Yarmouth, Queenborough, Castle Rising, East*

Certain boroughs to cease to send Members to Parliament.

b

2 WILLIAM IV. CHAP. 45.

Grinstead, Higham Ferrars, Wendover, Weobly, Winchelsea, Tregony, Haslemere, Saltash, Orford, Callington, Newton, Ilchester, Boroughbridge, Stockbridge, New Romney, Hedon, Plympton, Seaford, Heytesbury, Steyning, Whitchurch, Wootton Bassett, Downton, Fowey, Milborne Port, Aldeburgh, Minehead, Bishop's Castle, Okehampton, Appleby, Lostwithiel, Brackley, and *Amersham,* shall from and after the end of this present Parliament cease to return any member or members to serve in Parliament.

Certain boroughs to return One Member only.

II. And be it enacted, That each of the boroughs enumerated in the Schedule marked (B.) to this act annexed, (that is to say,) *Petersfield, Ashburton, Eye, Westbury, Wareham, Midhurst, Woodstock, Wilton, Malmesbury, Liskeard, Reigate, Hythe, Droitwich, Lyme Regis, Launceston, Shaftesbury, Thirsk, Christchurch, Horsham, Great Grimsby, Calne, Arundel, St. Ives, Rye, Clitheroe, Morpeth, Helston, North Allerton, Wallingford,* and *Dartmouth,* shall from and after the end of this present Parliament return one member and no more to serve in Parliament.

New boroughs hereafter to return Two Members.

III. And be it enacted, That each of the places named in the Schedule marked (C.) to this act annexed, (that is to say,) *Manchester, Birmingham, Leeds, Greenwich Sheffield, Sunderland, Devonport, Wolverhampton, Tower Hamlets, Finsbury, Mary-le-bone, Lambeth, Bolton, Bradford, Blackburn, Brighton, Halifax, Macclesfield, Oldham, Stockport, Stoke-upon-Trent,* and *Stroud,* shall for the purposes of this act be a borough, and shall as such borough include the place or places respectively which shall be comprehended within the boundaries of such borough, as such boundaries shall be settled and described by an act to be passed for that purpose in this present Parliament, which act, when passed, shall be deemed and taken to be part of this act as fully and effectually as if the same were incorporated herewith; and that each of the said boroughs named in the

2 WILLIAM IV. CHAP. 45.

iii

said Schedule (C.) shall from and after the end of this present Parliament return two members to serve in Parliament.

IV. And be it enacted, That each of the places named in the Schedule marked (D.) to this act annexed, (that is to say,) *Ashton-under-Lyne, Bury, Chatham, Cheltenham, Dudley, Frome, Gateshead, Huddersfield, Kidderminster, Kendal, Rochdale, Salford, South Shields, Tynemouth, Wakefield, Walsall, Warrington, Whitby, Whitehaven,* and *Merthyr Tydvil,* shall for the purposes of this act be a borough, and shall as such borough include the place or places respectively which shall be comprehended within the boundaries of such borough, as such boundaries shall be settled and described by an act to be passed for that purpose in this present Parliament, which act, when passed, shall be deemed and taken to be part of this act as fully and effectually as if the same were incorporated herewith; and that each of the said boroughs named in the said Schedule (D.) shall from and after the end of this present Parliament return one member to serve in Parliament.

New boroughs hereafter to return One Member.

V. And be it enacted, That the borough of *New Shoreham* shall for the purposes of this act include the whole of the rape of *Bramber* in the county of *Sussex*, save and except such parts of the said rape as shall be included in the borough of *Horsham* by an act to be passed for that purpose in this present Parliament; and that the borough of *Cricklade* shall for the purposes of this act include the hundreds and divisions of *Highworth, Cricklade, Staple, Kingsbridge,* and *Malmsbury* in the county of *Wilts*, save and except such parts of the said hundred of *Malmsbury* as shall be included in the borough of *Malmsbury* by an act to be passed for that purpose in this present Parliament; and that the borough of *Aylesbury* shall for the purposes of this act include the three hundreds of *Aylesbury* in the county of *Buckingham;* and

The boroughs of Shoreham, Cricklade, Aylesbury, and East Retford shall include certain adjacent districts.

b 2

iv 2 WILLIAM IV. CHAP. 45.

that the borough of *East Retford* shall for the purposes of this act include the hundred of *Bassetlaw* in the county of *Nottingham*, and all places locally situate within the outside boundary or limit of the hundred of *Bassetlaw*, or surrounded by such boundary and by any part of the county of *Lincoln* or county of *York*.

Weymouth and Melcombe Regis to return Two Members only, &c.

VI. And be it enacted, That the borough of *Weymouth* and *Melcombe Regis* shall from and after the end of this present Parliament return Two Members, and no more, to serve in Parliament; and that the borough of *Penryn* shall for the purposes of this Act include the town of *Falmouth ;* and that the borough of *Sandwich* shall for the purposes of this Act include the parishes of *Deal* and *Walmer*.

Boundaries of existing boroughs in England to be settled.

VII. And be it enacted, That every city and borough in *England* which now returns a member or members to serve in Parliament, and every place sharing in the election therewith, (except the several boroughs enumerated in the said Schedule (A.), and except the several boroughs of *New Shoreham, Cricklade, Aylesbury*, and *East Retford*,) shall, and each of the said boroughs of *Penryn* and *Sandwich* also shall, for the purposes of this Act, include the place or places respectively which shall be comprehended within the boundaries of every such city, borough or place, as such boundaries shall be settled and described by an Act to be passed for that purpose in this present Parliament, which Act, when passed, shall be deemed and taken to be part of this Act as fully and effectually as if the same were incorporated herewith.

Places in Wales to have a share in Elections for the shire. towns.

VIII. And be it enacted, That each of the places named in the first column of the Schedule (E.) to this Act annexed, shall have a share in the election of a member to serve in all future Parliaments for the shire-town or borough which is mentioned in

2 WILLIAM IV. CHAP. 45.

v

conjunction therewith, and named in the second column of the said Schedule (E.)

IX. And be it enacted, That each of the places named in the first column of the said Schedule (E.), and each of the shire-towns or boroughs named in the second column of the said Schedule (E.), and the borough of *Brecon*, shall for the purposes of this Act include the place or places respectively which shall be comprehended within the boundaries of each of the said places, shire-towns, and boroughs respectively, as such boundaries shall be settled and described by an Act to be passed for that purpose in this present Parliament, which Act, when passed, shall be deemed and taken to be part of this Act as fully and effectually as if the same were incorporated herewith.

Boundaries of shire-towns and places in Wales to be settled.

X. And be it enacted, That each of the towns of *Swansea, Loughor, Neath, Aberavon*, and *Ken-fig* shall for the purposes of this Act include the place or places respectively which shall be comprehended within the boundaries of each of the said towns, as such boundaries shall be settled and described by an Act to be passed for that purpose in this present Parliament, which Act, when passed, shall be deemed and taken to be part of this Act as fully and effectually as if the same were incorporated herewith; and that the said five towns, so including as aforesaid, shall for the purposes of this Act be one borough, and shall as such borough, from and after the end of this present Parliament, return One Member to serve in Parliament; and that the Portreeve of *Swansea* shall be the returning officer for the said borough ; and that no person, by reason of any right accruing in any of the said five towns, shall have any vote in the election of a member to serve in any future Parliament for the borough of *Cardiff*.

Swansea, Loughor, Neath, Aberavon, and Ken-fig to form One borough, and Electors thereof not to vote for a member for Cardiff.

XI. And be it enacted, That the persons respec-

Description of the returning officers for the new boroughs.

vi

2 WILLIAM IV. CHAP. 45.

tively described in the said Schedules (C.) and (D.)
shall be the returning officers at all elections of a
member or members to serve in Parliament for the
boroughs in conjunction with which such persons are
respectively mentioned in the said Schedules (C.)
and (D.); and that for those boroughs in the said
Schedules for which no persons are mentioned in
such Schedules as returning officers, the sheriff for
the time being of the county in which such boroughs
are respectively situate shall, within two months
after the passing of this Act, and in every succeeding
respective year in the month of March, by writing
under his hand, to be delivered to the Clerk of the
Peace of the county within one week, and to be by
such Clerk of the Peace filed and preserved with
the records of his office, nominate and appoint for
each of such boroughs a fit person, being resident
therein, to be, and such person so nominated and
appointed shall accordingly be, the returning officer
for each of such boroughs respectively until the
nomination to be made in the succeeding March;
and in the event of the death of any such person, or
of his becoming incapable to act by reason of sickness or other sufficient impediment, the sheriff for
the time being shall on notice thereof forthwith
nominate and appoint in his stead a fit person, being
so resident as aforesaid, to be, and such person so nominated and appointed shall accordingly be, the returning
officer for such borough for the remainder of the then
current year; and no person, having been so nominated
and appointed as returning officer for any borough,
shall after the expiration of his office be compellable
at any time thereafter to serve again in the said
Who disqua- office for the same borough : Provided always, that
lified. no person being in holy orders, nor any churchwarden or overseer of the poor within any such borough,
shall be nominated or appointed as such returning
officer for the same ; and that no person nominated
and appointed as returning officer for any borough
now sending or hereafter to send members to Par-

2 WILLIAM IV. CHAP. 45.

vii

liament shall be appointed a churchwarden or overseer of the poor therein during the time for which he shall be such returning officer : Provided also, *Who exempt* that no person qualified to be elected to serve as a member in Parliament shall be compellable to serve as returning officer for any borough for which he shall have been nominated and appointed by the sheriff as aforesaid, if within one week after he shall have received notice of his nomination and appointment as returning officer he shall make oath of such qualification before any justice of the peace, and shall forthwith notify the same to the sheriff: Pro- *Proviso.* vided also, that in case His Majesty shall be pleased to grant His Royal Charter of Incorporation to any of the boroughs named in the said Schedules (C.) and (D.) which are not now incorporated, and shall by such charter give power to elect a mayor or other chief municipal officer for any such borough, then and in every such case such mayor or other chief municipal officer for the time being shall be the only returning officer for such borough ; and the provisions hereinbefore contained with regard to the nomination and appointment of a returning officer for such borough shall thenceforth cease and determine.

XII. And be it enacted, That in all future Parlia- *Six Knights* ments there shall be six knights of the shire, instead *of the Shire for Yorkshire* of four, to serve for the county of *York*, (that is to *Two for each* say,) two knights for each of the three ridings of the *riding.* said county, to be elected in the same manner, and by the same classes and descriptions of voters, and in respect of the same several rights of voting, as if each of the three ridings were a separate county; and that the court for the election of knights of the shire for the North riding of the said county shall be holden at the city of *York*, and the court for the election of knights of the shire for the West riding of the said county shall be holden at *Wakefield*, and the court for the election of knights of the shire for viii

2 WILLIAM IV. CHAP. 45.

the East riding of the said county shall be holden at *Beverly.*

Four Knights of the Shire for Lincoln-shire; two for the parts of Lindsey, two for Kesteven and Holland.

XIII. And be it enacted, That in all future Parliaments there shall be four knights of the shire, instead of two, to serve for the county of *Lincoln,* (that is to say,) two for the parts of *Lindsey* in the said county, and two for the parts of *Kesteven* and *Holland* in the same county; and that such four knights shall be chosen in the same manner, and by the same classes and descriptions of voters, and in respect of the same several rights of voting, as if the said parts of *Lindsey* were a separate county, and the said parts of *Kesteven* and *Holland* together were also a separate county; and that the court for the election of knights of the shire for the parts of *Lindsey* in the said county shall be holden at the city of *Lincoln,* and the court for the election of knights of the shire for the parts of *Kesteven* and *Holland* in the said county shall be holden at *Sleaford.*

Certain counties to be divided, and to return Two Knights of the Shire for each division.

XIV. And be it enacted, That each of the counties enumerated in the Schedule marked (F.) to this act annexed shall be divided into two divisions, which divisions shall be settled and described by an act to be passed for that purpose in this present Parliament; which act, when passed, shall be deemed and taken to be part of this act as fully and effectually as if the same were incorporated herewith; and that in all future Parliaments there shall be four knights of the shire, instead of two, to serve for each of the said counties, (that is to say,) two knights of the shire for each division of the said counties; and that such knights shall be chosen in the same manner, and by the same classes and descriptions of voters, and in respect of the same several rights of voting, as if each of the said divisions were a separate county; and that the court for the election of knights of the shire for each division of the said counties shall be holden at the place to be named for that

2 William IV. Chap. 45.

ix

purpose in the act so to be passed as aforesaid, for settling and describing the divisions of the said counties.

XV. And be it enacted, That in all future Parliaments there shall be three knights of the shire, instead of two, to serve for each of the counties enumerated in the Schedule marked (F. 2.) to this act annexed, and two knights of the shire, instead of one, to serve for each of the counties of *Carmarthen*, *Denbigh*, and *Glamorgan*.

Certain counties to return Three Knights of the Shire.

XVI. And be it enacted, That the *Isle of Wight* in the county of *Southampton* shall for the purposes of this act be a county of itself, separate and apart from the county of *Southampton*, and shall return one knight of the shire to serve in every future Parliament; and that such knight shall be chosen by the same classes and descriptions of voters, and in respect of the same several rights of voting, as any knight of the shire shall be chosen in any county in *England;* and that all elections for the said county of the *Isle of Wight* shall be holden at the town of *Newport* in the *Isle of Wight*, and the sheriff of the *Isle of Wight*, or his deputy, shall be the returning officer at such elections.

Isle of Wight severed from Hampshire, to return a member.

XVII. And be it enacted, That for the purpose of electing a knight or knights of the shire to serve in any future Parliament, the East riding of the county of *York*, the North riding of the county of *York*, the parts of *Lindsey* in the county of *Lincoln*, and the several counties at large enumerated in the second column of the Schedule marked (G.) to this Act annexed, shall respectively include the several cities and towns, and counties of the same, which are respectively mentioned in conjunction with such ridings, parts, and counties at large, and named in the first column of the said Schedule (G.)

Towns which are counties of themselves to be included in adjoining counties for county elections.

b 5

2 WILLIAM IV. CHAP. 45.

Limitation on the right of voting for counties and for cities being counties of themselves, in respect of freeholds for life.

XVIII. And be it enacted, That no person shall be entitled to vote in the election of a knight or knights of the shire to serve in any future Parliament, or in the election of a member or members to serve in any future Parliament for any city or town being a county of itself, in respect of any freehold lands or tenements whereof such person may be seised for his own life, or for the life of another, or for any lives whatsoever, except such person shall be in the actual and bonâ fide occupation of such lands or tenements, or except the same shall have come to such person by marriage, marriage settlement, devise, or promotion to any benefice or to any office, or except the same shall be of the clear yearly value of not less than Ten Pounds above all rents and charges payable out of or in respect of the same; any statute or usage to the contrary notwithstanding: Provided always, that nothing in this Act contained shall prevent any person now seised for his own life, or for the life of another, or for any lives whatsoever, of any freehold lands or tenements in respect of which he now has, or but for the passing of this Act might acquire, the right of voting in such respective elections, from retaining or acquiring, so long as he shall be so seised of the same lands or tenements, such right of voting in respect thereof, if duly registered according to the respective provisions hereinafter contained.

Right of voting in counties extended to copyholders.

XIX. And be it enacted, That every male person of full age, and not subject to any legal incapacity, who shall be seised at law or in equity of any lands or tenements of copyhold or any other tenure whatever except freehold, for his own life, or for the life of another, or for any lives whatsoever, or for any larger estate, of the clear yearly value of not less than Ten Pounds over and above all rents and charges payable out of or in respect of the same, shall be entitled to vote in the election of a knight or knights of the shire to serve in any future Par-

2 William IV. Chap. 45.

xi

liament for the county, or for the riding, parts, or division of the county, in which such lands or tenements shall be respectively situate.

XX. And be it enacted, That every male person of full age, and not subject to any legal incapacity, who shall be entitled, either as lessee or assignee, to any lands or tenements, whether of freehold or of any other tenure whatever, for the unexpired residue, whatever it may be, of any term originally created for a period of not less than sixty years, (whether determinable on a life or lives, or not,) of the clear yearly value of not less than ten pounds over and above all rents and charges payable out of or in respect of the same, or for the unexpired residue, whatever it may be, of any term originally created for a period of not less than twenty years, (whether determinable on a life or lives, or not,) of the clear yearly value of not less than fifty pounds over and above all rents and charges payable out of or in respect of the same, or who shall occupy as tenant any lands or tenements for which he shall be bonâ fide liable to a yearly rent of not less than fifty pounds, shall be entitled to vote in the election of a knight or knights of the shire to serve in any future Parliament for the county, or for the riding, parts, or division of the county, in which such lands or tenements shall be respectively situate: Provided always, that no person, being only a sub-lessee, or the assignee of any underlease, shall have a right to vote in such election in respect of any such term of sixty years or twenty years as aforesaid, unless he shall be in the actual occupation of the premises.

Right of voting in counties extended to leaseholders and occupiers of premises of certain value above charges.

. XXI. And be it declared and enacted, That no public or parliamentary tax, nor any church rate, county rate, or parochial rate, shall be deemed to be any charge payable out of or in respect of any lands or tenements within the meaning of this Act.

What not to be deemed charges.

2 WILLIAM IV. CHAP. 45.

xii

County voters need not be assessed to the land-tax.

XXII. And be it enacted, That in order to entitle any person to vote in any election of a knight of the shire or other member to serve in any future Parliament, in respect of any messuages, lands, or tenements, whether freehold or otherwise, it shall not be necessary that the same shall be assessed to the land-tax; any statute to the contrary notwithstanding.

Provision as to trustees and mortgagees.

XXIII. And be it enacted, That no person shall be allowed to have any vote in the election of a knight or knights of the shire for or by reason of any trust estate or mortgage, unless such trustee or mortgagee be in actual possession or receipt of the rents and profits of the same estate, but that the mortgagor or cestuique trust in possession shall and may vote for the same estate notwithstanding such mortgage or trust.

No person to vote for a county in respect of any freehold house, &c. occupied by himself, which would confer a vote for a borough.

XXIV. And be it enacted, That notwithstanding any thing hereinbefore contained no person shall be entitled to vote in the election of a knight or knights of the shire to serve in any future Parliament in respect of his estate or interest as a freeholder in any house, warehouse, counting-house, shop, or other building occupied by himself, or in any land occupied by himself together with any house, warehouse, counting-house, shop, or other building, such house, warehouse, counting-house, shop, or other building being, either separately or jointly with the land so occupied therewith, of such value as would, according to the provisions hereinafter contained, confer on him the right of voting for any city or borough, whether he shall or shall not have actually acquired the right to vote for such city or borough in respect thereof.

No person to vote for a county in respect of certain copyholds and leaseholds in a borough.

XXV. And be it enacted, That notwithstanding any thing hereinbefore contained, no person shall be entitled to vote in the election of a knight or knights

2 WILLIAM IV. CHAP. 45.

xiii

of the shire to serve in any future Parliament in respect of his estate or interest as a copyholder or customary tenant, or tenant in ancient demesne, holding by copy of court roll, or as such lessee or assignee, or as such tenant and occupier as aforesaid, in any house, warehouse, counting-house, shop, or other building, or in any land occupied together with a house, warehouse, counting-house, shop, or other building, such house, warehouse, counting-house, shop, or other building being, either separately or jointly with the land so occupied therewith, of such value as would, according to the provisions hereinafter contained, confer on him or on any other person the right of voting for any city or borough, whether he or any other person shall or shall not have actually acquired the right to vote for such city or borough in respect thereof.

XXVI. And be it enacted, That notwithstanding any thing hereinbefore contained no person shall be entitled to vote in the election of a knight or knights of the shire to serve in any future Parliament, unless he shall have been duly registered according to the provisions hereinafter contained; and that no person shall be so registered in any year in respect of his estate or interest in any lands or tenements, as a freeholder, copyholder, customary tenant, or tenant in ancient demesne, unless he shall have been in the actual possession thereof, or in the receipt of the rents and profits thereof for his own use, for six calendar months at least next previous to the last day of July in such year; which said period of six calendar months shall be sufficient, any statute to the contrary notwithstanding; and that no person shall be so registered in any year in respect of any lands or tenements held by him as such lessee or assignee, or as such occupier and tenant as aforesaid, unless he shall have been in the actual possession thereof, or in the receipt of the rents and profits thereof for his own use, as the case may require, for

Possession for a certain time, and registration, essential to the right of voting for a county.

xiv

2 William IV. Chap. 45.

Exception in case of property coming by descent, &c.

twelve calendar months next previous to the last day of July in such year: Provided always, that where any lands or tenements, which would otherwise entitle the owner, holder, or occupier thereof to vote in any such election, shall come to any person, at any time within such respective periods of six or twelve calendar months, by descent, succession, marriage, marriage settlement, devise, or promotion to any benefice in a church, or by promotion to any office, such person shall be entitled in respect thereof to have his name inserted as a voter in the election of a knight or knights of the shire in the lists then next to be made by virtue of this Act as hereinafter mentioned, and, upon his being duly registered according to the provisions hereinafter contained, to vote in such election.

Right of voting in boroughs to be enjoyed by occupiers of houses, &c. of the annual value of 10l.

XXVII. And be it enacted, That in every city or borough which shall return a member or members to serve in any future Parliament, every male person of full age, and not subject to any legal incapacity, who shall occupy, within such city or borough, or within any place sharing in the election for such city or borough, as owner or tenant, any house, warehouse, counting-house, shop, or other building, being, either separately, or jointly with any land within such city, borough, or place occupied therewith by him as owner, or occupied therewith by him as tenant under the same landlord, of the clear yearly value of not less than ten pounds, shall, if duly registered according to the provisions herein-after contained, be entitled to vote in the election of a member or members to serve in any future Parlia-

No occupiers to vote unles rated to the poor rate.

ment for such city or borough: Provided always, that no such person shall be so registered in any year unless he shall have occupied such premises as aforesaid for twelve calendar months next previous to the last day of July in such year, nor unless such person, where such premises are situate in any parish or township in which there shall be a rate for

2 WILLIAM IV. CHAP. 45.

XV

the relief of the poor, shall have been rated in respect of such premises to all rates for the relief of the poor in such parish or township made during the time of such his occupation so required as aforesaid, nor unless such person shall have paid, on or before the twentieth day of July in such year, all the poor's rates and assessed taxes which shall have become payable from him in respect of such premises previously to the sixth day of April then next preceding: Provided also, that no such person shall be so registered in any year unless he shall have resided for six calendar months next previous to the last day of July in such year within the city or borough, or within the place sharing in the election for the city or borough, in respect of which city, borough, or place respectively he shall be entitled to vote, or within seven statute miles thereof or of any part thereof.

Rate and assessed taxes must be paid.

Residence also required.

XXVIII. And be it enacted, That the premises in respect of the occupation of which any person shall be entitled to be registered in any year, and to vote in the election for any city or borough as aforesaid, shall not be required to be the same premises, but may be different premises occupied in immediate succession by such person during the twelve calendar months next previous to the last day of July in such year, such person having paid, on or before the twentieth day of July in such year, all the poor's rates and assessed taxes which shall previously to the sixth day of April then next preceding have become payable from him in respect of all such premises so occupied by him in succession.

Provision as to premises occupied in succession.

XXIX. And be it enacted, That where any premises as aforesaid, in any such city or borough, or in any place sharing in the election therewith, shall be jointly occupied by more persons than one as owners or tenants, each of such joint occupiers shall, subject to the conditions herein-before contained as

As to joint occupiers.

xvi   2 WILLIAM IV. CHAP. 45.

to persons occupying premises in any such city,
borough, or place, be entitled to vote in the election
for such city or borough, in respect of the premises
so jointly occupied, in case the clear yearly value
of such premises shall be of an amount which, when
divided by the number of such occupiers, shall give
a sum of not less than ten pounds for each and every
such occupier, but not otherwise.

Occupiers
may demand
to be rated.

XXX. And be it enacted, That in every city or
borough which shall return a member or members
to serve in any future Parliament, and in every
place sharing in the election for such city or borough,
it shall be lawful for any person occupying any
house, warehouse, counting-house, shop, or other
building, either separately, or jointly with any land
occupied therewith by him as owner, or occupied
therewith by him as tenant under the same landlord,
in any parish or township in which there shall be a
rate for the relief of the poor, to claim to be rated
to the relief of the poor in respect of such premises,
whether the landlord shall or shall not be liable to
be rated to the relief of the poor in respect thereof;
and upon such occupier so claiming and actually
paying or tendering the full amount of the rate or
rates, if any, then due in respect of such premises,
the overseers of the parish or township in which
such premises are situate are hereby required to put
the name of such occupier upon the rate for the
time being; and in case such overseers shall neglect
or refuse so to do, such occupier shall nevertheless
for the purposes of this Act be deemed to have been
rated for the relief of the poor in respect of such
premises from the period at which the rate shall
have been made in respect of which he shall have
so claimed to be rated as aforesaid : Provided always,
that where by virtue of any Act of Parliament the
landlord shall be liable to the payment of the rate
for the relief of the poor in respect of any premises
occupied by his tenant, nothing herein contained

2 WILLIAM IV. CHAP. 45.

xvii

shall be deemed to vary or discharge the liability of such landlord; but that in case the tenant who shall have been rated for such premises in consequence of any such claim as aforesaid shall make default in the payment of the poor's rate due in respect thereof, such landlord shall be and remain liable for the payment thereof in the same manner as if he alone had been rated in respect of the premises so occupied by his tenant.

XXXI. And be it enacted, that in every city or town being a county of itself, in the election for which freeholders or burgage tenants, either with or without any superadded qualification, now have a right to vote, every such freeholder or burgage tenant shall be entitled to vote in the election of a member or members to serve in all future Parliaments for such city or town, provided he shall be duly registered according to the provisions hereinafter contained; but that no such person shall be so registered in any year in respect of any freehold or burgage tenement, unless he shall have been in the actual possession thereof, or in the receipt of the rents and profits thereof, for his own use, for twelve calendar months next previous to the last day of July in such year, (except where the same shall have come to him, at any time within such twelve months, by descent, succession, marriage, marriage settlement, devise, or promotion to any benefice in a church, or to any office,) nor unless he shall have resided for six calendar months next previous to the last day of July in such year within such city or town, or within seven statute miles thereof or of any part thereof: Provided always, that nothing in this enactment contained shall be deemed to vary or abridge the provisions herein-before made relative to the right of voting for any city or town being a county of itself, in respect of any freehold for life or lives: Provided also, that every freehold or burgage tenement which may be situate without the

Provision as to freeholders voting for cities and towns being counties of themselves.

To extend to freeholds within the new boundaries.

2 WILLIAM IV. CHAP. 45.

xviii

present limits of any such city or town being a county of itself, but within the limits of such city or town, as the same shall be settled and described by the Act to be passed for that purpose as herein-before mentioned, shall confer the right of voting in the election of a member or members to serve in any future Parliament for such city or town in the same manner as if such freehold or burgage tenement were situate within the present limits thereof.

Freemen not to vote in boroughs, unless resident, &c.

XXXII. And be it enacted, That every person who would have been entitled to vote in the election of a member or members to serve in any future Parliament for any city or borough not included in the Schedule marked (A.) to this Act annexed, either as a burgess or freeman, or in the city of *London* as a freeman and liveryman, if this act had not been passed, shall be entitled to vote in such election, provided such person shall be duly registered according to the provisions herein-after contained; but that no such person shall be so registered in any year, unless he shall, on the last day of July in such year, be qualified in such manner as would entitle him then to vote if such day were the day of election, and this Act had not been passed, nor unless, where he shall be a burgess or freeman or freeman and liveryman of any city or borough, he shall have resided for six calendar months next previous to the last day of July in such year within such city or borough, or within seven statute miles from the place where the poll for such city or borough shall heretofore have been taken, nor unless, where he shall be a burgess or freeman of any place sharing in the election for any city or borough, he shall have resided for six calendar months next previous to the last day of July in such year within such respective place so sharing as aforesaid, or within seven statute miles of the place mentioned in conjunction with such respective place so sharing as aforesaid and named in the second column of the Schedule marked

2 William IV. Chap. 45.

xix

(E. 2.) to this Act annexed: Provided always, that no person who shall have been elected, made, or admitted a burgess or freeman since the first day of March one thousand eight hundred and thirty-one, otherwise than in respect of birth or servitude, or who shall hereafter be elected, made, or admitted a burgess or freeman, otherwise than in respect of birth or servitude, shall be entitled to vote as such in any such election for any city or borough as aforesaid or to be so registered as aforesaid: Provided also, that no person shall be so entitled as a burgess or freeman in respect of birth unless his right be originally derived from or through some person who was a burgess or freeman, or entitled to be admitted a burgess or freeman, previously to the first day of March in the year one thousand eight hundred and thirty-one, or from or through some person who since that time shall have become or shall hereafter become a burgess or freeman in respect of servitude: Provided also, that every person who would have been entitled, if this Act had not been passed, to vote as a burgess or freeman of *Swansea, Loughor, Neath, Aberavon,* or *Ken-fig,* in the election of a member to serve in any future Parliament for the borough of *Cardiff,* shall cease to vote in such election, and shall instead thereof be entitled to vote as such burgess or freeman in the election of a member to serve in all future Parliaments for the borough composed of the towns of *Swansea, Loughor, Neath, Aberavon,* and *Ken-fig,* subject always to the provisions herein-before contained with regard to a burgess or freeman of any place sharing in the election for any city or borough.

Exclusion of freemen created since the 1st of March, 1831.

Exception.

Provision as to the freemen of Swansea, Loughor, Neath, Aberavon, and Ken-fig.

XXXIII. And be it enacted, That no person shall be entitled to vote in the election of a member or members to serve in any future Parliament for any city or borough, save and except in respect of some right conferred by this Act, or as a burgess or freeman, or as a freeman and liveryman, or, in the case

Reservation of other rights of voting in boroughs.

2 William IV. Chap. 45.

of a city or town being a county of itself, as a free-holder or burgage tenant, as hereinbefore mentioned: Provided always, that every person now having a right to vote in the election for any city or borough (except those enumerated in the said Schedule A.) in virtue of any other qualification than as a burgess or freeman, or as a freeman and liveryman, or, in the case of a city or town being a county of itself, as a freeholder or burgage tenant, as hereinbefore mentioned, shall retain such right of voting so long as he shall be qualified as an elector according to the usages and customs of such city or borough, or any law now in force, and such person shall be entitled to vote in the election of a member or members to serve in any future Parliament for such city or borough, if duly registered according to the provisions herein-after contained; but that no such person shall be so registered in any year unless he shall, on the last day of July in such year, be qualified as such elector in such manner as would entitle him then to vote if such day were the day of election and this Act had not been passed, nor unless such person, where his qualification shall be in any city or borough, shall **Residence, &c. required.** have resided for six calendar months next previous to the last day of July in such year within such city or borough, or within seven statute miles from the place where the poll for such city or borough shall heretofore have been taken, nor unless such person, where his qualification shall be within any place sharing in the election for any city or borough, shall have resided for six calendar months next previous to the last day of July in such year within such re-spective place so sharing as aforesaid, or within seven statute miles of the place mentioned in con-junction with such respective place so sharing as aforesaid, and named in the second column of the Schedule marked (E. 2.) to this Act annexed: Pro-vided nevertheless, that every such person shall for ever cease to enjoy such right of voting for any such city or borough as aforesaid if his name shall have

2 William IV. Chap. 45.

xxi

been omitted for two successive years from the Register of such voters for such city or borough hereinafter directed to be made, unless he shall have been so-omitted in consequence of his having received parochial relief within twelve calendar months next previous to the last day of July in any year, or in consequence of his absence on the naval or military service of his Majesty.

XXXIV. And be it enacted, That every person now having a right to vote for the borough of *New Shoreham*, or of *Cricklade, Aylesbury*, or *East Retford*, respectively, in respect of any freehold, wheresoever the same may be situate, shall retain such right of voting, subject always to the same provisions as are hereinbefore mentioned with regard to persons whose right of voting for any borough is saved and reserved by this Act, save and except that such persons now having a right to vote for the borough of *New Shoreham*, or of *Cricklade, Aylesbury*, or *East Retford* respectively, shall not be registered in any year unless they shall have resided for six calendar months next previous to the last day of July in such year within the borough of *New Shoreham*, or of *Cricklade, Aylesbury*, or *East Retford* respectively, as defined by this Act, or within seven statute miles of such respective borough, or of any part thereof; and that for the purpose of the registration hereinafter required, all persons now having a right to vote for the borough of *New Shoreham* in respect of any freeholds which may be situate in the borough of *Horsham*, or for the borough of *Cricklade* in respect of any freeholds which may be situate in the borough of *Malmsbury*, as such boroughs of *Horsham* or *Malmsbury* may respectively be defined by the Act to be passed for that purpose as hereinbefore mentioned, shall be inserted in the list of voters hereinafter directed to be made by the overseers of that parish or township within the borough of *New Shoreham* or the borough of *Cricklade* re-

Provision as to persons now entitled to vote for New Shoreham, Cricklade, Aylesbury or East Retford, in respect of freeholds.

xxii   2 WILLIAM IV. CHAP. 45.

spectively, as defined by this Act, which shall be
next adjoining to the parish or township in which
any such freeholds shall respectively be situate; and
if the parish or township in which any such freeholds shall be situate shall adjoin two or more
parishes or townships within either of the said
boroughs of *New Shoreham* or *Cricklade,* the person
so having a right to vote in respect of such freeholds
shall be inserted in the list of voters to be made by
the overseers of the least populous of such adjoining
parishes or townships, according to the last Census
for the time being.

Exclusion of certain rights of voting in boroughs acquired since the 1st of March, 1831.
XXXV. Provided nevertheless, and be it enacted,
That notwithstanding anything hereinbefore contained, no person shall be entitled to vote in the
election of a member or members to serve in any
future Parliament for any city or borough (other
than a city or town being a county of itself, in the
election for which freeholders or burgage tenants
have a right to vote as hereinbefore mentioned) in
respect of any estate or interest in any burgage tenement or freehold which shall have been acquired by
such person since the first day of March, one thousand eight hundred and thirty-one, unless the same
shall have come to or been acquired by such person
since that day, and previously to the passing of this
Act, by descent, succession, marriage, marriage settlement, devise, or promotion to any benefice in a
church, or by promotion to any office.

As to receipt of parochial relief.
XXXVI. And be it enacted, That no person shall
be entitled to be registered in any year as a voter in
the election of a member or members to serve in any
future Parliament for any city or borough who shall
within twelve calendar months next previous to the
last day of July in such year have received parochial
relief or other alms which by the law of Parliament
now disqualify from voting in the election of members to serve in Parliament.

2 WILLIAM IV. CHAP. 45.

xxiii

XXXVII. And whereas it is expedient to form a Register of all persons entitled to vote in the election of a knight or knights of the shire to serve in any future Parliament, and that for the purpose of forming such Register the overseers of every parish and township should annually make out lists in the manner hereinafter mentioned; be it therefore enacted, That the overseers of the poor of every parish and township shall on the twentieth day of June in the present and in every succeeding year, cause to be fixed on or near the doors of all the churches and chapels within such parish or township, or if there be no church or chapel therein, then to be fixed in some public and conspicuous situation within the same respectively, a notice according to the Form numbered 1, in the Schedule (H.) to this Act annexed, requiring all persons who may be entitled to vote in the election of a knight or knights of the shire to serve in any future Parliament, in respect of any property situate wholly or in part in such parish or township, to deliver or transmit to the said overseers on or before the twentieth day of July in the present and in every succeeding year, a notice of their claim as such voters according to the Form numbered 2, in the said Schedule (H.), or to the like effect: Provided always, that after the formation of the Register to be made in each year, as hereinafter mentioned, no person whose name shall be upon such Register for the time being shall be required thereafter to make any such claim as aforesaid, so long as he shall retain the same qualification, and continue in the same place of abode described in such Register.

Overseers to give notice annually, requiring county voters to send in their claims.

Persons once on the Register not required to make any subsequent claim.

XXXVIII. And be it enacted, That the overseer of the poor of every parish and township shall, on or before the last day of July in the present year, make out, or cause to be made out, according to the Form numbered 3, in the said Schedule (H.), an alphabetical list of all persons who shall claim as aforesaid to be inserted in such list as voters in the election of a

Overseers to prepare lists of county voters, and to publish them every year.

xxiv

2 WILLIAM IV. CHAP. 45.

knight or knights of the shire to serve for the county, or for the riding, parts, or division of the county wherein such parish or township lies, in respect of any lands or tenements situate wholly or in part within such parish or township; and that the said overseers shall, on or before the last day of July in every succeeding year, make out, or cause to be made out a like list, containing the names of all persons who shall be upon the Register for the time being as such voters, and also the names of all persons who shall claim as aforesaid to be inserted in such last-mentioned list as such voters; and in every list so to be made by the overseers as aforesaid, the Christian name and surname of every person shall be written at full length, together with the place of his abode, the nature of his qualification, and the local or other description of such lands or tenements, as the same are respectively set forth in his claim to vote, and the name of the occupying tenant, if stated in such

Overseers to have power of objecting to any name inserted in the lists;

claim; and the said overseers, if they shall have reasonable cause to believe that any person so claiming as aforesaid, or whose name shall appear in the Register for the time being, is not entitled to vote in the election of a knight or knights of the shire for the county, or for the riding, parts, or division of the county in which their parish or township is situate, shall have power to add the words " objected to " opposite the name of every such person on the mar-

to keep co-pies of lists for inspec-tion.

gin of such list; and the said overseers shall sign such list, and shall cause a sufficient number of copies of such list to be written or printed, and to be fixed on or near the doors of all the churches and chapels within their parish or township, or if there be no church or chapel therein, then to be fixed up in some public and conspicuous situation within the same respectively, on the two Sundays next after such list shall have been made; and the said over-seers shall likewise keep a true copy of such list, to be perused by any person, without payment of any fee, at all reasonable hours during the two first

2 William IV. Chap. 45.

XXV

weeks after such list shall have been made: Pro- *Provision as to places having no overseers.*
vided always, that every precinct or place, whether
extra-parochial or otherwise, which shall have no
overseers of the poor, shall, for the purpose of
making out such list as aforesaid, be deemed to be
within the parish or township adjoining thereto, such
parish or township being situate within the same
county, or the same riding, parts, or division of a
county, as such precinct or place ; and if such precinct or place shall adjoin two or more parishes or
townships so situate as aforesaid, it shall be deemed
to be within the least populous of such parishes or
townships, according to the last Census for the time
being ; and the overseers of the poor of every such
parish or township shall insert in the list for their
respective parish or township the names of all persons who shall claim as aforesaid to be inserted
therein as voters in the election of a knight or knights
of the shire to serve for the county, or for the riding,
parts, or division of the county in which such precinct or place as aforesaid lies, in respect of any
lands or tenements situate wholly or in part within
such precinct or place.

XXXIX. And be it enacted, That every person *Notice of ob-jection by third parties to persons not entitled to be retained in the county lists.*
who shall be upon the Register for the time being of
voters for any county, or for any riding, parts or
division of a county, or who shall have claimed to be
inserted in any list for the then current year of
voters for any county, or any riding, parts or division of a county, may object to any person as not
having been entitled on the last day of July then
next preceding to have his name inserted in any list
of voters for such county, riding, parts or division so
to be made out as aforesaid ; and every person so
objecting (save and except overseers objecting in the
manner hereinbefore mentioned) shall, on or before
the twenty-fifth day of August in the present and in
every succeeding year, give or cause to be given a
notice in writing according to the Form numbered 4,

c

xxvi

2 WILLIAM IV. CHAP. 45.

in the said Schedule (H.), or to the like effect, to the overseers who shall have made out the list in which the name of the person so objected to shall have been inserted; and the person so objecting shall also, on or before the twenty-fifth day of August in the present and in every succeeding year, give to the person objected to, or leave at his place of abode as described in such list, or personally deliver to his tenant in occupation of the premises described in such list, a notice in writing according to the Form numbered 5, in the said Schedule (H.), or to the like effect; and the overseers shall include the names of all persons so objected to in a list according to the Form numbered 6 in the said Schedule (H.), and shall cause copies of such list to be fixed on or near the doors of all the churches and chapels within their parish or township, or if there be no church or chapel therein, then to be fixed in some public and conspicuous situation within the same respectively, on the two Sundays next preceding the fifteenth day of September in the present and in every succeeding year; and the overseers shall likewise keep a copy of the names of all the persons so objected to, to be perused by any person, without payment of any fee, at all reasonable hours during the ten days next preceding the said fifteenth day of September in the present and in every succeeding year.

Lists of persons objected to by third parties to be published, &c.

Lists of county voters to be forwarded to the clerks of the peace.

XL. And be it enacted, That on the twenty-ninth day of August in the present and in every succeeding year, the overseers of every parish and township shall deliver the list of voters so made out as aforesaid, together with a written statement of the number of persons objected to by the overseers and by other persons, to the high constable or high constables of the hundred or other like district in which such parish or township is situate; and such high constable or high constables shall forthwith deliver all such lists, together with such statements as aforesaid, to the clerk of the peace of the county, riding

2 William IV. Chap. 45.

xxvii

or parts, who shall forthwith make out an abstract of the number of persons objected to by the overseers and by other persons in each parish and township, and transmit the same to the barrister or barristers appointed as hereinafter mentioned, to revise such lists, in order that the said barrister or barristers may fix proper times and places for holding his or their courts for the revision of the said lists.

XLI. And be it enacted, That the Lord Chief Justice of the Court of King's Bench for the time being shall, in the month of July or August in the present and in every succeeding year, nominate and appoint for *Middlesex*, and the senior judge for the time being in the commission of assize for every other county shall, when travelling the summer circuit, in the present and in every succeeding year, nominate and appoint for every such county, or for each of the ridings, parts, or divisions of such county, a barrister or barristers to revise the lists of voters in the election of a knight or knights of the shire; and such barrister or barristers so appointed as aforesaid shall give public notice, as well by advertisement in some of the newspapers circulating within the county, riding, parts, or division, as also by a notice to be fixed in some public and conspicuous situation at the principal place of election for the county, riding, parts, or division, (such lastmentioned notice to be given three days at the least before the commencement of his or their circuit,) that he or they will make a circuit of the county, riding, parts, or division for which he or they shall be so appointed, and of the several times and places at which he or they will hold courts for that purpose, such times being between the fifteenth day of September inclusive and the twenty-fifth day of October inclusive in the present and in every succeeding year, and he or they shall hold open courts for that purpose at the times and places so to be announced; and where two or more barristers shall be

Judges of assize to name barristers, who shall revise the lists of county voters.

Period for revision.

c 2

xxviii

2 WILLIAM IV. CHAP. 45.

appointed for the same county, riding, parts, or division, they shall attend at the same places together, but shall sit apart from each other, and hold separate courts at the same time for the despatch of business: Provided always, that no member of Parliament, nor any person holding any office or place of profit under the crown, shall be appointed such barrister, and that no barrister so appointed as aforesaid shall be eligible to serve in Parliament for eighteen months from the time of such his appointment for the county, riding, parts, or division for which he shall be so appointed.

Clerk of the peace and overseers to attend before the barristers, who shall retain on the county lists all names not objected to, and shall expunge those whose qualification, if objected to, shall not be proved.

XLII. And be it enacted, That the clerk of the peace shall at the opening of the first court to be held by every such barrister for any county, or for any riding, parts, or division of a county, produce or cause to be produced before him, the several lists of voters for such county, riding, parts, or division, which shall have been delivered to such clerk of the peace by the high constables as aforesaid; and the overseers of every parish and township who shall have made out the lists of voters shall attend the court to be held by every such barrister at the place appointed for revising the lists relating to such parish or township respectively, and shall also deliver to such barrister a copy of the list of the persons objected to, so made out by them as aforesaid; and the said overseers shall answer upon oath all such questions as such barrister may put to them or any of them touching any matter necessary for revising the lists of voters; and every such barrister shall retain on the lists of voters the names of all persons to whom no objection shall have been made by the overseers, or by any other person, in the manner hereinbefore mentioned; and he shall also retain on the list of voters the name of every person who shall have been objected to by any person other than the overseers, unless the party so objecting shall appear by himself or by some one on his behalf in support of

2 William IV. Chap. 45.

xxix

such objection; and where the name of any person inserted in the list of voters shall have been objected to by the overseers, or by any other person, in the manner hereinbefore mentioned, and such person so objecting shall appear by himself or by some one on his behalf in support of such objection, every such barrister shall require it to be proved that the person so objected to was entitled on the last day of July then next preceding to have his name inserted in the list of voters in respect of the qualification described in such list; and in case the same shall not be proved to the satisfaction of such barrister, or in case it shall be proved that such person was then incapacitated by any law or statute from voting in the election of members to serve in Parliament, such barrister shall expunge the name of every such person from the said lists; and he shall also expunge from the said lists the name of every person who shall be proved to him to be dead; and shall correct any mistake which shall be proved to him to have been made in any of the said lists as to any of the particulars by this Act required to be inserted in such lists; and where the Christian name of any person, or his place of abode, or the nature of his qualification, or the local or other description of his property, or the name of the tenant in the occupation thereof, as the same respectively are required to be inserted in any such list, shall be wholly omitted therefrom, such barrister shall expunge the name of every such person from such list, unless the matter or matters so omitted be supplied to the satisfaction of such barrister before he shall have completed the revision of such list, in which case he shall then and there insert the same in such list: Provided always, that no person's name shall be expunged from any such list, except in case of his death or of his being objected to on the margin of the list by the overseers as aforesaid, or except in case of any such omission or omissions as hereinbefore last mentioned, unless such notice

Power to rectify mistakes and supply omissions in the lists.

Proviso.

XXX

2 WILLIAM IV. CHAP. 45.

as is hereinbefore required in that behalf shall have
been given to the overseers, nor unless such notice
as is hereinbefore required in that behalf shall have
been given to such person, or left at his place of
abode, or delivered to his tenant as hereinbefore
mentioned.

Barrister to have power to insert in the county lists the names of claimants omitted by the overseers on proof of claim and qualification.

XLIII. Provided also and be it enacted, That if
it shall happen that any person who shall have given
to the overseers of any parish or township due notice of his claim to have his name inserted in the
list of voters in the election of a knight or knights
of the shire shall have been omitted by such overseers from such list, it shall be lawful for the barrister, upon the revision of such list, to insert therein
the name of the person so omitted, in case it shall be
proved to the satisfaction of such barrister that such
person gave due notice of such his claim to the said
overseers, and that he was entitled on the last day
of July then next preceding to be inserted in the
list of voters in the election of a knight or knights of
the shire for the county, or for the riding, parts, or
division of the county, wherein the parish or township of such overseers may be situate, in respect of
any lands or tenements within such parish or township.

Overseers to prepare lists of persons (other than freemen) en-titled to vote in boroughs, and to pub-lish them.

XLIV. And be it enacted, That the overseers of
the poor of every parish and township, either wholly
or in part situate within any city or borough, or
place sharing in the election for any city or borough,
which shall return a member or members to serve
in any future Parliament, shall, on or before the last
day of July in the present and in each succeeding
year, make out or cause to be made out, according
to the Form numbered 1, in the Schedule marked (I.)
to this Act annexed, an alphabetical list of all persons who may be entitled by virtue of this Act
to vote in the election of a member or members to
serve in any future Parliament for such city or bo-

2 WILLIAM IV. CHAP. 45.

xxxi

rough in respect of the occupation of premises of the clear yearly value of not less than ten pounds as hereinbefore mentioned, situate wholly or in part within such parish or township, and another alphabetical list, according to the Form numbered 2 in the said Schedule (I.) of all other persons (except freemen) who may be entitled to vote in the election for such city or borough by virtue of any other right whatsoever; and in each of the said lists the Christian name and surname of every person shall be written at full length, together with the nature of his qualification; and where any person shall be entitled to vote in respect of any property, then the name of the street, lane, or other description of the place where such property may be situate shall be specified in the list; and where any person shall be entitled to vote otherwise than in respect of any property, then the name of the street, lane, or other description of the place of such person's abode shall be specified in the list; and the overseers shall sign each of such lists, and shall cause a sufficient number of copies of such lists to be printed, and to be fixed on or near the doors of all the churches and chapels in their several parishes and townships, or if there be no church or chapel therein, then to be fixed up in some public and conspicuous situation within the same respectively, on the two Sundays next after such lists shall have been made; and the said overseers shall likewise keep true copies of such lists, to be perused by any person, without payment of any fee, at all reasonable hours during the two first weeks after such lists shall have been made.

Copies of lists to be kept for inspection.

XLV. And be it enacted, That every precinct or place, whether extra-parochial or otherwise, having no overseers of the poor, which now is or hereafter may be within any city or borough, or within any place sharing in the election for any city or borough, shall, for the purpose of making out the list of voters for such city or borough, be deemed to be

Provision for places within boroughs having no overseers.

xxxii   2 WILLIAM IV. CHAP. 45.

within the parish or township adjoining thereto, and situate wholly or in part within such city or borough, or within such place sharing in the election therewith; and if such precinct or place shall adjoin two or more parishes or townships so situate as aforesaid, it shall be deemed to be within the least populous of such parishes or townships according to the last census for the time being; and the overseers of every such parish or township shall insert in the list for their respective parish or township the names of all persons who may be entitled to vote in the election of a member or members to serve in any future Parliament for any such city or borough in respect of any property occupied by such persons within such city or borough, or within any place sharing in the election therewith, such property being situate wholly or in part within such precinct or place as aforesaid.

Town clerks to prepare and publish the lists of freemen.

XLVI. And be it enacted, That the town clerk of every city or borough shall, on or before the last day of July in the present and in each succeeding year, make out or cause to be made out, according to the Form numbered 3 in the said Schedule (I.) an alphabetical list of all the freemen of such city or borough who may be entitled to vote in the election of a member or members to serve in any future Parliament for such city or borough, together with the respective places of their abode; and the town clerk of every place sharing in the election for any city or borough shall, at the respective times aforesaid, make out or cause to be made out a like list of all the freemen of such place who may be entitled to vote in the election of a member or members to serve in any future Parliament for such city or borough; and every such town clerk shall cause a copy of every such list to be fixed on or near the door of the town-hall, or in some public and conspicuous situation within such respective city, borough, or place as aforesaid, on the two Sundays

2 WILLIAM IV. CHAP. 45.

xxxiii

next after such list shall have been made, and shall likewise keep a true copy of such list, to be perused by any person, without payment of any fee, at all reasonable hours during the two first weeks after such list shall have been made: Provided always, that where there shall be no town clerk for such city, borough, or place as aforesaid, or where the town clerk shall be dead or incapable of acting, all matters by this Act required to be done by and with regard to the town clerk shall be done by and with regard to the person executing duties similar to those of the town clerk, and if there be no such person, then by and with regard to the chief civil officer of such city, borough, or place.

XLVII. And be it enacted, That every person whose name shall have been omitted in any such list of voters for any city or borough so to be made out as hereinbefore mentioned, and who shall claim to have his name inserted therein as having been entitled on the last day of July then next preceding, shall, on or before the twenty-fifth day of August in the present, and in every succeeding year, give or cause to be given a notice in writing, according to the Form numbered 4 in the said Schedule (I.), or to the like effect, to the overseers of that parish or township in the list whereof he shall claim to have his name inserted, or if he shall claim as a freeman of any city or borough, or place sharing in the election therewith, then to the town clerk of such city, borough, or place; and every person whose name shall have been inserted in any list of voters for any city or borough may object to any other person as not having been entitled on the last day of July then next preceding to have his name inserted in any list of voters for the same city or borough, and every person so objecting shall, on or before the twenty-fifth day of August in the present and in every succeeding year, give or cause to be given a notice in writing, according to the Form numbered 5 in the

Persons omitted in the borough lists to give notice of their claims.

Notices as to persons not entitled to be retained in the lists.

c 5

xxxiv

2 William IV. Chap. 45.

said Schedule (I.), or to the like effect, to the overseers who shall have made out the list in which the name of the person so objected to shall have been inserted, or if the person objected to shall have been inserted in the list of freemen of any city, borough, or place as aforesaid, then to the town clerk of such city, borough, or place ; and the overseers shall include the names of all persons so claiming as aforesaid in a list according to the Form numbered 6 in the said Schedule (I.), and the names of all persons so objected to as aforesaid in a list according to the Form numbered 7 in the said Schedule (I.), and shall cause copies of such two lists to be fixed on or near the doors of all the churches and chapels within their parish or township, or if there be no church or chapel therein, then to be fixed in some public and conspicuous situation within the same respectively, on the two Sundays next preceding the fifteenth day of September in the present and in every succeeding year; and every town clerk shall include the names of all persons so claiming as freemen in a list according to the Form numbered 8 in the said Schedule (I.), and the names of all persons so objected to as freemen in a list according to the Form numbered 9 in the said Schedule (I.), and shall cause copies of such two lists to be fixed on or near the doors of the Town Hall, or in some public and conspicuous situation, within his respective city, borough, or place as aforesaid, on the two Sundays hereinbefore last mentioned in the present and in every succeeding year ; and the overseers and town clerks shall likewise keep a copy of the names of all the persons so claiming as aforesaid, and also a copy of the names of all persons so objected to as aforesaid, to be perused by any person, without payment of any fee, at all reasonable hours during the ten days next preceding the said fifteenth day of September in the present and in every succeeding year, and shall deliver a copy of each of such lists to any person requiring the same, on payment of one shilling for each copy.

Lists of claimants, and of persons objected to, to be published, &c.

2 William IV. Chap. 45.

XXXV

XLVIII. And be it enacted, That for providing a list of such of the freemen of the city of *London* as are liverymen of the several companies entitled to vote in the election of a member or members to serve in any future Parliament for the city of *London*, the returning officer or officers of the said city shall, on or before the last day of July in the present and in each succeeding year, issue precepts to the clerks of the said livery companies, requiring them forthwith to make out or cause to be made out, at the expense of the respective companies, an alphabetical list, according to the Form in the Schedule (K.) to this Act annexed, of the freemen of *London* being liverymen of the said respective companies and entitled to vote in such election; and every such clerk shall sign such list, and transmit the same, with two printed copies thereof, to such returning officer or officers, who shall forthwith fix one such copy in the *Guildhall* and one in the *Royal Exchange* of the said city, there to remain fourteen days in the present and in every subsequent year; and the clerks of the said livery companies shall cause a sufficient number of such lists of freemen and liverymen of their respective companies to be printed at the expense of the respective companies, and shall keep the same, to be perused by any person, without payment of any fee, at all reasonable hours during the two first weeks after such lists shall have been printed; and every person whose name shall have been omitted in any such list of freemen and liverymen, and who shall claim to have his name inserted therein as having been entitled on the last day of July then next preceding, shall, on or before the twenty-fifth day of August in the present and in every succeeding year, give or cause to be given a notice in writing according to the Form numbered 1 in the said Schedule (K.), or to the like effect, to the returning officer or officers, and to the clerk of that company in the list whereof he shall claim to have his name inserted; and the returning officer or offi-

List of livery-men of London to be transmitted to the returning officer.

Notices to be given of omissions and objections in list of liverymen.

xxxvi

2 WILLIAM IV. CHAP. 45.

cers shall include the names of all persons so claiming as aforesaid in a list according to the Form numbered 2 in the said Schedule (K.), and shall cause such last-mentioned list to be fixed in the *Guildhall* and *Royal Exchange* of the said city on the two Mondays next preceding the fifteenth day of September in the present and in every succeeding year; and the said returning officer or officers, and clerks of the said companies, shall likewise keep a copy of the names of all the persons so claiming as aforesaid, to be perused by any person, without payment of any fee, at all reasonable hours during the ten days next preceding the said fifteenth day of September in the present and in every succeeding year; and every person who shall object to any other person as not having been entitled on the last day of July then next preceding to have his name inserted in any such livery list shall, on or before the twenty-fifth day of August in the present and in every succeeding year, give to such other person, or leave at his usual place of abode, a notice in writing according to the Form numbered 3 in the said Schedule (K.), or to

Poll of livery-men to be taken at Guildhall. the like effect; and in the city of *London* the returning officer or officers shall take the poll or votes of such freemen of the said city being liverymen of the several companies as are entitled to vote at such election in the *Guildhall* of the said city; and the said returning officer or officers shall not be required to provide any booth or compartments, but shall appoint or take one poll for the whole number of such liverymen at the same place.

Judges of assize to name barristers, who shall revise the lists of borough voters. XLIX. And be it enacted, That the Lord Chief Justice of the Court of King's Bench for the time being shall, in the month of July or August in the present and in every succeeding year, nominate and appoint so many barristers as the said Lord Chief Justice shall deem necessary, to revise the respective lists of voters for the city of *London*, and for the city of *Westminster*, and for the several boroughs in

2 WILLIAM IV. CHAP. 45.

xxxvii

the county of *Middlesex*; and that the senior judge for the time being in the commission of assize for every other county shall, when travelling the Summer circuit, in the present and in every succeeding year, nominate and appoint so many barristers as the said judge shall deem necessary, to revise the respective lists of voters, as well for the several cities and boroughs in every such county, as for every city and town, and county of a city and town, next adjoining to any such county; and the town and county of the town of *Kingston-upon-Hull* shall for this purpose be considered as next adjoining to the county of *York*, and the town and county of the town of *Newcastle-upon-Tyne* as next adjoining to the county of *Northumberland*, and the city and county of the city of *Bristol* as next adjoining to the county of *Somerset*; and the said Lord Chief Justice and judge respectively shall have power to nominate and appoint one or more barristers to revise the lists for the same city or borough or other place as aforesaid, or one barrister only, to revise the lists for several cities, boroughs, and other places as aforesaid : Provided always, that no Member of Parliament, nor any person holding any office or place of profit under the crown, shall be appointed as such barrister as aforesaid, and that no barrister so appointed as aforesaid shall be eligible to serve in Parliament for eighteen months from the time of his appointment for any city, borough, or other place as aforesaid for which he shall be so appointed : Provided also, that nothing herein contained shall prevent the same barrister from being appointed to revise the lists for two or more counties, ridings, parts, or divisions, or for any county, riding, parts, or division, and any one or more of the cities or boroughs therein.

Proviso.

L. And be it enacted, That the barrister or barristers so appointed to revise the lists of voters for any city or borough shall hold an open court or

Barrister to revise lists of borough voters, and upon due proof to insert and expunge names.

xxxviii

2 WILLIAM IV. CHAP. 45.

courts for that purpose within such city or borough,
and also within every place sharing in the election
for such city or borough, at some time between the
fifteenth day of September inclusive and the twenty-
fifth day of October inclusive in the present and in
every succeeding year, having first given three clear
days' notice of the holding of such court or courts,
to be fixed on the doors of all the churches and
chapels within such city, borough, or place respectively, or if there be no church or chapel therein,
then to be fixed in some public and conspicuous
situation within the same respectively; and the
overseers and town clerks who shall have made out
the lists of voters as aforesaid, and in the case of the
city of *London* the returning officer or officers of the
said city, shall, at the opening of the first court to be
held by every such barrister for revising such lists,
produce their respective lists before him; and the
said overseers and town clerks shall also deliver to
such barrister a copy of the list of the persons
objected to, so made out by them as aforesaid; and
the clerks of the several livery companies of the
city of *London*, and the town clerk of every other
city or borough, or place sharing in the election
therewith, and the several overseers within every
city, borough, or place as aforesaid, shall attend the
court to be held by every such barrister for any such
city, borough, or place as aforesaid, and shall answer
upon oath all such questions as such barrister may
put to them, or any of them, touching any matter
necessary for revising the lists of voters; and every
such barrister shall insert in such lists the name of
every person who shall be proved to his satisfaction
to have been entitled on the last day of July then
next preceding to have his name inserted in any such
list of voters for such city or borough; and such
barrister shall retain on the lists of voters for such
city or borough the names of all persons to whom
no objection shall have been made in the manner
hereinbefore mentioned, and he shall also retain on

2 WILLIAM IV. CHAP. 45.

xxxix

the said lists the name of every person who shall
have been objected to by any person, unless the
party so objecting shall appear by himself, or by
some one on his behalf, in support of such objection;
and where the name of any person inserted in the
list of voters for such city or borough shall have
been objected to in the manner hereinbefore mentioned, and the person so objecting shall appear by
himself, or by some one on his behalf, in support of
such objection, every such barrister shall require it
to be proved that the person so objected to was
entitled on the last day of July then next preceding
to have his name inserted in the list of voters for
such city or borough in respect of the qualification
described in such list, and in case the same shall not
be proved to the satisfaction of such barrister, or in
case it shall be proved that such person was then
incapacitated by any law or statute from voting in
the election of members to serve in Parliament, such
barrister shall expunge the name of every such person from the said lists, and he shall also expunge
from the said lists the name of every person who
shall be proved to him to be dead, and shall correct
any mistake which shall be proved to him to have
been made in any of the said lists as to any of the
particulars by this Act required to be inserted in
such lists; and where the Christian name, or the
place of abode, or the nature of the qualification, or
the local description of the property of any person
who shall be included in any such list shall be wholly
omitted in such list in any case where the same is by
this Act directed to be specified therein, such barrister shall expunge the name of every such person
from such list, unless · the matter or matters so
omitted be supplied to the satisfaction of such barrister before he shall have completed the revision of
such list, in which case he shall then and there insert
the same in such list: Provided always, that no person's name shall be inserted by such barrister in any
such list for any city or borough, or shall be ex-

*Power to rec-
tify mistakes
and supply
omissions in
the lists.*

2 WILLIAM IV. CHAP. 45.

xl

punged therefrom, except in the case of death, or of such omission or omissions as hereinbefore last-mentioned, unless such notice shall have been given as is hereinbefore required in each of the said cases.

Power of inspecting tax assessments and rate books.

LI. And be it enacted, That the overseers of every parish or township shall, for their assistance in making out the lists in pursuance of this Act, (upon request made by them or any of them, at any reasonable time between the first day of June and the last day of July in the present and in any succeeding year, to any assessor or collector of taxes, or to any other officer having the custody of any duplicate or tax assessment for such parish or township,) have free liberty to inspect any such duplicate or tax assessment, and to extract from thence such particulars as may appear to such overseer or overseers to be necessary ; and every barrister appointed under this Act shall have power to require any assessor, collector of taxes, or other officer having the custody of any duplicate or tax assessment, or any overseer or overseers having the custody of any poor rate, to produce the same respectively before him at any court to be held by him, for the purpose of assisting him in revising the lists to be by him revised in pursuance of this Act.

Barrister, on revising the lists, to have power of adjonrning, of administering oaths, &c. ;

LII. And be it enacted, That every barrister holding any court under this Act as aforesaid shall have power to adjourn the same from time to time, and from any one place to any other place or places within the same county, riding, parts, or division, or within the same city or borough, or within any place sharing in the election for such city or borough, but so as that no such adjourned court shall be held after the twenty-fifth day of October in any year ; and every such barrister shall have power to administer an oath (or, in the case of a Quaker or Moravian, an affirmation,) to all persons making objection to the insertion or omission of

2 William IV. Chap. 45.   xli

any name in any of such lists as aforesaid, and to all persons objected to or claiming to be inserted in any of such lists, or claiming to have any mistake corrected or any omission supplied in any of such lists, and to all witnesses who may be tendered on either side; and that if any person taking any oath or making any affirmation under this Act shall wilfully swear or affirm falsely, such person shall be deemed guilty of perjury, and shall be punished accordingly; and that at the holding of such respective courts the parties shall not be attended by counsel; and that every such barrister shall, upon the hearing in open court, finally determine upon the validity of such claims and objections, and shall for that purpose have the same powers and proceed in the same manner (except where otherwise directed by this Act) as the returning officer of any county, city, or borough according to the laws and usages now observed at elections; and such barrister shall *and to settle* in open court write his initials against the names re- *and sign the lists in open* spectively struck out or inserted, and against any *court.* part of the said lists in which any mistake shall have been corrected or any omission supplied, and shall sign his name to every page of the several lists so settled.

LIII. And be it enacted, That notwithstanding *Judges to ap-* any thing hereinbefore contained, if it shall be made *point addi- tional barris-* to appear to the Lord Chief Justice or Judge who *ters in case* shall have appointed any barrister or barristers *of need.* under this Act, to revise the list of voters, that by reason of the death, illness, or absence of any such barrister or barristers, or by reason of the insufficiency of the number of such barristers, or from any other cause, such lists cannot be revised within the period directed by this Act, it shall be lawful for such Lord Chief Justice or Judge, and he is hereby required, to appoint one or more barrister or barristers to act in the place of or in addition to the barrister or barristers originally appointed; and

xlii

2 William IV. Chap. 45.

such barrister or barristers so subsequently appointed shall have the same powers and authorities in every respect as if they had been originally appointed by such Lord Chief Justice or Judge.

County lists to be transmitted to clerk of the peace; borough lists to be kept by returning officer, and handed to his successor.

Lists to be copied into books, with the names numbered.

LIV. And be it enacted, That the lists of voters for each county, or for the riding, parts, or division of each county, so signed as aforesaid by any such barrister, shall be forthwith transmitted by him to the clerk of the peace of the county, riding, or parts for which such barrister shall have been appointed; and the clerk of the peace shall keep the said lists among the records of the sessions, arranged with every hundred in alphabetical order, and with every parish and township within such hundred likewise in alphabetical order, and shall forthwith cause the said lists to be fairly and truly copied in the same order in a book to be by him provided for that purpose, and shall prefix to every name so copied out its proper number, beginning the numbers from the first name, and continuing them in a regular series down to the last name, and shall complete and deliver such book on or before the last day of October in the present and in every succeeding year to the sheriff of the county, or his under-sheriff, who shall safely keep the same, and shall at the expiration of his office deliver over the same to the succeeding sheriff or his under-sheriff; and the lists of voters for each city or borough, so signed as aforesaid by any such barrister, shall be forthwith delivered by him to the returning officer for such city or borough, who shall safely keep the same, and shall cause the said lists to be fairly and truly copied in a book to be by him provided for that purpose, with every name therein numbered according to the directions aforesaid, and shall cause such book to be completed on or before the last day of October in the present and in every succeeding year, and shall deliver over such book, together with the lists, at the expiration of his office, to the person succeeding him in such

2 WILLIAM IV. CHAP. 45.

xliii

office; and every such book, to be so completed on *Such books to be the register of electors.* or before the last day of October in the present year, shall be deemed the register of the electors to vote, after the end of this present Parliament, in the choice of a member or members to serve in Parliament for the county, riding, parts, or division of a county, city, or borough to which such register shall relate, at any election which may take place after the said last day of October in the present year and before the first day of November in the year one thousand eight hundred and thirty-three; and every *Register how long to be in force.* such book to be so completed on or before the last day of October in the year one thousand eight hundred and thirty-three, and in every succeeding year, shall be the register of electors to vote at any election which shall take place between the first day of November inclusive in the year wherein such respective register shall have been made and the first day of November in the succeeding year.

LV. And be it enacted, That the overseers of *Copies of the lists and of the registers to be printed for sale.* every parish and township shall cause to be written or printed copies of the lists so by them to be made in the present and in every succeeding year, and shall deliver such copies to all persons applying for the same, on payment of a reasonable price for each copy; and the monies arising from the sale thereof shall be accounted for by the said overseers, and applied to the same purposes as monies collected for the relief of the poor; and the clerks of the peace shall cause to be written or printed copies of the registers of the electors for their respective counties, ridings, or parts, or for the divisions of their respective counties; and the returning officer of every city or borough shall cause to be written or printed copies of the register of the electors for such city or borough; and every such clerk of the peace, and every such returning officer, shall deliver such respective copies to all persons applying for the same, on payment of a reasonable price for each

xliv   2 WILLIAM IV. CHAP. 45.

copy; and the monies arising from the sale of all such copies shall be accounted for to the treasurer of the county, riding, or parts.

Expenses of overseers, clerks of the peace, &c. how to be defrayed.

LVI. And be it enacted, That for the purpose of defraying the expenses to be incurred by the overseers of the poor and by the clerk of the peace in carrying into effect the several provisions of this Act, so far as relates to the electors for any county, or for any riding, parts, or division of a county, every person, upon giving notice of his claim as such elector to the overseers, as hereinbefore mentioned, shall pay or cause to be paid to the said overseers the sum of one shilling; and such notice of claim shall not be deemed valid until such sum shall have been paid; and the overseers of each parish or township shall add all monies so received by them to the money collected or to be collected for the relief of the poor in such parish or township, and such monies so added shall be applicable to the same purposes as monies collected for the relief of the poor; and that for the purpose of defraying the expenses to be incurred by the returning officer of every city and borough, and by the overseers of the several parishes and townships in every city and borough, and place sharing in the election therewith, in carrying into effect the provisions of this Act, so far as relates to the electors for such city or borough, every such elector whose name shall be upon the register of voters for such city or borough for the time being shall be liable to the payment of one shilling annually, which sum shall be levied and collected from each elector in addition to and as part of the money payable by him as his contribution to the rate for the relief of the poor, and such sum shall be applicable to the same purposes as money collected for the relief of the poor; and that the expenses incurred by the overseers of any parish or township in making out, printing, and publishing the several lists and notices directed by this Act, and all other expenses

2 WILLIAM IV. CHAP. 45.

xlv

incurred by them in carrying into effect the provisions of this Act, shall be defrayed out of the money collected or to be collected for the relief of the poor in such parish or township; and that all expenses incurred by the returning officer of any city or borough in causing the lists of the electors for such city or borough to be copied out and made into a register, and in causing copies of such register to be written or printed, shall be defrayed by the overseers of the poor of the several parishes and townships within such city or borough, or place sharing in the election therewith, out of the money collected or to be collected for the relief of the poor in such parishes and townships, in proportion to the number of persons placed on the register of voters for each parish or township; and that all expenses incurred by the clerk of the peace of any county, riding, or parts, in causing the lists of the electors for such county, riding or parts, or for any division of such county, to be copied out and made into a register, and in causing copies of such register to be written or printed, and in otherwise carrying into effect the provisions of this Act, shall be defrayed by the treasurer of such county, riding, or parts out of any public money in his hands, and he shall be allowed all such payments in his accounts: Provided always, that no expenses incurred by any clerk of the peace under this Act shall be so defrayed unless the account shall be laid before the justices of the peace at the next quarter sessions after such expenses shall have been incurred, and allowed by the Court.

LVII. And be it enacted, That every barrister appointed to revise any lists of voters under this Act shall be paid at the rate of five guineas for every day that he shall be so employed, over and above his travelling and other expenses: and every such barrister, after the termination of his last sitting, shall lay or cause to be laid before the lords commissioners of his majesty's treasury for the time

Remuneration of the barristers for revising the lists.

xlvi

2 WILLIAM IV. CHAP. 45.

being a statement of the number of days during which he shall have been so employed, and an account of the travelling and other expenses incurred by him in respect of such employment; and the said lords commissioners shall make an order for the amount to be paid to such barrister.

No inquiry at the time of election, except as to the identity of the voter, the continuance of his qualification, and whether he has voted before at same election.

LVIII. And be it enacted, That in all elections whatever of members to serve in any future Parliament no inquiry shall be permitted at the time of polling, as to the right of any person to vote, except only as follows; that is to say, that the returning officer or his respective deputy shall, if required on behalf of any candidate, put to any voter at the time of his tendering his vote, and not afterwards, the following questions, or any of them, and no other:

Form of questions as to these points.

1. Are you the same person whose name appears as *A. B.* on the register of voters now in force for the county of   [*or* for the   riding, parts, *or* division, *&c. or* for the city, *&c. as the case may be*]?

2. Have you already voted, either here or elsewhere, at this election for the county of   [*or* for the   riding, parts, *or* division of the county of   , *or* for the city *or* borough of   *as the case may be*]?

3. Have you the same qualification for which your name was originally inserted in the register of voters now in force for the county of, *&c.* [*or* for the   riding, *&c.,* or for the city, *&c., as the case may be, specifying in each case the particulars of the qualification as described in the register*]?

And if any person shall wilfully make a false answer to any of the questions aforesaid, he shall be deemed guilty of an indictable misdemeanor, and shall be punished accordingly; and the returning officer or his deputy, or a commissioner or commis-

2 William IV. Chap. 45.   xlvii

sioners to be for that purpose by him or them ap- Oath to be
pointed, shall (if required on behalf of any candidate administered
at the time aforesaid) administer an oath (or, in case
of a Quaker or Moravian, an affirmation) to any
voter in the following form ; (that is to say,)

' You do swear, [or *being a Quaker or Moravian*, do Form of oath.
' affirm,] That you are the same person whose name
' appears as *A. B.* on the register of voters now in
' force for the county of   [*or* for the
' riding, parts, *or* division of the county of
' *or* for the city *or* borough of   *as the case*
' *may be*], and that you have not before voted, either
' here or elsewhere, at the present election for the said
' county [*or* for the said riding, parts, *or* division of
' the said county, *or* for the said city *or* borough, *as*
' *the case may be*].   So help you GOD.'

And no elector shall hereafter at any such election No other
be required to take any oath or affirmation, except oath as to
as aforesaid, either in proof of his freehold or of his qualification.
residence, age, or other qualification or right to vote,
any law or statute, local or general, to the contrary
notwithstanding ; and no person claiming to vote at
any such election shall be excluded from voting
thereat, except by reason of its appearing to the
returning officer or his respective deputy, upon put-
ting such questions as aforesaid, or any of them,
that the person so claiming to vote is not the same
person whose name appears on such register as
aforesaid, or that he has previously voted at the
same election, or that he has not the same qualification for which his name was originally inserted in
such register, or except by reason of such person
refusing to take the said oath or make the said
affirmation or to take or make the oath or affirmation against bribery, or any other oath or affirmation
now required by law, and not hereby dispensed
with ; and no scrutiny shall hereafter be allowed by No scrutiny
or before any returning officer with regard to any by returning
votes given or tendered at any election of a member

xlviii

2 WILLIAM IV. CHAP. 45.

or members to serve in any future Parliament ; any law, statute, or usage to the contrary notwithstanding.

Persons excluded from the register by the barrister may tender their votes at elections.

LIX. Provided always, and be it enacted, That any person whose name shall have been omitted from any register of voters in consequence of the decision of the barrister who shall have revised the lists from which such register shall have been formed may tender his vote at any election at which such register shall be in force, stating at the time the name or names of the candidate or candidates for whom he tenders such vote, and the returning officer or his deputy shall enter upon the poll book every vote so tendered, distinguishing the same from the votes admitted and allowed at such election.

Tender to be recorded.

Correctness of the register to be questionable before a committee of the House of Commons.

LX. Provided also, and be it enacted, That, upon petition to the House of Commons, complaining of an undue election or return of any member or members to serve in Parliament, any petitioner, or any person defending such election or return, shall be at liberty to impeach the correctness of the register of voters in force at the time of such election, by proving that in consequence of the decision of the barrister who shall have revised the lists of voters from which such register shall have been formed the name of any person who voted at such election was improperly inserted or retained in such register, or the name of any person who tendered his vote at such election improperly omitted from such register ; and the select committee appointed for the trial of such petition shall alter the poll taken at such election according to the truth of the case, and shall report their determination thereupon to the House, and the House shall thereupon carry such determination into effect, and the return shall be amended, or the election declared void, as the case may be, and the register corrected accordingly, or such other order shall be made as to the House shall seem proper.

2 William IV. Chap. 45. xlix

LXI. And be it enacted, That the sheriffs of *Yorkshire* and *Lincolnshire*, and the sheriffs of the counties divided by this Act, shall duly cause proclamation to be made of the several days fixed for the election of a knight or knights of the shire for the several ridings, parts, and divisions of their respective counties, and shall preside at the election by themselves or their lawful deputies.

Sheriffs of the divided counties to fix the time and preside at elections.

LXII. And be it enacted, That at every contested election of a knight or knights to serve in any future Parliament for any county, or for any riding, parts, or division of a county, the polling shall commence at nine o'clock in the forenoon of the next day but two after the day fixed for the election, unless such next day but two shall be Saturday or Sunday, and then on the Monday following, at the principal place of election, and also at the several places to be appointed as hereinafter directed for taking polls; and such polling shall continue for two days only, such two days being successive days; that is to say, for seven hours on the first day of polling, and for eight hours on the second day of polling; and no poll shall be kept open later than four o'clock in the afternoon of the second day; any statute to the contrary notwithstanding.

Commencement and continuance of polls at county elections.

LXIII. And be it enacted, That the respective counties in *England* and *Wales*, and the respective ridings, parts, and divisions of counties, shall be divided into convenient districts for polling, and in each district shall be appointed a convenient place for taking the poll at all elections of a knight or knights of the shire to serve in any future Parliament, and such districts and places for taking the poll shall be settled and appointed by the Act to be passed in this present Parliament for the purpose of settling and describing the divisions of the counties enumerated in the Schedule marked (F.) to this Act annexed; provided that no county, nor any

Counties to be divided into districts for polling.

d

2 WILLIAM IV. CHAP. 45.

riding, parts or division of a county, shall have more than fifteen districts and respective places appointed for taking the poll for such county, riding, parts, or division.

As to booths at the polling places for counties.

LXIV. And be it enacted, That at every contested election for any county, or riding, parts, or division of a county, the sheriff, under-sheriff, or sheriff's deputy shall, if required thereto by or on behalf of any candidate, on the day fixed for the election, and if not so required may, if it shall appear to him expedient, cause to be erected a reasonable number of booths for taking the poll at the principal place of election, and also at each of the polling places so to be appointed as aforesaid, and shall cause-to be affixed on the most conspicuous part of each of the said booths the names of the several parishes, townships and places for which such booth is respectively allotted; and no person shall be admitted to vote at any such election in respect of any property situate in any parish, township, or place, except at the booth so allotted for such parish, township, or place; and if no booth shall be so allotted for the same, then at any of the booths for the same district; and in case any parish, township, or place shall happen not to be included in any of the districts to be appointed, the votes in respect of property situate in any parish, township, or place so omitted shall be taken at the principal place of election for the county, or riding, parts, or division of the county, as the case may be.

No voter to poll out of the district where his property lies.

Provision as to sheriff's deputies, the custody of poll books, and final declaration of the poll for counties.

LXV. And be it enacted, That the sheriff shall have power to appoint deputies to preside and clerks to take the poll at the principal place of election, and also at the several places appointed for taking the poll for any county, or any riding, parts, or division of a county; and that the poll clerks employed at those several places shall, at the close

2 William IV. Chap. 45.

of each day's poll, enclose and seal their several
books, and shall publicly deliver them, so enclosed
and sealed, to the sheriff, under-sheriff, or sheriff's
deputy presiding at such poll, who shall give a receipt for the same, and shall, on the commencement
of the poll on the second day, deliver them back, so
enclosed and sealed, to the persons from whom he
shall have received them; and on the final close of
the poll every such deputy who shall have received
any such poll books shall forthwith deliver or
transmit the same, so enclosed and sealed, to the sheriff or his under-sheriff, who shall receive and keep
all the poll books unopened until the re-assembling
of the court on the day next but one after the close
of the poll, unless such next day but one shall be
Sunday, and then on the Monday following, when
he shall openly break the seals thereon, and cast up
the number of votes as they appear on the said several books, and shall openly declare the state of
the poll, and shall make proclamation of the member or members chosen, not later than two o'clock
in the afternoon of the said day.

LXVI. And be it enacted, That in all matters
relative to the election of knights or a knight of the
shire to serve in any future Parliament for any
county, or for any riding, parts, or division of a
county, the sheriff of the county, his under-sheriff,
or any lawful deputy of such sheriff, shall have
power to act in all places having any exclusive jurisdiction or privilege whatsoever, in the same manner
as such sheriff, under-sheriff or deputy may act within
any part of such sheriff's ordinary jurisdiction.

Sheriff in county elections may act in places of exclusive jurisdiction.

LXVII. And be it enacted, That at every contested election of a member or members to serve in
any future Parliament for any city or borough in
England, except the borough of *Monmouth*, the poll
shall commence on the day fixed for the election, or
on the day next following, or at the latest on the

Commence-ment and continuance of polls at borough elections in England.

lii

2 WILLIAM IV. CHAP. 45.

third day, unless any of the said days shall be Saturday or Sunday, and then on the Monday following, the particular day for the commencement of the poll to be fixed by the returning officer; and such polling shall continue for two days only, such two days being successive days, (that is to say), for seven hours on the first day of polling, and for eight hours on the second day of polling; and that the poll shall on no account be kept open later than four o'clock in the afternoon of such second day; any statute to the contrary notwithstanding.

Polling for boroughs in England to be at several booths, not more than 600 voting at one compartment in a booth.

LXVIII. And be it enacted, That at every contested election of a member or members to serve in any future Parliament for any city or borough in England, except the borough of *Monmouth*, the returning officer shall, if required thereto by or on behalf of any candidate, on the day fixed for the election, and if not so required may, if it shall appear to him expedient, cause to be erected for taking the poll at such election different booths for different parishes, districts, or parts of such city or borough, which booths may be situated either in one place or in several places, and shall be so divided and allotted into compartments as to the returning officer shall seem most convenient, so that no greater number than six hundred shall be required to poll at any one compartment; and the returning officer shall appoint a clerk to take the poll at each compartment, and shall cause to be affixed on the most conspicuous part of each of the said booths the names of the several parishes, districts, and parts for which such booth is respectively allotted;

Each person to vote at the booth appointed for his parish or district.

and no person shall be admitted to vote at any such election, except at the booth allotted for the parish, district, or part wherein the property may be situate in respect of which he claims to vote, or in case he does not claim to vote in respect of property, then wherein his place of abode as described in the register may be; but in case no booth shall happen

2 William IV. Chap. 45.

liii

to be provided for any particular parish, district, or part as aforesaid, the votes of persons voting in respect of property situate in any parish, district, or part so omitted, or having their place of abode therein, may be taken at any of the said booths, and the votes of freemen residing out of the limits of the city or borough may be taken at any of the said booths; and public notice of the situation, division, and allotment of the different booths shall be given two days before the commencement of the poll by the returning officer; and in case the booths shall *If the booths* be situated in different places, the returning officer *are in different places,* may appoint a deputy to preside at each place; and *a deputy to* at every such election the poll clerks at the close of *preside at* each day's poll shall enclose and seal their several *As to custody of poll* poll books, and shall publicly deliver them, so en- *books and* closed and sealed, to the returning officer or his *final declaration of poll* deputy, who shall give a receipt for the same, and *for boroughs.* shall, on the commencement of the poll on the second day, deliver them back, so enclosed and sealed, to the persons from whom he shall have received the same; and every deputy so receiving any such poll books, on the final close of the poll shall forthwith deliver or transmit the same, so enclosed and sealed, to the returning officer, who shall receive and keep all the poll books unopened until the following day, unless such day be Sunday, and then till the Monday following, when he shall openly break the seals thereon, and cast up the number of votes as they appear on the said several books, and shall openly declare the state of the poll, and make proclamation of the member or members chosen, not later than two o'clock in the afternoon of the said day: provided always, that the returning officer, or his lawful deputy, may, if he think fit, declare the final state of the poll, and proceed to make the return immediately after the poll shall have been lawfully closed: provided also, that no nomination shall be made or election holden of any member for liv

2 WILLIAM IV. CHAP. 45.

any city or borough in any church, chapel, or other
place of public worship.

Polling districts to be appointed for Shoreham, Cricklade, Aylesbury, and East Retford. LXIX. Provided always, and be it enacted, That
so far as relates to the several boroughs of *New
Shoreham, Cricklade, Aylesbury,* and *East Retford,* as
defined by this Act, the said several boroughs shall
be divided into convenient districts for polling, and
there shall be appointed in each district a convenient place for taking the poll at all elections of
members to serve in any future Parliament for each
of the said boroughs, which districts and places for
taking the poll shall be settled and appointed by an
Act to be passed in this present Parliament.

When returning officers may close the poll before the expiration of the time fixed.

Adjournment of poll in case of riot. LXX. And be it enacted, That nothing in this
Act contained shall prevent any sheriff or other re-
turning officer, or the lawful deputy of any returning officer, from closing the poll previous to the
expiration of the time fixed by this Act, in any case
where the same might have been lawfully closed
before the passing of this Act; and that where the
proceedings at any election shall be interrupted or
obstructed by any riot or open violence, the sheriff
or other returning officer, or the lawful deputy of
any returning officer, shall not for such cause finally
close the poll, but, in case the proceedings shall be
so interrupted or obstructed at any particular polling
place or places, shall adjourn the poll at such place
or places only until the following day, and if necessary shall further adjourn the same until such interruption or obstruction shall have ceased, when the
returning officer or his deputy shall again proceed
to take the poll at such place or places; and any
day whereon the poll shall have been so adjourned
shall not, as to such place or places, be reckoned
one of the two days of polling at such election within the meaning of this Act; and wherever the poll
shall have been so adjourned by any deputy of any
sheriff or other returning officer, such deputy shall

2 William IV. Chap. 45.

forthwith give notice of such adjournment to the sheriff or returning officer, who shall not finally declare the state of the poll, or make proclamation of the member or members chosen, until the poll so adjourned at such place or places as aforesaid shall have been finally closed, and delivered or transmitted to such sheriff or other returning officer; any thing herein-before contained to the contrary notwithstanding.

LXXI. And be it enacted, That from and after the end of this present Parliament all booths erected for the convenience of taking polls shall be erected at the joint and equal expence of the several candidates, and the same shall be erected by contract with the candidates, if they shall think fit to make such contract, or if they shall not make such contract, then the same shall be erected by the sheriff or other returning officer at the expence of the several candidates as aforesaid, subject to such limitation as is herein-after next mentioned; (that is to say,) that the expence to be incurred for the booth or booths to be erected at the principal place of election for any county, riding, parts, or division of a county, or at any of the polling places so to be appointed as aforesaid, shall not exceed the sum of forty pounds in respect of any one such principal place of election, or any one such polling place ; and that the expence to be incurred for any booth or booths to be erected for any parish, district, or part of any city or borough shall not exceed the sum of twenty-five pounds in respect of any one such parish, district, or part; and that all deputies appointed by the sheriff or other returning officer shall be paid each two guineas by the day, and all clerks employed in taking the poll shall be paid each one guinea by the day, at the expence of the candidates at such election: Provided always, that if any person shall be proposed without his consent, then the person so proposing him shall be liable to defray his

Candidates or persons proposing a candidate without his consent, to be at the expence of booths and poll clerks.

Limitation of expence.

lvi
2 WILLIAM IV. CHAP. 45.

Houses may be hired for polling in, instead of booths.

share of the said expences in like manner as if he had been a candidate; provided also, that the sheriff or returning officer may, if he shall think fit, instead of erecting such booth or booths as aforesaid, procure or hire and use any houses or other buildings for the purpose of taking the poll therein, subject always to the same regulations, provisions, liabilities, and limitations of expence as are herein-before mentioned with regard to booths for taking the poll.

Certified copies of the register of voters for each booth.

LXXII. And be it enacted, That the sheriff or other returning officer shall, before the day fixed for the election, cause to be made, for the use of each booth or other polling place at such election, a true copy of the register of voters, and shall under his hand certify every such copy to be true.

Powers of deputies of returning officers.

LXXIII. And be it enacted, That every deputy of a sheriff or other returning officer shall have the same power of administering the oaths and affirmations required by law, and of appointing commissioners for administering such oaths and affirmations as may by law be administered by commissioners, as the sheriff or other returning officer has by virtue of this or any other Act, and subject to the same regulations and provisions in every respect as such sheriff or other returning officer.

Regulations respecting polling, &c. for the borough of Monmouth, and for the contributory boroughs in Wales.

LXXIV. And be it enacted, That from and after the end of this present Parliament, every person who shall have a right to vote in the election of a member for the borough of *Monmouth*, in respect of the towns of *Newport* or *Usk*, shall give his vote at *Newport* or *Usk* respectively before the deputy for each of such towns, whom the returning officer of the borough of *Monmouth* is hereby authorized and required to appoint; and every person who shall have a right to vote in the election of a member for any shire-town or borough, in respect of any place

2 WILLIAM IV. CHAP. 45.

lvii

named in the first column of the schedule marked (E.) to this Act annexed, shall give his vote at such place before the deputy for such place whom the returning officer of the shire-town or borough is hereby authorized and required to appoint; and every person who shall have a right to vote in the election of a member for the borough composed of the towns of *Swansea, Loughor, Neath, Aberavon*, and *Ken-fig* shall give his vote at the town in respect of which he shall be entitled to vote, (that is to say,) at *Swansea* before the portreeve of *Swansea*, and at each of the other towns before the deputy of such town whom the said portreeve is hereby authorized and required to appoint; and at every contested election for the borough of *Monmouth*, or for any shire-town or borough named in the second column of the said Schedule (E.), or for the borough composed of the said five towns, or for the borough of *Brecon*, the polling shall commence on the day next after the day fixed for the respective election, unless such next day be Saturday or Sunday, and then on the Monday following, as well at *Monmouth* as at *Newport* and *Usk* respectively, and as well at the shire-town or borough as at each of the places sharing in the election therewith respectively, and as well at *Swansea* as at each of the four other towns respectively; and such polling shall continue for two days only, such two days being successive days, (that is to say,) for seven hours on the first day of polling, and for eight hours on the second day of polling, and that the poll shall on no account be kept open later than four o'clock in the afternoon of such second day ; and the returning officer of the borough of *Monmouth* shall give to the deputies for *Newport* and *Usk* respectively, and the returning officer of every shire-town or borough named in the second column of the said Schedule (E.) shall give to the deputy for each of the places sharing in the election for such shire-town or borough, notice of the day fixed for such respective election and shall be-

d 5

lviii

2 WILLIAM IV. CHAP. 45.

fore the day fixed for such respective election cause to be made, and to be delivered to every such deputy, a true copy of the register of voters for the borough of *Monmouth*, or for such shire-town or borough, as the case may be, and shall under his hand certify every such copy to be true; and the portreeve of the town of *Swansea* shall give notice of the day of election to the deputy for each of the towns of *Loughor*, *Neath*, *Aberavon*, and *Ken-fig*, and shall in like manner cause to be made, and to be delivered to every such deputy, a true and certified copy of the register of voters for the borough composed of the said five towns; and the respective deputies for *Newport* and *Usk*, and for the respective places named in the first column of the said Schedule (E.) as well as for the towns of *Loughor*, *Neath*, *Aberavon*, and *Ken-fig*, shall respectively take and conduct the poll and deliver or transmit the poll books in the same manner as the deputies of the returning officers of the cities and boroughs in *England* are herein-before directed to do, and shall have the same powers and perform the same duties in every respect as are respectively conferred and imposed

As to appointment of deputies in Wales.

on the said deputies by this Act: Provided always, that where there shall be a mayor, portreeve, or other chief municipal officer in any town or place for which the returning officer or the portreeve of *Swansea* is required to appoint a deputy as aforesaid, such returning officer or the portreeve of *Swansea*, as the case may be, is hereby required to appoint such chief municipal officer for the time being to be such deputy for such town or place.

All election laws to remain in force, except where superseded by this Act.

LXXV. And be it enacted, That all laws, statutes, and usages now in force respecting the election of members to serve in parliament for that part of the United Kingdom called *England* and *Wales* shall be and remain, and are hereby declared to be and remain, in full force, and shall apply to the election of members to serve in parliament for all

2 WILLIAM IV. CHAP. 45.

lix

the counties, ridings, parts, and divisions of counties, cities, and boroughs, hereby empowered to return members, as fully and effectually as if the same respectively had heretofore returned members, except so far as any of the said laws, statutes, or usages are repealed or altered by this Act, or are inconsistent with the provisions thereof.

LXXVI. And be it enacted, That if any sheriff, returning officer, barrister, overseer, or any person whatsoever shall wilfully contravene or disobey the provisions of this Act or any of them, with respect to any matter or thing which such sheriff, returning officer, barrister, overseer, or other person is hereby required to do, he shall for such his offence be liable to be sued in an action of debt in any of his Majesty's courts of record at *Westminster* for the penal sum of five hundred pounds, and the jury before whom such action shall be tried may find their verdict for the full sum of five hundred pounds, or for any less sum which the said jury shall think it just that he should pay for such his offence; and the defendant in such action, being convicted, shall pay such penal sum so awarded, with full costs of suit, to the party who may sue for the same: Provided always, that no such action shall be brought except by a person being an elector or claiming to be an elector, or a candidate, or a member actually returned, or other party aggrieved: Provided also, that the remedy hereby given against the returning officer shall not be construed to supersede any remedy or action against him according to the law now in force.

Penalties on officers for breach of duty.

LXXVII. And be it enacted, That all writs to be issued for the election of members to serve in all future Parliaments, and all mandates, precepts, instruments, proceedings, and notices consequent upon such writs, shall be and the same are hereby authorized to be framed and expressed in such man-

Writs, &c. to be made conformable to this Act.

lx

2 William IV. Chap. 45.

ner and form as may be necessary for the carrying the provisions of this Act into effect.

This Act not to extend to Universities of Oxford and Cambridge. LXXVIII. Provided always, and be it enacted, That nothing in this Act contained shall extend to or in anywise affect the election of members to serve in Parliament for the Universities of *Oxford* or *Cambridge*, or shall entitle any person to vote in the election of members to serve in Parliament for the city of *Oxford* or town of *Cambridge* in respect of the occupation of any chambers or premises in any of the colleges or halls of the Universities of *Oxford* or *Cambridge*.

Of the sense in which words in this Act are to be understood: " city or borough:" LXXIX. And be it enacted, That throughout this Act, wherever the words " city or borough," " cities or boroughs," may occur, those words shall be construed to include, except there be something in the subject or context manifestly repugnant to such construction, all towns corporate, cinque ports, districts, or places within *England* and *Wales* which shall be entitled, after this Act shall have passed, to return a member or members to serve in Parliament, other than counties at large, and ridings, parts, and divisions of counties at large, and shall also include the town of *Berwick-upon-Tweed;* and *" Returning officer:"* the words " returning officer" shall apply to every person or persons to whom, by virtue of his or their office, either under the present Act, or under any former law, custom, or statute, the execution of any writ or precept doth or shall belong for the election of a member or members to serve in Parliament, by whatever name or title such person or persons *" Parish or township:"* may be called ; and the words " parish or township" shall extend to every parish, township, vill, hamlet, district, or place maintaining its own poor; and the *" Overseer's of the poor:"* words " overseers of the poor" shall extend to all persons who by virtue of any office or appointment shall execute the duties of overseers of the poor, by whatever name or title such persons may be called,

2 WILLIAM IV. CHAP. 45.

lxi

and in whatsoever manner they may be appointed, and that all matters by this Act directed to be done by the overseers of a parish or township may be lawfully done by the major part of such overseers, and that wherever any notice is by this Act required to be given to the overseers of any parish or township, it shall be sufficient if such notice shall be delivered to any one of such overseers, or shall be left at his place of abode, or at his office or other place for transacting parochial business, or shall be sent by the post, addressed by a sufficient direction, to the overseers of the particular parish or township, or to any one of them, either by their or his Christian name and surname, or by their or his name of office; and that all provisions in this Act relative to any matters to be done by or with regard *" Justices of* to justices of the peace for counties, or sessions of *the peace for counties,"* the peace for counties, or clerks of the peace for *&c.* counties, or treasurers of counties, shall extend to the justices, sessions, clerks of the peace, and treasurers of the several ridings of *Yorkshire* and parts of *Lincolnshire*, and that the clerk of the peace for the time being for the borough of *Newport* in the *Isle of Wight* shall for the purposes of this Act be deemed and taken to be the clerk of the peace for the county of the *Isle of Wight*, and that all the said respective justices, sessions, and clerks of the peace shall have power to do the several matters required by this Act, as well within places of exclusive jurisdiction as without; and that no misnomer or inac- *Misnomer* curate description of any person or place named or *not to vitiate.* described in any schedule to this Act annexed, or in any list or register of voters, or in any notice required by this Act, shall in anywise prevent or abridge the operation of this Act with respect to such person or place, provided that such person or place shall be so designated in such schedule, list, register, or notice as to be commonly understood.

LXXX. And whereas it may happen that the *In case the* Act or Acts for settling the boundaries of cities, *proposed Boundary Act*

lxii   2 WILLIAM IV. CHAP. 45.

shall not pass before the 20th of June, 1832, the preparations for first registration to be deferred; but if the Boundary Act pass after that day, the periods preparatory to and connected with the first registration to be settled by an order in council.

boroughs, and other places, and the divisions of counties, as herein-before mentioned, may not be passed within such time as will allow the several provisions of this Act relative to the list of voters within such respective boundaries and divisions, and the various notices and proceedings preparatory to and connected with such lists, to be carried into effect within the several periods in the present year herein-before specified and limited in that behalf; and it is therefore expedient in such event as aforesaid to appoint other periods for the purposes aforesaid; be it therefore enacted, That if the Act or Acts for settling the boundaries and divisions herein-before mentioned shall not be passed before the twentieth day of *June* in the present year, then and in such case the notice herein-before required to be given on the said twentieth day of *June* shall not be given on that day, and the list of voters, and the notices and other proceedings preparatory to and connected with such lists, shall not be made out, given, or had upon or within the several days or times in the present year herein-before specified in that behalf; but if the Act or Acts for settling the boundaries of cities, boroughs, and other places, and the divisions of counties, as herein-before mentioned, shall be passed in the present year subsequently to the twentieth day of *June*, then and in such case his Majesty shall, by an order made with the advice of his most honourable privy council, appoint, in lieu of the day for the present year herein-before specified in that behalf, a certain other day, before or upon which the respective lists of voters shall be made out, and shall also appoint, in lieu of the several days and times for the present year herein-before specified or limited in that behalf, certain other days and times upon or within which all notices, claims, objections, and other matters whatsoever by this Act required to be given, delivered, transmitted, done, or performed in relation to such lists, either before or after the

2 WILLIAM IV. CHAP. 45.

lxiii

making out of such lists, shall be respectively given, delivered, transmitted, done, and performed; and his Majesty shall also by such order appoint, in lieu of the period for the present year, herein-before limited in that behalf, a certain other period for the revision of the respective lists of voters by the barristers, and shall also appoint within what time, in lieu of the time for the present year herein-before limited in that behalf, such respective lists shall be copied out into books, and, where necessary, delivered to the sheriff or under-sheriff, and from what day, in lieu of the day for the present year herein-before specified in that behalf, such respective books shall begin to be in force as the registers of voters; and his Majesty may also by such order in council appoint any days and times for doing the several other matters required or authorized by this Act, in lieu of the several days and times for the present year herein-before specified; and all days and times so appointed by his Majesty as aforesaid shall be deemed to be of the same force and effect as if they had in every instance been mentioned in this Act in lieu of the days and times for the present year herein-before specified in that behalf: Provided always, that nothing herein contained shall authorize his Majesty to appoint any days or times in lieu of the days and times mentioned in this Act, except for the purpose of carrying into effect the first registration of voters under this Act: Provided also, that no person shall be entitled to be included in such first registration of voters unless he would have been entitled on the last day of *July* in the present year to have his name inserted in some list of voters if such list had been made out on the said last day of *July*.

Proviso.

LXXXI. Provided always, and be it enacted, That if a dissolution of the present Parliament shall take place after the passing of this Act, and after the passsing of the Act or Acts for settling the

In case of a dissolution of Parliament after the passing of the pro-

lxiv

2 WILLIAM IV. CHAP. 45.

posed Boundary Act, and before registration, the rights of voting shall take effect without registration.

boundaries of cities, boroughs, and other places, and the divisions of counties, as herein-before mentioned, but before the day at and from which the registers of voters to be first made by virtue of this Act shall begin to be in force, in such case such persons only shall be entitled to vote in the election of members to serve in a new Parliament for any county, or for any riding, parts, or division of a county, or for any city or borough, as would be entitled to be inserted in the respective lists of voters for the same directed to be made under this Act if the day of election had been the day for making out such respective lists; and such persons shall be entitled to vote in such election although they may not be registered according to the provisions of this Act, any thing herein contained notwithstanding; and the polling at such election for any county, or for any riding, parts, or division of a county, may be continued for fifteen days, and the polling at such election for any city or borough may be continued for eight days, any thing herein contained notwithstanding.

In case of a dissolution of Parliament before the passing of the proposed Boundary Act, counties not to be divided.

LXXXII. Provided also, and be it enacted, That if a dissolution of the present Parliament shall take place after the passing of this Act, and before the passing of the Act or Acts for settling respectively the boundaries of cities, boroughs, and other places, and the divisions of counties, as herein-before mentioned, then and in such case the election of members to serve in a new Parliament shall, both as to the persons entitled to vote, and otherwise, be regulated according to the provisions of this Act, save and except as herein-after mentioned : (that is to say,) that as to the several counties enumerated in the Schedule (F.) to this Act annexed, all persons entitled by virtue of this Act in respect of property therein to vote in the election of knights of the shire shall be entitled to vote for Four Knights of the Shire to serve in such new Parlia-

2 William IV. Chap. 45.

lxv

ment for each of the said counties, and not for Two Knights to serve for any division of the said counties; and that as to the several boroughs enumerated in the Schedules (C.) and (D.) to this Act annexed, each of the said boroughs shall, for the purpose of electing a member or members to serve in such new Parliament, be deemed to include such places as are specified and described in conjunction with the name of each of the said boroughs in the Schedule marked (L.) to this Act annexed; and that as to the several cities and boroughs in *England* and *Wales* not included in the Schedule (A.) to this Act annexed, and now returning a member or members to serve in Parliament, and the places sharing in the election for such cities and boroughs, each of such cities, boroughs, and places respectively shall, for the purpose of electing a member or members to serve in such new Parliament as aforesaid, be deemed to be comprehended within the same limits as before the passing of this Act, and not otherwise; and that no place named in the first column of the Schedule (E.) to this Act annexed, which before the passing of this Act did not share in the election of a member for any shire-town or borough named in the second column of the said Schedule (E.), shall share in the election of a member for any shire-town or borough to serve in such new Parliament, any thing hereinbefore contained to the contrary notwithstanding; and that the borough composed of the towns of *Swansea, Longhor, Neath, Aberavon,* and *Ken-fig* shall not return a member to serve in such new Parliament, but shall instead thereof share in the election of a member to serve in such new Parliament for the borough of *Cardiff*, any thing herein-before contained to the contrary notwithstanding; and that in the event of such dissolution of Parliament so taking place as last aforesaid, such persons only shall be entitled to vote in the election of members to serve in such new Parliament as aforesaid for the

Boundaries of new boroughs defined.

Boundaries of old boroughs to remain;

and the rights of voting to take effect without registration.

lxvi

2 WILLIAM IV. CHAP. 45.

counties, ridings, parts, cities and boroughs which in such event shall return members to serve in such new Parliament, as would be entitled to be inserted in the respective lists of voters directed to be made under this Act if the day of election had been the day for making out such respective lists; and such persons shall be entitled to vote in such election, although they may not be registered according to the provisions of this Act, any thing herein-before contained to the contrary notwithstanding; and the polling at such election for any county, or for any riding of *Yorkshire* or parts of *Lincolnshire*, may be continued for fifteen days, and the polling at such election for any city or borough may be continued for eight days, any thing herein-before contained to the contrary notwithstanding.

2 WILLIAM IV. CHAP. 45.

lxvii

SCHEDULES to which the foregoing Act refers.

SCHEDULE (A).

Boroughs.	County.	Boroughs.	County.
Old Sarum	Wiltshire.	Winchelsea	Sussex.
Newtown	Isle of Wight.	Tregony	Cornwall.
St. Michael's or Midshall	Cornwall.	Haslemere	Surrey.
		Saltash	Cornwall.
Gatton	Surrey.	Orford.	Suffolk.
Bramber	Sussex.	Callington	Cornwall.
Bossiney	Cornwall.	Newton	Lancashire.
Dunwich	Suffolk.	Ilchester	Somersetshire.
Ludgershall	Wiltshire.	Boroughbridge	Yorkshire.
St. Mawe's	Cornwall.	Stockbridge	Hampshire.
Beeralston	Devonshire.	Romney (New)	Kent.
West Looe	Cornwall.	Hedon	Yorkshire.
St. Germain's	Cornwall.	Plympton	Devonshire.
Newport	Cornwall.	Seaford	Sussex.
Blechingley	Surrey.	Heytesbury	Wiltshire.
Aldborough	Yorkshire.	Steyning	Sussex.
Camelford	Cornwall.	Whitchurch	Hampshire.
Hindon	Wiltshire.	Wootton Bassett	Wiltshire.
East Looe	Cornwall.	Downton	Wiltshire.
Corfe Castle	Dorsetshire.	Fowey	Cornwall.
Bedwin (Great)	Wiltshire.	Milborne Port	Somersetshire.
Yarmouth	{ Isle of Wight, Hampshire.	Aldeburgh	Suffolk.
		Minehead	Somersetshire.
Queenborough	Kent.	Bishop's Castle	Shropshire.
Castle Rising	Norfolk.	Okehampton	Devonshire.
East Grinstead	Sussex.	Appleby	Westmoreland.
Higham Ferrers	Northamptonshire.	Lostwithiel	Cornwall.
Wendover	Buckinghamshire.	Brackley	Northamptonshire.
Weobly	Herefordshire.	Amersham	Buckinghamshire.

lxviii　　　2 WILLIAM IV. CHAP. 45.

SCHEDULE (B).

Boroughs.	County.	Boroughs.	County.
Petersfield	Hampshire.	Shaftesbury	Dorsetshire.
Ashburton	Devonshire.	Thirsk	Yorkshire.
Eye	Suffolk.	Christchurch . . .	Hampshire.
Westbury	Wiltshire.	Horsham	Sussex.
Wareham	Dorsetshire.	Great Grimsby .	Lincolnshire.
Midhurst	Sussex.	Calne	Wiltshire.
Woodstock	Oxfordshire.	Arundel	Sussex.
Wilton	Wiltshire.	St. Ives	Cornwall.
Malmesbury . . .	Wiltshire.	Rye	Sussex.
Liskeard	Cornwall.	Clitheroe	Lancashire.
Reigate	Surrey.	Morpeth	Northumberland.
Hythe	Kent.	Helston	Cornwall.
Droitwich	Worcestershire.	North Allerton . .	Yorkshire.
Lyme Regis	Dorsetshire.	Wallingford	Berkshire.
Launceston	Cornwall.	Dartmouth	Devonshire.

2 WILLIAM IV. CHAP. 45.   lxix

SCHEDULE (C).

Principal Places to be Boroughs.	Returning Officers.
Manchester (Lancashire)	The Boroughreeve and Constables of Manchester.
Birmingham (Warwickshire)	The two Bailiffs of Birmingham.
Leeds (Yorkshire).............	The Mayor of Leeds.
Greenwich (Kent).	
Sheffield (Yorkshire)	The Master Cutler.
Sunderland (Durham).	
Devonport (Devonshire).	
Wolverhampton (Staffordshire) ..	Constable of the Manor of the Deanery of Wolverhampton.
Tower Hamlets (Middlesex).	
Finsbury (Middlesex).	
Mary-le-bone (Middlesex).	
Lambeth (Surrey).	
Bolton (Lancashire)..........	The Boroughreeves of Great and Little Bolton.
Bradford (Yorkshire).	
Blackburn (Lancashire).	
Brighton (Sussex).	
Halifax (Yorkshire).	
Macclesfield (Cheshire)	The Mayor of Macclesfield.
Oldham (Lancashire).	
Stockport (Cheshire)...........	The Mayor of Stockport.
Stoke-upon-Trent (Staffordshire).	
Stroud (Gloucestershire)	

SCHEDULE (D).

Principal Places to be Boroughs.	Returning Officers.
Ashton-under-Lyne (Lancashire)..	The Mayor of Ashton-under-Lyne.
Bury (Lancashire).	
Chatham (Kent).	
Cheltenham (Gloucestershire).	
Dudley (Worcestershire).	
Frome (Somersetshire).	
Gateshead (Durham).	
Huddersfield (Yorkshire).	
Kidderminster (Worcestershire) ..	The High Bailiff of Kidderminster.
Kendal (Westmoreland)	The Mayor of Kendal.
Rochdale (Lancashire).	
Salford (Lancashire)...........	The Boroughreeve of Salford.
South Shields (Durham).	
Tynemouth (Northumberland).	
Wakefield (Yorkshire).	
Walsall (Staffordshire)	The Mayor of Walsall.
Warrington (Lancashire).	
Whitby (Yorkshire).	
Whitehaven (Cumberland).	
Merthyr Tydvil (Glamorganshire).	

lxx   2 WILLIAM IV. CHAP. 45.

SCHEDULE (E).

Places sharing in the Election of Members.	Shire-Towns or Principal Boroughs.	County in which such Boroughs are situated.
Amlwch . . . . ⎫ Holyhead, and . . . . ⎬ sharing with Llangefni . . . . ⎭	Beaumaris	Anglesey.
Aberystwith . . . . . . ⎫ Lampeter, and . . . . ⎬ sharing with Adpar . . . . ⎭	Cardigan	Cardiganshire.
Llanelly . . . . sharing with	Caermarthen . . .	Caermarthenshire.
Pwllheli . . . . ⎫ Nevin . . . . ⎪ Conway . . . . ⎬ sharing with Bangor . . . . ⎪ Criccieth . . . . ⎭	Caernarvon	Caernarvonshire.
Ruthin . . . . ⎫ Holt . . . . ⎬ sharing with Town of Wrexham . ⎭	Denbigh	Denbighshire.
Rhyddlan . . . . ⎫ Overton . . . . ⎪ Caerwis . . . . ⎪ Caergwrley . . . . . . ⎬ sharing with St. Asaph . . . . ⎪ Holywell . . . . ⎪ Mold . . . . ⎭	Flint	Flintshire.
Cowbridge . . . . ⎫ Llantrissent . . . . . . ⎬ sharing with	Cardiff	Glamorganshire.
Llanidloes . . . . ⎫ Welsh Pool . . . . . . ⎪ Machynlleth . . . . . . ⎬ sharing with Llanfyllin . . . . ⎪ Newtown . . . . ⎭	Montgomery . . .	Montgomeryshire.
Narberth . . . . ⎫ Fishguard . . . . ⎬ sharing with	Haverfordwest . .	Pembrokeshire.
Tenby . . . . ⎫ Wiston . . . . ⎬ sharing with Town of Milford . . . ⎭	Pembroke	Pembrokeshire.
Knighton . . . . ⎫ Rhayder . . . . ⎪ Kevinleece . . . . ⎬ sharing with Knucklas . . . . ⎪ Town of Presteigne ⎭	Radnor	Radnorshire.

2 WILLIAM IV. CHAP. 45.

lxxi

SCHEDULE (E. 2.)

Places sharing in the Election of Members.	Places therein from which the Seven Miles are to be calculated.
Newport	The Market Place.
Usk	The Town Hall.
Aberystwith	The Bridge over the Rheidal.
Lampeter	The Parish Church.
Adpar	The Bridge over the Teivi.
Pwllheli	The Guildhall.
Nevin	The Parish Church.
Conway	The Parish Church.
Criccieth	The Castle.
Ruthin	The Parish Church called St. Peter's.
Holt	The Parish Church.
Rhyddlan	The Parish Church.
Overton	The Parish Church.
Caerwis	The Parish Church.
Caergwrley	The Parish Church of Hope.
Cowbridge	The Town Hall.
Llautrissent	The Town Hall.
Tenby	The Parish Church.
Wiston	The Parish Church.
Knighton	The Parish Church. .
Rhayder	The Market Place.
Kevinleece	The Parish Church.
Knucklas	The Site of the ancient Castle of Cnweglas.
Swansea	The Town Hall.
Loughor	The Parish Church.
Neath	The Town Hall.
Aberavon	The Bridge over the Avon.
Ken-fig	The Parish Church of Lower Ken-fig.

lxxii   2 WILLIAM IV. CHAP. 45.

SCHEDULE (F.)

COUNTIES to be DIVIDED.

Cheshire.	Northumberland.
Cornwall.	Northamptonshire.
Cumberland.	Nottinghamshire.
Derbyshire.	Shropshire.
Devonshire.	Somersetshire.
Durham.	Staffordshire.
Essex.	Suffolk.
Gloucestershire.	Surrey.
Kent.	Sussex.
Hampshire.	Warwickshire.
Lancashire.	Wiltshire.
Leicestershire.	Worcestershire.
Norfolk.	

SCHEDULE (F. 2.)

COUNTIES to return THREE MEMBERS each.

Berkshire.	Herefordshire.
Buckinghamshire.	Hertfordshire.
Cambridgeshire.	Oxfordshire.
Dorsetshire.	

SCHEDULE (G.)

Cities and Towns and Counties thereof.	Counties at large in which Cities and Towns and Counties thereof are to be included.
Caermarthen	Caermarthenshire.
Canterbury..	Kent.
Chester	Cheshire.
Coventry	Warwickshire.
Gloucester	Gloucestershire.
Kingston-upon-Hull	East Riding of Yorkshire.
Lincoln	The Parts of Lindsey, Lincolnshire.
London	Middlesex.
Newcastle-upon-Tyne	Northumberland.
Poole	Dorsetshire.
Worcester	Worcestershire.
York and Ainsty	North Riding of Yorkshire.
Southampton	Hampshire.

2 William IV. Chap. 45. lxxiii

Schedule (H).

FORMS OF LISTS AND NOTICES APPLICABLE TO COUNTIES.
No. 1.

Notice of the making out of the Lists to be given by the Overseers.

We hereby give notice, that we shall, on or before the last day of July in this year, make out a list of all persons entitled to vote in the election of a knight or knights of the shire for the county of   [*or* for the   riding, parts, *or* division of the county of   *as the case may be,*] in respect of property situate wholly or in part within this parish [*or* township]; and all persons so entitled are hereby required to deliver or transmit to us, on or before the twentieth day of July in this year, a claim in writing, containing their Christian name and surname, their place of abode, the nature of their qualification, and the name of the street, lane, or other like place wherein the property in respect of which they claim to vote is situated; and if the property be not situated in any street, lane, or other like place, then such claim must describe the property by the name by which it is usually known, or by the name of the tenant occupying the same; and each of such persons so claiming must also at the same time pay to us the sum of one shilling. Persons omitting to deliver or transmit such claim or to make such payment will be excluded from the register of voters for this county [*or* riding, parts, *or* division, *as the case may be*]. [*In subsequent years after one thousand eight hundred and thirty-two, add the following words,* " But persons whose names are now on the register are not required to make a fresh claim so long as they retain the same qualification and continue in the same place of abode as described in the Register."]

(Signed)   A. B. ⎫ Overseers of the parish
                C. D. ⎬ [*or* township] of
                E. F. ⎭

——————

No. 2.
Notice of Claim to be given to the Overseers.

I hereby give you notice, that I claim to be inserted in the list of voters for the county of   [*or* for the   riding, parts, *or* division of the county of   *as the case may be,*] and that the particulars of my place of abode and qualification are stated below. Dated the   day of   in the year

(Signed)   John Adams.

Place of abode, Cheapside, London.

Nature of qualification, Freehold house, [*or* warehouse, stable, land, field, annuity, rent-charge, &c. *as the case may be, giving such a description of the property as may serve to identify it*].

Where situate in this parish [*or* township], King Street. [*If the property be not situate in any street, lane, or other like place, then say,* Name of the property, High Field Farm; *or,* Name of the occupying tenant, John Edwards.]

e

lxxiv

2 WILLIAM IV. CHAP. 45.

No. 3.

County of   to wit, [or Riding, Parts, or Division of the County of   as the case may be.] } THE LIST of PERSONS entitled to vote in the Election of a Knight [or Knights] of the Shire for the County of   [or for the   Riding, Parts, or Division of the County of   as the case may be,] in respect of Property situate within the Parish of   [or Township, as the case may be].

Christian name and surname of each voter at full length.	Place of abode.	Nature of qualification.	Street, lane, or other like place in this parish [or township] where the property is situate, or name of the property, or name of the tenant.
Adams, John .	Cheapside, London.	Freehold house.	King Street.
Alley, James .	Long Lane, in this parish.	Copyhold field.	John Edwards, tenant.
Ball, William	Market Street, Lancaster.	Lease of warehouse for years.	Duke Street.
Boyce, Henry	Church Street, in this parish.	Fifty Acres of Land as occupier.	High Field Farm.

(Signed)   A. B. } Overseers of the
C. D. } said parish
E. F. } [or township].

No. 4.

Notice of objection to be given to the Overseers.

To the overseers of the parish of   [or township, *as the case may be*].

I hereby give you notice, that I object to the name of William Ball being retained in the List of Voters for the county of   [or for the   riding, parts, or division of the county of   ]. Dated the   day of   in the year

(Signed)   A. B. of [*Place of abode*].

2 WILLIAM IV. CHAP. 45.

lxxv

No. 5.

Notice of Objection to Parties inserted in the List.

To Mr. William Ball.

I hereby give you notice, that I object to your name being retained in the List of Voters for the county of [*or* for the riding, parts, *or* division of the county of], and that you will be required to prove your qualification at the time of the revising of the said list. Dated the day of in the year

(Signed)   **A. B.** of [*Place of abode*].

No. 6.

List of Persons objected to, to be published by the Overseers.

The following Persons have been objected to as not being entitled to have their Names retained in the List of Voters for the County of [*or* for the Riding, Parts, *or* Division of the County of].

Christian name and sur-name of each person objected to.	Place of abode.	Nature of the supposed qualification.	Street, lane, or other like place in this parish [*or* township] where the property is situate, or name of the property, or name of the tenant.
Alley, James .	Long Lane, in this parish.	Copyhold field.	John Edwards, tenant.
Ball, William	Market Street, Lancaster.	Lease of warehouse for years.	Duke Street.

(Signed)   A. B. ⎫ Overseers of the parish
C. D. ⎬ of   [*or* township,
E. F. ⎭ *as the case may be*].

e 2

lxxvi   2 WILLIAM IV. CHAP. 45.

SCHEDULE (I).

FORMS OF LISTS AND NOTICES APPLICABLE TO CITIES AND BOROUGHS.

No. 1.

THE LIST of PERSONS entitled to vote in the Election of a Member [or Members] for the City [or Borough] of   in respect of Property occupied within the Parish [or Township] of   by virtue of an Act passed in the Second Year of the Reign of King William the Fourth, intituled, " An Act to amend the Representation of the People in England and Wales."

Christian Name and Surname of each Voter at full length.	Nature of Qualification.	Street, Lane, or other Place in this Parish where the Property is situate.
Ashton, John	House...............	Church Street.
Atkinson, William.....	Warehouse...........	Bolt Court, Fleet Street.
Bates, Thomas	Shop	Castle Street.
Bull, Thomas.........	Counting-house	Lord Street.

(Signed)   A. B. ⎫ Overseers of the
              C. D. ⎬   said Parish
              E. F. ⎭ [or Township].

No. 2.

THE LIST of all PERSONS (not being Freemen) entitled to vote in the Election of a Member [or Members] for the City [or Borough] of   in respect of any Rights other than those conferred by an Act passed in the Second Year of the Reign of King William the Fourth, intituled " An Act to amend the Representation of the People in England and Wales."

Christian Name and Surname of each Voter at full length.	Nature of Qualification.	Street, Lane, or other Place in this Parish where the Property is situate. *If the Right of voting does not depend on Property, then state the Place of Abode.*

(Signed)   A. B. ⎫ Overseers of the Parish o:
              C. D. ⎬   [or Township] within
              E. F. ⎭ the said City [or Borough]

2 WILLIAM IV. CHAP. 45.

lxxvii

No. 3.

THE LIST of the FREEMEN of the City [or Borough] of   [or of   being a Place sharing in the Election with the City [or Borough] of   ] entitled to vote in the Election of a Member [or Members] for the said City [or Borough.]

Christian Name and Surname of each Freeman, at full length.	Place of his Abode.

(Signed)   A. B. ⎰ Town Clerk of the said City
                      ⎱ [or Borough, or Place.]

No. 4.

Notice of Claim.

To the Overseers of the Parish [or Township] of   or to the Town Clerk of the City [or Borough] of   or otherwise, as the case may be].

I hereby give you notice, That I claim to have my Name inserted in the List made by you of Persons entitled to vote in the Election of a Member [or Members] for the City [or Borough] of   and that my qualification consists of a House in Duke Street in your Parish, or otherwise [as the case may be]; and in the case of a Freeman, say, and that my qualification is as a Freeman of   and that I reside in Lord Street in this City or Borough]. Dated the   day of   one thousand eight hundred and thirty   .
(Signed)   John Allen of [Place of Abode].

No. 5.

Notice of Objection.

To the Overseers of the Parish [or Township] of   [or to the Town Clerk of the City [or Borough] of   or otherwise, as the case may be].

I hereby give you notice, that I object to the name of Thomas Bates being retained in the List of Persons entitled to vote in the Election of a Member [or Members] for the City [or Borough] of   and that I shall bring forward such objection at the time of the revising of such List. Dated the   day of   the year   .
(Signed)   A. B. of [Place of Abode].

lxxviii   2 WILLIAM IV. CHAP. 45.

No. 6.

List of Claimants to be published by the Overseers.

The following Persons claim to have their Names inserted in the List of Persons entitled to vote in the Election of a Member [*or* Members] for the City [*or* Borough of   .

Christian Name and Surname of each Claimant at full length.	Nature of Qualification.	Street, Lane, or other Place in this Parish where the Property is situate. *If the Right does not depend on Property, state the Place of Abode.*
Allen, John.	House.	Duke Street.

      (Signed)   A . B.
                    C. D. } Overseers of, &c.
                    E. F.

No. 7.

List of Persons objected to, to be published by the Overseers.

The following Persons have been objected to as not being entitled to have their Names retained in the List of Persons qualified to vote in the Election of a Member [*or* Members] for the City [*or* Borough of   .

Christian Name and Surname of each Person objected to.	Nature of the supposed Qualification.	Street, Lane, or other Place in this Parish where the Property is situate. *If the Right does not depend on Property, state the Place of Abode.*
Bates, Thomas.	Shop.	Castle Street.

      (Signed)   A . B.
                    C. D. } Overseers of, &c.
                    E. F.

2 William IV. Chap. 45.

lxxix

No. 8.

List of Claimants to be published by the Town Clerks.

The following Persons claim to have their Names inserted in the List of the Freemen of the City [*or* Borough] of   [*or* of   being a Place sharing in the Election with the City [*or* Borough] of   ], entitled to vote in the Election of a Member [*or* Members] for the said City [*or* Borough].

Christian Name and Surname of each Claimant at full length.	Place of his Abode.

(Signed)   A. B. ⎰ Town Clerk of the said City
                     ⎱ [*or* Borough *or* Place].

No. 9.

The List of Persons objected to, to be published by the Town Clerks.

The following Persons have been objected to as having no Right to be retained on the List of the Freemen of the City [*or* Borough] of   [*or* of   being a Place sharing in the Election with the City [*or* Borough] of   ], entitled to vote in the Election of a Member [*or* Members] for the said City [*or* Borough].

Christian and Surname of each Person objected to.	Place of his Abode.

(Signed)   A. B. ⎰ Town Clerk of the said City
                     ⎱ [*or* Borough *or* Place].

lxxx   2 WILLIAM IV. CHAP. 45.

SCHEDULE (K).

A LIST of such of the FREEMEN of LONDON as are Liverymen of the Company
of   entitled to vote in the Election of Members for the City of
London.

Christian Name and Surname of the Voter, at full length.	Street, Lane, or other Description of his Place of Abode.

(Signed)   A. B. Clerk.

No. 1.

Notice of Claim to be given to the Returning Officer or Officers of the City of London, and to the Clerks of the respective Livery Companies.

To the Returning Officer or Officers of the City of London [*or* to the Clerk of the Company of   .

I hereby give you Notice, That I claim to have my Name inserted in the List made by the Clerk of the Company of   [*or, in case of Notice to the Clerk, say,* made by you] of the Liverymen of the said Company [*or, in case of Notice to the Clerk, say,* of the Liverymen of the Company of   ] entitled to vote in the Election of Members for the City of London.   Dated the   day of   .

(Signed)   A. B. { Place of Abode.
{ Name of Company.

2 WILLIAM IV. CHAP. 45.

lxxxi

No. 2.

LIST of CLAIMANTS to be published by the RETURNING OFFICER or OFFICERS of the City of London.

The following persons claim to have their names inserted in the List of persons entitled to vote as Freemen of the City of London and Liverymen of the several Companies herein specified, in the election of Members for the City of London.

Christian Name and Surname of Claimants, at full length.	Place of Abode.

No. 3.

NOTICE of OBJECTION to PARTIES inserted in the LIST of the LIVERY.

To Mr. William Baker.

I hereby give you notice, That I object to your name being retained in the List of persons entitled to vote as Freemen of the City of London and Liverymen of the Company of   in the election of Members for the said City, and that I shall bring forward such objection at the time of revising the said list.   Dated the   day of

(Signed)   A. B. [*Place of Abode.*]

lxxxii   2 WILLIAM IV. CHAP. 45.

(L.) SCHEDULE

Boroughs.	Temporary Contents and Boundary.
Ashton-under-Lyne......	The Division of the parish of Ashton-under-Lyne, called the Town's Division.
Birmingham ..	Parishes of Birmingham and Edgbaston, and Townships of Bordesley, Deritend, and Duddeston with Nechels.
Blackburn	Township of Blackburn.
Bolton	Townships of Great Bolton, Haulgh, and Little Bolton, except the detached part of the township of Little Bolton which lies to the North of the town of Bolton.
Bradford	Township of Bradford.
Brighthelmstone	Parishes of Brighthelmstone and Hove.
Bury..........	Township of Bury.
Chatham......	From the Easternmost point at which the boundary of the City of Rochester meets the Right Bank of the River Medway, Southward along the boundary of the City of Rochester, to the Boundary Stone of the said city marked 5; thence in a straight line to the Windmill in the parish of Chatham on the top of Chatham Hill; thence in a straight line to the Oil Windmill in the parish of Gillingham, between the village of Gillingham and the Fortifications; thence in a straight line through Gillingham Fort to the Right Bank of the River Medway; thence along the Right Bank of the River Medway to the point first described.
Cheltenham ...	Parish of Cheltenham.
Devonport	Parish of Stoke Damerill and township of East Stonehouse.
Dudley	Parish of Dudley.
Finsbury......	Parishes of St. Giles in the Fields; St. George, Bloomsbury; St. George the Martyr; St. Andrew above Bars; St. Luke; St. Sepulchre, except so much as is in the city of London; St. James, Clerkenwell, except so much as is locally in the parish of Hornsey; Ecclesiastical districts of Trinity, St. Paul, and St. Mary, in the parish of St. Mary, Islington; Liberties of Saffron Hill, Hatton Garden, and Ely Rents; Ely Place; the Rolls; Glasshouse Yard; Precinct of the Charter-house; Lincoln's Inn; Gray's Inn; so much of Furnival's Inn and Staple's Inn as is not within the city of London.
Frome........	Town of Frome as within the limits now assigned to the town of Frome by the trustees under the provisions of an Act passed in the first and second years of his present Majesty, intituled, " An Act for better repairing and improving several Roads leading to and from the town of Frome, in the county of Somerset."
Gateshead.....	Parish of Gateshead.

2 WILLIAM IV. CHAP. 45.   lxxxi

Boroughs.	Temporary Contents and Boundary.
Greenwich	Parishes of St. Paul and St. Nicholas, Deptford, and so much of the parishes of Greenwich, Charlton, and Woolwich as lie between the Thames and the Dovor Road.
Halifax	Township of Halifax.
Huddersfield ...	Township of Huddersfield.
Kendal........	Townships of Kendal and Kirkland, and all such parts of the township of Nethergaveship as adjoin the township of Kendal.
Kidderminster ..	Borough of Kidderminster.
Lambeth	Parishes of St. Mary, Newington ; St. Giles, Camberwell, except the Manor and Hamlet of Dulwich ; Precinct of the Palace ; and so much of the parish of Lambeth as is North of the Ecclesiastical division of Brixton.
Leeds	Borough of Leeds.
Macclesfield ...	Borough of Macclesfield.
Manchester....	Townships of Manchester, Chorlton Row, Ardwick, Hulme, Beswick, Cheetham, Bradford, Newton, and Harpur Hey.
Marylebone....	Parishes of St. Marylebone and Paddington, and so much of the parish of St. Pancras as is South of the Regent's Canal.
Merthyr Tydvil	Parishes of Merthyr Tydvil and Aberdare.
Oldham.......	Township of Oldham.
Rochdale	Town of Rochdale, as within the provisions of an Act passed in the sixth year of his late Majesty, intituled, " An Act for lighting, cleansing, watching, and regulating the Town of Rochdale, in the County Palatine of Lancaster."
Salford	Townships of Salford, Pendleton, and Broughton.
Sheffield	Townships of Sheffield, Attercliffe-cum-Darnall, Brightside Bierlow, and Nether Hallam.
South Shields ..	Townships of South Shields and Westoe.
Stockport......	Borough of Stockport ; Hamlets of Brinksway and Edgeley.
Stoke-upon-Trent	Townships of Tunstall, Burslem, Hanley, Shelton, Penkhull with Boothen, Lane End, Longton, Fenton Vivian, Fenton Culvert ; Hamlet of Sneyd ; and Vill of Rushton Grange.
Stroud........	Parishes of Stroud, Bisley, Painswick, Pitchcomb, Randwick, Stonehouse, Eastington, Leonard Stanley except Lorridge's Farm ; King's Stanley, Rodborough, Minchinhampton, Woodchester, Avening, Horsley.
Sunderland....	Parish of Sunderland ; Townships of Bishop Wearmouth, Bishop Wearmouth Panns, Monk Wearmouth, Monk Wearmouth Shore, and Southwick.
Tower Hamlets	Liberties of the Tower, and Tower division of Ossulston Hundred, except the parishes of St. John, Hackney ; St. Mary, Stratford-le-Bow ; and St. Leonard, Bromley.

lxxxiv   2 WILLIAM IV. CHAP. 45.

Boroughs.	Temporary Contents and Boundary.
Tynemouth	Townships of Tynemouth, North Shields, Chirton, Preston, and Cullercoats.
Wakefield	Township of Wakefield.
Walsall........	Borough of Walsall, except the parts detached from the borough of Walsall.
Warrington....	Township of Warrington.
Whitehaven ...	Township of Whitehaven.
Whitby	Township of Whitby.
Wolverhampton	Townships of Wolverhampton, Bilston, Wednesfield, and Willenhall; and parish of Sedgeley.

THE BOUNDARY ACT,

2 & 3 WM. IV. CAP. LXIV.

f—B

CONTENTS.

Divisions of Counties, and where Courts for Election of Knights of the Shire are to be held.

			Page				Page
Cheshire	..	..	7	Northampton	..	..	22
Cornwall	..	..	9	Northumberland	..	..	22
Cumberland	..	..	14	Nottingham	..	..	23
Derby	..	..	14	Salop	..	..	23
Devon	..	..	15	Somerset	..	..	24
Durham	..	..	16	Stafford	..	..	25
Essex	..	..	16	Suffolk	..	..	26
Gloucester	..	..	17	Surrey	..	..	26
Hants	..	..	18	Sussex	..	..	27
Kent	..	..	19	Warwick	..	..	27
Lancaster	..	..	20	Wilts	..	..	28
Leicester	..	..	20	Worcester	..	..	29
Norfolk	..	..	21				

Provision for detached Parts of Counties   30

Provision for the detached Parts of Hundreds, &c.   30

Provision for Liberties, &c.   31

County Polling Places shall be such as are mentioned in Schedule (N.)   31

Polling Districts for Counties to be settled by Justices   ..   33

In what Counties, &c. Places having separate Jurisdiction are to be considered   33

Polling Places for New Shoreham, &c.   34

Polling Districts for New Shoreham, &c. to be settled by Justices   34

Election or Poll may take place at Places in the Neighbourhood of those named   35

Contents and Boundaries shall be such as are set forth in Schedule (O.)   35

Rules for the Construction of the Descriptions contained in Schedule (O.)   37

Provision as to detached Parts of Parishes, &c. and for Extra-parochial Places   39

Misnomer not to vitiate, and the Descriptions in Schedule (O.) to be considered as existing on the 1st Oct. 1831   ..   40

Act may be amended this Session   41

2 & 3 WILLIAM IV. CAP. 64.

3

Schedule (M.)—Counties and Divisions to which isolated Parts are annexed for the Purposes of Elections .. *page* 42

Schedule (N.)—Polling Places for Counties and Divisions of Counties 50

Schedule (N. 2.)—Polling Places for certain Boroughs .. 61

Schedule (O.)—Boundaries of the several Counties, Cities, Boroughs, and Places in England and Wales, for the purpose of the Election of Members to serve in Parliament :

County of Bedford—(Bedford) 61

County of Berks—(Abingdon, Reading, Wallingford, New Windsor,) 62

County of Buckingham—(Buckingham, Great Marlow, Chipping Wycombe,) 63

County of Cambridge—(Cambridge,) 63

County of Chester.
Northern Division—(Macclesfield, Stockport,) .. 65
Southern Division—(Chester) 64

County of Cornwall.
Eastern Division—(Bodmin, Launceston, Liskeard,) .. 65
Western Division—(Helston, St. Ives, Penryn and Falmouth, Truro,) 65

County of Cumberland.
Eastern Division—(Carlisle,) 67
Western Division—(Cockermouth, Whitehaven,) .. 67

County of Derby.
Southern Division—(Derby) 68

County of Devon.
Northern Division—(Barnstaple, Tiverton,) 68
Southern Division—Ashburton, Dartmouth, Devonport, Exeter, Honiton, Plymouth, Tavistock, Totness,) .. 69

County of Dorset—(Bridport, Dorchester, Lyme Regis, Poole, Shaftesbury, Wareham, Weymouth and Melcombe Regis,) 70

County of Durham.
Northern Division—(Durham, Gateshead, South Shields, Sunderland,) 73

County of Essex.
Northern Division—(Colchester, Harwich,) 74
Southern Division—(Maldon,) 74

County of Gloucester.
Eastern Division—(Cheltenham, Cirencester, Gloucester, Stroud, Tewkesbury,) 74

·4   2 & 3 WILLIAM IV. CAP. 64.

Schedule (O.)—*continued*.

County of Hants.   *page*
    Northern Division—(Andover, Petersfield, Winchester,) 75
    Southern Division—(Christchurch, Lymington, Ports-
    mouth, Southampton,)   76

County of Hereford—(Hereford, Leominster,)   76

County of Hertford—(St. Alban's, Hertford)   77

County of Huntingdon—(Huntingdon,)   77

County of Kent.
    Eastern Division—(Canterbury, Dovor, Hythe, Sandwich,) 77
    Western Division—(Chatham, Greenwich, Maidstone,
    Rochester,)   79

County of Lancaster.
    Northern Division—(Blackburn, Clitheroe, Lancaster,
    Preston,)   80
    Southern Division—(Ashton-under-Lyne, Bolton Le
    Moors, Bury, Liverpool, Manchester, Oldham, Roch-
    dale, Salford, Warrington, Wigan,)   81

County of Leicester.
    Southern Division—(Leicester,)   83

County of Lincoln.
    Parts of Lindsey—(Lincoln, Great Grimsby,)   83
    Parts of Kesteven and Holland—(Boston, Grantham,
    Stamford,)   83

County of Middlesex—(Finsbury, London, Marylebone, Tower
    Hamlets, Westminster,)   84

County of Monmouth.
    Monmouth District—(Monmouth, Newport, Usk,)   ..   85

County of Norfolk.
    Eastern Division—(Norwich, Great Yarmouth,)   ..   86
    Western Division—(King's Lynn, Thetford,)   86

County of Northampton.
    Northern Division—(Peterborough,)   86
    Southern Division—(Northampton,)   86

County of Northumberland.
    Northern Division—(Berwick-upon-Tweed, Morpeth,) ..   87
    Southern Division—(Newcastle-upon-Tyne, Tynemouth
    and North Shields,)   87

County of Nottingham.
    Northern Division—(Nottingham,)   87
    Southern Division—(Newark-upon-Trent,)   87

County of Oxford—(Banbury, Oxford, New Woodstock,)   ..   87

2 & 3 WILLIAM IV. CAP. 64. 5

Schedule (O.)—*continued.*

County of Salop.
    Northern Division—(Shrewsbury,) .. .. *page* 88
    Southern Division—(Bridgenorth, Ludlow, Wenlock,) .. 89

County of Somerset.
    Eastern Division—(Bath, Bristol, Frome, Wells,) .. 90
    Western Division—(Bridgwater, Taunton,) 92

County of Stafford.
    Northern Division—(Newcastle-under-Lyme, Stafford,
      Stoke-upon-Trent,) 94
    Southern Division—(Lichfield, Tamworth, Walsall, Wol-
      verhampton,) 95

County of Suffolk.
    .Eastern Division—(Ipswich,) 95
    Western Division—(Bury St. Edmunds, Eye, Sudbury,) 95

County of Surrey.
    Eastern Division—(Lambeth, Reigate, Southwark,) .. 96
    Western Division—(Guildford,) 96

County of Sussex.
    Eastern Division—(Brighthelmstone, Hastings, Lewes,
      Rye,) 97
    Western Division—(Arundel, Chichester, Horsham, Mid-
      hurst,) 97

County of Warwick.
    Northern Division—(Birmingham, Coventry,) 99
    Southern Division—(Warwick,) 99
County of Westmorland—(Kendal,) 99

Isle of Wight—(Newport,) 99

County of Wilts.
    Northern Division—(Calne, Chippenham, Devizes, Malms-
      bury, Marlborough,) 99
    Southern Division—(Salisbury, Westbury, Wilton,) .. 100

County of Worcester.
    Eastern Division—(Droitwich, Dudley, Evesham,) .. 101
    Western Division—(Bewdley, Kidderminster, Worcester,) 102

County of York.
    North Riding—(Malton, Northallerton, Richmond, Scar-
      borough, Thirsk, Whitby, York,) 104
    East Riding—(Beverley, Kingston-upon-Hull,) .. 105
    West Riding—(Bradford, Halifax, Huddersfield, Knares-
      borough, Leeds, Pontefract, Ripon, Sheffield, Wake-
      field,) 105

2 & 3 WILLIAM IV. CAP. 64.

WALES.

Schedule (O.)—continued.

County of Anglesea.
 Beaumaris District — (Amlwch, Beaumaris, Holyhead, Llangefni,) .. .. *page* 108

County of Brecon—(Brecon,) 110

County of Caermarthen.
 Caermarthen District—(Caermarthen, Llanelly,) .. 110

County of Cardigan.
 Cardigan District—(Aberystwith, Adpar, Cardigan, Lampeter,) 111

County of Carnarvon.
 Carnarvon District—(Bangor, Carnarvon, Conway, Cricceith, Nevin, Pwllheli,) 112

County of Denbigh.
 Denbigh District—(Denbigh, Holt, Ruthin, Wrexham,) 113

County of Flint.
 Flint District—St. Asaph, Caergwyle, Caerwys, Flint, Holywell, Mold, Overton, Rhuddlan,) 113

County of Glamorgan—(Merthyr Tydvil,) 115
 Cardiff District—(Cardiff, Cowbridge, Llantrissent,) .. 116
 Swansea District—(Aberavon, Kenfig, Loughor, Neath, Swansea,) 116

County of Montgomery.
 Montgomery District—(Llanfyllin, Llanidloes, Machynlleth, Montgomery, Newtown, Welshpool,) 118

County of Pembroke.
 Haverfordwest District—(Fishguard, Haverfordwest, Narberth,) 121
 Pembroke District—(Milford, Pembroke, Tenby, Wiston,) 123

County of Radnor.
 Radnor District—(Cefn Llys, Knighton, Knucklas, Prestein, New Radnor, Rhaydrgwy,) 124

2 & 3 WILLIAM IV.

CAP. LXIV.

BEING

An Act to settle and describe the Divisions of Counties, and the Limits of Cities and Boroughs, in *England* and *Wales*, in so far as respects the Election of Members to serve in Parliament.

[July 11, 1832.]

WHEREAS by an Act passed in this present 2 W. 4, c. 45, Session of Parliament, and intituled *An Act to amend the Representation of the People in* England *and* Wales, it is (amongst other things) provided, that each of the counties enumerated in the Schedule Sec. 14. marked (F) thereto annexed should be divided into Two Divisions, which Divisions should be settled and described by an Act to be passed for that purpose in this present Parliament, which Act, when passed, should be deemed and taken to be part of the Act now in recital as fully and effectually as if incorporated therewith; and that Two Knights of the Shire should be chosen for each Division of the said Counties; and that the Court for the election of such knights of the shire should be held at the place to be named for that purpose in the Act so to be passed for settling and describing the divisions

8   2 & 3 WILLIAM IV. CAP. 64.

of the said counties: And whereas the Act so to be passed for settling and describing the Divisions of the said Counties, as in the said recited Act is mentioned, is this present Act: And whereas the several Counties enumerated in the said Schedule marked (F.) to the said recited Act annexed are the several Counties whereof the Divisions are herein-after settled and described: Be it therefore enacted by the King's most excellent Majesty, by and with the advice and consent of the Lords spiritual and temporal, and Commons, in this present Parliament assembled, and by the authority of the same, That Divisions of Cheshire. the Two Divisions of the county of CHESTER shall respectively be called the *Northern Division* and the *Southern Division*; and that such Northern Division shall include the whole of the respective hundreds of

MACCLESFIELD
and
BUCKLOW;

and that such Southern Division shall include the whole of the several hundreds of

BROXTON,
EDDISBURY,
NANTWICH,
NORTHWICH,
and
WIRRALL;

and also the city and county of the city of Chester;
Courts. and that the Court for the election of knights of the shire shall be held for such Northern Division at the town of Knutsford, and for such Southern Division at the city of Chester.

2 & 3 WILLIAM IV. CAP. 64. 9

II. And be it enacted, That the Two Divisions **Divisions of Cornwall.** of the county of CORNWALL shall respectively be called the *Eastern Division* and the *Western Division;* and that such Eastern Division shall include the whole of the several hundreds called

EAST,	STRATTON,
WEST,	and
LESNEWTH,	TRIGG ;

and also the following parishes and places in the hundred of POWDER; (that is to say,)

St. Austell,	*Luxulion,*
St. Blazey,	*Mevagissey,*
St. Denis,	*St. Mewan,*
St. Ewe,	*St. Michael Carhaise,*
Fowey,	*Roach,*
Gorran,	*St. Sampson's,*
Ladock,	*St. Stephen's* in *Brannel,*
Lanlivery,	and
Lostwithiel,	*Tywardreth.*

together with all such part of the hundred of PYDAR as will not be included in the Western Divisions of the county of Cornwall next hereinafter described ;

and that such Western Division shall include the whole of the respective hundreds of

KERRIER and PENWITH ;

all such part of the hundred of POWDER as will not be included in the Eastern Division of the county of Cornwall, hereinbefore described ; the following parishes in the hundred of PYDAR, (that is to say,)

St. Agnes,	*Newlyn,*
Crantock,	*St. Enoder,* and
Cubert,	*Perranzabuloe,*

and the SCILLY ISLANDS ;

14   2 & 3 WILLIAM IV. CAP. 64.

Courts.

and that the Court for the election of knights of the shire shall be held for such Eastern Division at the borough of Bodmin, and for such Western Division at the borough of Truro.

Divisions of Cumberland.

III. And be it enacted, That the Two Divisions of the County of CUMBERLAND shall respectively be called the *Eastern Division* and the *Western Division;* and that such Eastern Division shall include the whole of the several wards of

CUMBERLAND,   and
ESKDALE,   LEATH;

and that such Western Division shall include the whole of the respective wards of

ALLERDALE above DERWENT, and
ALLERDALE below DERWENT;

Courts.

and that the Court for the election of knights of the shire shall be held for such Eastern Division at the city of Carlisle, and for such Western Division at the borough of Cockermouth.

Divisions of Derby.

IV. And be it enacted, That the two Divisions of the County of DERBY shall respectively be called the *Northern Division* and the *Southern Division;* and that such Northern Division shall include the whole of the respective hundreds of

HIGH PEAK, and SCARSDALE;

and also so much of the wapentake of Wirksworth as, by virtue of the Order made at the Quarter Sessions of the Peace for the county of Derby held at the borough of Derby on the twenty-eighth day June one thousand eight hundred and thirty-one, is comprised in the Bakewell Division, as established by such Order;

2 & 3 WILLIAM IV. CAP. 64.

15

and that such Southern Division shall include the whole of the several hundreds of

APPLETREE, MORLESTON and LITCHURCH, and REPTON and GRESLEY;

and all such parts of the wapentake of WIRKS-WORTH as will not be included within the Northern Division of the County of Derby last hereinbefore described;

and that the Court for the election of knights of the shire shall be held for such Northern Division at the town of Bakewell, and for such Southern Division at the county hall in Derby.

Courts.

V. And be it enacted, That the Two Divisions of the County of DEVON shall respectively be called the *Northern Division* and the *Southern Division;* and that such Northern Division shall include the whole of the several hundreds of

Divisions of Devon.

BAMPTON,	NORTH TAWTON and
BLACK TORRINGTON,	WINKLEIGH,
BRAUNTON,	SHEBBEAR,
CREDITON,	SHERWILL,
FREMINGTON,	SOUTH MOLTON,
HALBERTON,	TIVERTON,
HARTLAND,	WITHERIDGE,
HAYRIDGE,	and
HEMYOCK,	WEST BUDLEIGH;

and that such Southern Division shall include the whole of the several hundreds of

AXMINSTER,	LIFTON,
CLYSTON,	EXMINSTER,
COLYTON,	TEIGNBRIDGE,
OTTERY ST. MARY,	HAYTOR,
EAST BUDLEIGH,	COLERIDGE,

16   2 & 3 WILLIAM IV. CAP. 64.

STANBOROUGH,   ROBOROUH, and
ERMINGTON,   TAVISTOCK;
PLYMPTON,

and also the CASTLE OF EXETER;
and the hundred of WONFORD, except such parts
of that hundred as are included in the limits of
the city of Exeter, as hereinafter described;

Courts. and that the Court for the election of knights of the
shire shall be held for such Northern Division at
the town of South Molton, and for such Southern
Division at the city of Exeter.

Divisions of Durham. VI. And be it enacted, that the Two Divisions
of the County of DURHAM shall respectively be
called the *Northern Division* and the *Southern Division;* and that such Northern Division shall include
the whole of the respective wards of

CHESTER and EASINGTON;

and that such Southern Division shall include the
whole of the respective wards of

DARLINGTON and STOCKTON;

Courts. and that the Court for the election of knights of the
shire shall be held for such Northern Division at
the city of Durham, and for such Southern Division
at the town of Darlington.

Divisions of Essex. VII. And be it enacted, that the Two Divisions
of the County of ESSEX shall respectively be called
the *Northern Division* and the *Southern Division;*
and that such Northern Division shall include the
whole of the several hundreds of

CLAVERING,   HINCKFORD,
DUNMOW,   LEXDEN,
FRESHWELL,   TENDRING,

2 & 3 WILLIAM IV. CAP. 64.

THURSTABLE, WINSTREE, and
UTTLESFORD, WITHAM.

and that such Southern Division shall include the whole of the several hundreds of

BARSTABLE, HARLOW,
BECONTREE, ONGAR,
CHAFFORD, ROCHFORD,
CHELMSFORD, and
DENGIE, WALTHAM;

and of the liberty of HAVERING;
and that the Court for the election of knights of the Courts. shire shall be held for such Northern Division at the town of Braintree, and for such Southern Division at the town of Chelmsford.

VIII. And be it enacted, that the Two Divisions Divisions of of the County of GLOUCESTER shall respectively Gloucester. be called the *Eastern Division* and the *Western Division;* and that such Eastern Division shall include the whole of the several hundreds of

CROWTHORNE and WESTMINSTER,
 MINETY, DEERHURST,
BRIGHTWELL'S BAR- SLAUGHTER,
 ROW, CHELTENHAM,
BRADLEY, CLEEVE,
RAPSGATE. TIBALDSTON,
BISLEY, TEWKESBURY,
LONGTREE, and
WHITSTONE, DUDSTONE and KING'S
KIFTSGATE, BARTON;

and also the city and county of the city of GLOU-
 CESTER,
and the borough of CIRENCESTER;

C

18   2 & 3 WILLIAM IV. CAP. 64.

and that such Western Division shall include the whole of the several hundreds of

BERKLEY,	LANCASTER DUCHY,
THORNBURY,	BOTLOE,
LANGLEY and	ST. BRIARVEL'S,
SWINESHEAD,	WESTBURY,
GRUMBALD'S ASH.	and
PUCKLE CHURCH,	BLIDESLOE ;

and the hundreds of HENBURY and BARTON REGIS, except such parts of those hundreds as are included in the limits of the city of Bristol as hereinafter described ;

Courts. and that the Court for the election of knights of the shire shall be held for such Eastern Division at the city of Gloucester, and for such Western Division at the town of Dursley.

Divisions of Hants. IX. And be it enacted, That the Two Divisions of the County of HANTS shall respectively be called the *Northern Division* and the *Southern Division;* and that such Northern Division shall include the whole of the several now existing Divisions of

ALTON,	DROXFORD,
ANDOVER,	ODIHAM,
BASINGSTOKE,	PETERSFIELD, and
KING'S CLERE,	WINCHESTER,

as the same are now established by virtue of an Order made by his Majesty's justices of the peace for the county of Hants at the Midsummer Quarter Sessions for the said County held at Winchester on the twenty-eighth day of June, one thousand eight hundred and thirty-one; and also all such other places, if any, in the said county of Hants, as are locally situated within or are sur-

2 & 3 WILLIAM IV. CAP. 64.

rounded by the said sessional divisions or any of them, and are not mentioned in the said order.

and that such Southern Division shall include the whole of the several now existing Divisions of

FAREHAM,   ROMSEY,
LYMINGTON,   and
RINGWOOD,   SOUTHAMPTON,

as the same are now established by the Order aforesaid; and also all such other places, if any, in the said county of Hants, as are locally situated within or are surrounded by the said four last-mentioned sessional divisions of the said county or any of them, and are not mentioned in the said Order;

and also the town and county of the town of SOUTHAMPTON;

and that the Court for the election of knights of the shire shall be held for such Northern Division at the city of Winchester, and for such Southern Division at the borough of Southampton.

Courts.

X. And be it enacted, That the Two Divisions of the County of KENT shall respectively be called the *Eastern Division* and the *Western Division;* and that such Eastern Division shall include the whole of the respective lathes of

Divisions of Kent.

St. AUGUSTINE and SHEPWAY,

(including the liberty of ROMNEY MARSH,)

and of the Upper Division of the lathe of SCRAY;
and that such Western Division shall include the whole of the respective lathes of

SUTTON-AT-HONE and AYLESFORD,

and of the Lower Division of the lathe of SCRAY;
and that the Court for the election of knights of the

C 2

2 & 3 WILLIAM IV. CAP. 64.

shire shall be held for such Eastern Division at the city of Canterbury, and for such Western Division at the borough of Maidstone.

Divisions of Lancaster.

XI. And be it enacted, That the Two Divisions of the County of LANCASTER shall respectively be called the *Northern Division* and the *Southern Division;* and that such Northern Division shall include the whole of the several hundreds of

<blockquote>
LONSDALE,   LEYLAND, and
AMOUNDERNESS,   BLACKBURN;
</blockquote>

and that such Southern Division shall include the whole of the respective hundreds of

<blockquote>
SALFORD and WEST DERBY;
</blockquote>

Courts.

and that the Court for the election of knights of the shire shall be held for such Northern Division at the borough of Lancaster, and for such Southern Division at the town of Newton.

Divisions of Leicester.

XII. And be it enacted, That the Two Divisions of the County of LEICESTER shall respectively be called the *Northern Division* and the *Southern Division;* and that such Northern Division shall include the whole of the several hundreds of

<blockquote>
WEST GOSCOTE,   and
EAST GOSCOTE,   FRAMLAND;
</blockquote>

and also those two detached portions of the hundred of GARTREE which are situated on the east of the hundred of EAST GOSCOTE;

and that such Southern Division shall include the whole of the several hundreds of

<blockquote>
GARTREE (except as before-mentioned),
SPARKENHOE, and GUTHLAXTON;
</blockquote>

and also the borough of LEICESTER and the liberties thereof;

2 & 3 WILLIAM IV. CAP. 64. 21

and that the Court for the election of knights of the Courts. shire shall be held for such Northern Division at the town of Loughborough, and for such Southern Division at the borough of Leicester.

XIII. And be it enacted, That the Two Divisions Divisions of Norfolk. of the County of NORFOLK shall respectively be called the *Eastern Division* and the *Western Division;* and that such Eastern Division shall include the whole of the several hundreds of

BLOFIELD,	WEST FLEGG,
CLAVERING,	FOREHOE,
DEPWADE,	HAPPING,
DISS,	HENSTEAD,
EARSHAM,	HUMBLEYARD,
NORTH ERPINGHAM,	LODDON,
SOUTH ERPINGHAM,	TAVERSHAM,
EYNESFORD,	TUNSTEAD, and
EAST FLEGG,	WALSHAM;

and that such Western Division shall include the whole of the several hundreds of

FREEBRIDGE MARSH-LAND,	LAUNDITCH,
	SOUTH GREENHOE,
SMITHDON,	GRIMSHOE,
FREEBRIDGE LYNN,	NORTH GREENHOE,
CLACKCLOSE,	WAYLAND,
BROTHERCROSS,	SHROPHAM,
GALLOW,	GILT CROSS, and
HOLT,	MITFORD;

and that the Court for the election of knights of the Courts. shire shall be held for such Eastern Division at the city of Norwich, and for such Western Division at the town of Swaffham.

2 & 3 WILLIAM IV. CAP. 64.

Divisions of Northampton

XIV. And be it enacted, That the Two Divisions of the County of NORTHAMPTON shall respectively be called the *Northern Division* and the *Southern Division;* and that such Northern Division shall include the whole of the liberty of

PETERBOROUGH,

and of the several hundreds of

WILLYBROOK,	HIGHAM FERRERS,
POLEBROOK,	ROTHWELL,
HUXLOE,	HAMFORDSHOE,
NAVISFORD,	and
CORBY,	ORLINGBURY;

and that such Southern Division shall include the whole of the several hundreds of

KING'S SUTTON,	FAWSLEY,
CHIPPING WARDEN,	WYMERSLEY,
GREEN'S NORTON,	SPELHOE,
CLELEY,	NOBOTTLE GROVE, and
TOWCESTER,	GUILSBOROUGH;

Courts.

and that the Court for the election of knights of the shire shall be held for such Northern Division at the town of Kettering, and for such Southern Division at the borough of Northampton.

Divisions of Northumberland.

XV. And be it enacted, That the Two Divisions of the County of NORTHUMBERLAND shall respectively be called the *Northern Division* and the *Southern Division;* and that such Northern Division shall include the whole of the several wards of

BAMBOROUGH,	GLENDALE, and
COQUETDALE,	MORPETH,

and of the BERWICK BOUNDS;

and that such Southern Division shall include the whole of the respective wards of

2 & 3 WILLIAM IV. CAP. 64.

TYNEDALE and CASTLE,

and also the town and county of the town of

NEWCASTLE-UPON-TYNE;

and that the Court for the election of knights of the *Courts.*
shire shall be held for such Northern Division at the
town of Alnwick and for such Southern Division at
the town of Hexham.

XVI. And be it enacted, That the Two Divisions *Divisions of Nottingham.*
of the County of NOTTINGHAM shall respec-
tively be called the *Northern Division* and the
Southern Division ; and that such Northern Division
shall include the whole of the respective hundreds of

BASSETLAW and BROXSTOW;

and that such Southern Division shall include the
whole of the several hundreds of

RUSHCLIFFE,   NEWARK, and
BINGHAM,   THURGARTON;

and that the Court for the election of knights of the *Courts.*
shire shall be held for such Northern Division at the
town of Mansfield, and for such Southern Division
at the borough of Newark.

XVII. And be it enacted, That the Two Divi- *Divisions of Salop.*
sions of the County of SALOP shall respectively be
called the *Northern Division* and the *Southern Divi-*
sion ; and that such Northern Division shall include
the whole of the several hundreds of

OSWESTRY,   NORTH BRADFORD, and
PIMHILL,   SOUTH BRADFORD,

and of the liberty of SHREWSBURY;

and that such Southern Division shall include the
whole of the several hundreds of

24   2 & 3 William IV. Cap. 64.

Brimstrey,   Overs,
Chirbury,   Purslow, including Clun,
Condover,   and
Ford,   Stoddesdon,
Munslow,

and of the franchise of Wenlock ;

Courts. and that the Court for the election of knights of the shire shall be held for such Northern Division at the borough of Shrewsbury, and for such Southern Division at the town of Church Stretton.

Divisions of Somerset. XVIII. And be it enacted, That the Two Divisions of the County of SOMERSET shall respectively be called the *Eastern Division* and the *Western Division ;* and that such Eastern Division shall include the whole of the several hundreds or liberties of

Bath Forum,   Hampton and Cla-
Bempstone,   verton,
Brent and Wring-   Horethorne,
    ton,   Keynsham,
Bruton,   Kilmersdon,
Catsash,   Mells and Leigh,
Chew and Chewton,   Portbury,
Norton Ferris,   Wellow,
Frome,   Wells Forum,
Glaston Twelve   Whitstone,
    Hides,   Winterstoke, and
                        Witham Friary ;

and also the hundred of Hartcliffe with Bedminster, except such parts of that hundred as are included in the limits of the city of Bristol as herein-after described ;

2 & 3 WILLIAM IV. CAP. 64.

25

and that such Western Division shall include the whole of the several hundreds of

ABDICK & BULSTONE,	MILVERTON,
ANDERSFIELD,	NORTH PETHERTON,
CANNINGTON,	SOUTH PETHERTON,
CARHAMPTON,	PITNEY,
CREWKERNE,	SOMERTON,
NORTH CURRY,	STONE,
HOUNDSBOROUGH, BERWICK, & COKER,	TAUNTON and TAUNTON DEAN,
HUNTSPILL and PURITON,	TINTINHULL,
	WHITLEY, and
KINGSBURY, EAST,	WILLITON and FREEMANORS;
KINGSBURY, WEST,	
MARTOCK,	

and that the Court for the election of knights of the shire shall be held for such Eastern Division at the city of Wells, and for such Western Division at the borough of Taunton. Courts.

XIX. And be it enacted, That the Two Divisions of the county of STAFFORD shall respectively be called the *Northern Division* and the *Southern Division;* and that such Northern Division shall include the whole of the several hundreds of Divisions of Stafford.

PIREHILL,	NORTH OFFLOW;
TOTMONSLOW, and	

and that such Southern Division shall include the whole of the respective hundreds of

SOUTH OFFLOW,	CUTTLESTONE;
SEISDON, and	

and that the Court for the election of knights of the shire shall be held for such Northern Division at Courts.

C 5

26 2 & 3 WILLIAM IV. CAP. 64.

the borough of Stafford, and for such Southern Division at the city of Lichfield.

Divisions of Suffolk.

XX. And be it enacted, That the Two Divisions of the county of SUFFOLK shall respectively be called the *Eastern Division* and the *Western Division;* and that such Western Division shall include the whole of the liberty of

BURY ST. EDMUND'S

and of the respective hundreds of

HARTESMERE and STOW;

and that such Eastern Division shall include

all such parts of the county of Suffolk as are not comprised in the liberty of Bury St. Edmund's, or in either of the hundreds of Hartesmere and Stow;

Courts.

and that the Court for the election of knights of the shire shall be held for such Western Division at the borough of Bury St. Edmund's, and for such Eastern Division at the borough of Ipswich.

Divisions of Surrey.

XXI. And be it enacted, That the Two Divisions of the county of SURREY shall respectively be called the *Eastern Division* and the *Western Division;* and that such Eastern Division shall include the whole of the several hundreds of

BRIXTON,	TANDRIDGE,
KINGSTON,	and
REIGATE,	WALLINGTON;

and that such Western Division shall include the whole of the several hundreds of

BLACKHEATH,	ELMBRIDGE,
COPTHORNE,	FARNHAM,
EFFINGHAM,	GODALMING,

2 & 3 William IV. Cap. 64.

Godley and Chert- Woking, and
    sey,   Wotton ;
and that the Court for the election of knights of the Courts.
shire shall be held for such Eastern Division at the
town of Croydon, and for such Western Division at
the borough of Guildford.

XXII. And be it enacted, That the Two Divisions Divisions of
of the county of SUSSEX shall respectively be Sussex.
called the *Eastern Division* and the *Western Division ;*
and that such Eastern Division shall include the
whole of the several rapes of
    Lewes,   Pevensey ;
    Hastings, and
and that such Western Division shall include the
whole of the several rapes of
    Arundel,   Chichester ;
    Bramber, and
and that the Court for the election of knights of the Courts.
shire shall be held for such Eastern Division at the
borough of Lewes, and for such Western Division at
the city of Chichester.

XXIII. And be it enacted, That the Two Divi- Divisions of
sions of the county of WARWICK shall respectively Warwick.
be called the *Northern Division* and the *Southern
Division ;* and that such Northern Division shall include the whole of the hundred of
    Hemlingford,
and of the county of the city of
    Coventry,
and the *Rugby Division,* and the *Kirby Division*
of the hundred of Knightlow ;

28   2 & 3 WILLIAM IV. CAP. 64.

and that such Southern Division shall include the
whole of the respective hundreds of

BARLICHWAY and KINGTON,

and the *Kenilworth Division*, and the *Southam Division* of the hundred of KNIGHTLOW;

Courts.

and that the Court for the election of knights of the
shire shall be held for such Northern Division at
the town of Coleshill, and for such Southern Division at the borough of Warwick.

Divisions of Wilts.

XXIV. And be it enacted, That the Two Divisions of the county of WILTS shall respectively be
called the *Northern Division* and the *Southern Division;* and that such Northern Division shall include
the whole of the several hundreds of

CHIPPENHAM,	RAMSBURY,
NORTH DAMERHAM,	WHORWELSDOWN,
BRADFORD,	SWANBOROUGH,
MELKSHAM,	HIGHWORTH, CRICKLADE,
POTTERNE and CAN-NINGS,	and STAPLE, KINGSBRIDGE,
CALNE,	and
SELKLEY,	MALMSBURY;

and that such Southern Division shall include the
whole of the several hundreds of

KINWARDSTONE,	DOWNTON,
HEYTESBURY,	CHALK,
BRANCH and DOLE,	DUNWORTH,
ELSTUB and EVER-LEY,	CAWDEN and CADWORTH, FRUSTFIELD,
AMESBURY,	ALDERBURY,
WARMINSTER,	UNDERDITCH,
MERE,	and
SOUTH DAMERHAM,	WESTBURY;

2 & 3 WILLIAM IV. CAP. 64.

29

and that the Court for the election of knights of the *Courts.*
shire shall be held for such Northern Division at
the borough of Devizes, and for such Southern Division at the city of Salisbury.

XXV. And be it enacted, That the Two Divi- *Divisions of*
sions of the county of WORCESTER shall respec- *Worcester.*
tively be called the *Eastern Division* and the *Western
Division;* and that such Eastern Division shall include the whole of the several now existing divisions
of

STOURBRIDGE,	NORTHFIELD,
DUDLEY,	BLOCKLEY, and
DROITWICH,	PERSHORE,

as the same are established by an order made by
his Majesty's Justices of the Peace for the county
of Worcester at the Epiphany Quarter Sessions
for the year one thousand eight hundred and
thirty-one ;

and also the borough of EVESHAM : and also
all such other places, if any, in the said county
of Worcester, as are locally situated within or
are surrounded by the herein-before mentioned
sessional divisions thereof, or any of them, and
are not mentioned in the said order ;

and that such Western Division shall include the
whole of the several now existing divisions of

UPTON,	HUNDRED HOUSE, and
WORCESTER,	KIDDERMINSTER,

as the same are established by the last-mentioned
order ;

and also the city and county of the city of
WORCESTER ; and also all such other places, if
any, in the said county of Worcester, as are

2 & 3 WILLIAM IV. CAP. 64.

locally situated within or are surrounded by the four lastly herein-before mentioned sessional divisions thereof, or any of them, and are not mentioned in the said order;

Courts. and that the Court for the election of knights of the shire shall be held for such Eastern Division at the borough of Droitwich, and for such Western Division at the city of Worcester.

Provision for detached parts of counties. XXVI. And be it enacted, That the isolated parts of counties in England and Wales which are described in the Schedule to this Act annexed, marked (M.) shall, as to the election of members to serve in Parliament as Knights of the Shire, be considered as forming parts of the respective counties and divisions which are respectively mentioned in the fourth column of the said Schedule (M.) in conjunction with the names of such isolated parts respectively; and that every part of any county in England or Wales which is detached from the main body of such county, but for which no special provision is hereby made, shall be considered, for the purposes of the election of members to serve in Parliament as Knights of the Shire, as forming part of that county, (not being a county corporate,) and of that division, riding, or parts, whereby such detached part shall be surrounded; but if any such detached part shall be surrounded by two or more counties, or divisions, ridings, or parts, then as forming part of that county, or division, riding, or parts, with which such detached part shall have the longest common boundary.

Provision for the detached parts of hundreds, &c. XXVII. And be it further enacted, That as respects the counties of York and Lincoln, and also the counties herein-before divided, except the counties of Hants and Worcester, every portion of any hundred, ward, wapentake, rape, lathe, or liberty of any such county which is detached from the main body of such hundred, ward, wapentake, rape, lathe or liberty, and is also locally separated from that division of the county to which such main body is to belong under the provisions contained in this Act, or in the herein-before recited Act, but which is not subject to the provisions lastly herein-before contained, shall, for the purpose of the election of members to serve in Parliament as Knights of the Shire, be considered as forming part of that division, parts, or riding of the same county by which such detached portion is surrounded or to which it adjoins.

XXVIII. And be it enacted, That all liberties, franchises, and places having a separate jurisdiction, which are not herein-before expressly mentioned, (except the several cities and towns, and counties thereof respectively, of Bristol, Exeter, Lichfield, Norwich, and Nottingham, and except the several places by this Act comprised within the boundaries thereof respectively,) shall, as to the election of members to serve in Parliament as Knights of the Shire, respectively be considered as included within the respective divisions hereby established in which such liberties, franchises, and places having a separate jurisdiction shall be locally situated.

Provision for liberties, &c.

32   2 & 3 WILLIAM IV. CAP. 64.

County polling places shall be such as are mentioned in Schedule (N.) to this Act.

XXIX. And whereas by the herein-before recited Act it is also provided, that the respective counties in England and Wales, and the respective ridings, parts, and divisions of counties, should be divided into convenient districts for polling, and that in each district should be appointed a convenient place for taking the poll at all elections of a Knight or Knights of the Shire to serve in any future Parliament, and that such districts and places for taking the poll should be settled and appointed by the Act to be passed in this present Parliament for the purpose of settling and describing the divisions of the counties enumerated in the Schedule marked (F.) to the said recited Act annexed, provided that no county, nor any riding, parts, or division of a county, should have more than fifteen districts and respective places appointed for taking the poll for such county, riding, parts, or division; and by the said recited Act it is also provided that the several boroughs of New Shoreham, Cricklade, Aylesbury, and East Retford, as thereby defined, should be divided into convenient districts for polling, and that there should be appointed in each district a convenient place for taking the poll at all elections of members to serve in any future Parliament for each of the said boroughs, which districts and places for taking the poll should be settled and appointed by an Act to be passed in this present Parliament; be it therefore enacted, That the poll for election of Knights of the Shire shall be taken at such places as in the Schedule to this Act annexed, marked (N.) are mentioned in conjunction with the names of the

2 & 3 WILLIAM IV. CAP. 64.

counties, and of the ridings, parts, and divisions of counties, in which such places are respectively situated.

XXX. And be it enacted, That the Justices of the Peace for every county in England and Wales, and for each of the ridings of Yorkshire, and for the parts of Lindsey, and for the parts of Kesteven and Holland, in Lincolnshire, assembled at the Quarter Sessions to be holden in the month of October in the present year, or at some Special Sessions to be appointed by them so assembled as aforesaid which shall be holden on or before the last day of October in the present year, shall divide their respective counties, and ridings, parts, and divisions of counties, into convenient districts for polling, and shall assign one of such districts to every polling place mentioned in the said Schedule marked (N.) to this Act annexed ; and that a list describing the districts named in every such assignment, and naming the polling places to which such districts are respectively assigned, shall be lodged with the Clerk of the Peace of the county, riding, or parts, who shall forthwith cause copies of such list to be printed, and shall deliver a copy of such list to every person who shall apply for the same upon payment of one shilling for each copy.

Polling districts for counties to be settled by Justices.

XXXI. Provided always, and be it enacted, That for the purpose of assigning such districts to every polling place as aforesaid, every liberty, franchise, and place having a separate or exclusive jurisdiction shall be considered as being within that county, and within that division, riding, or parts, in which such

In what counties, &c. places having separate jurisdiction are to be considered.

liberty, franchise, or place is placed by this Act, or by the Act herein-before recited, or in which the same is locally situated : Provided nevertheless, that the Justices of the Peace for the Isle of Ely, assembled at the Quarter Sessions for the said Isle of Ely to be holden in the month of October in the present year, or at some Special Sessions to be appointed by them, so assembled as aforesaid, which shall be holden on or before the last day of October, in the present year, shall divide the said Isle of Ely into convenient districts for polling, and shall assign one of such districts to every polling place within the said Isle of Ely mentioned in the said Schedule (N.); and that a list, describing the districts named in such assignment, and naming the polling places to which such districts are respectively assigned, shall be lodged with the Clerk of the Peace for the said Isle of Ely, who shall allow the same, or a copy thereof, to be inspected at his office at all times.

Polling places for New Shoreham, &c.
XXXII. And be it enacted, That the poll for the election of members to serve in Parliament for the said several boroughs of New Shoreham, Cricklade. Aylesbury, and East Retford shall be taken at the place or places which in the Schedule to this Act annexed, marked (N. 2,) is or are mentioned in conjunction with the names of such several boroughs respectively.

Polling districts for New Shoreham, &c. to be settled by Justices.
XXXIII. And be it enacted, That the Justices of the Peace for the respective counties in which the boroughs of New Shoreham, Cricklade, and East Retford are situated, shall, at the Quarter Sessions to be holden in the month of October in

2 & 3 WILLIAM IV. CAP. 64.

the present year, divide the said boroughs of New Shoreham, Cricklade, and East Retford into convenient districts for polling, and shall assign one of such districts to every polling place for the said boroughs of New Shoreham, Cricklade, and East Retford, mentioned in the said Schedule to this Act annexed, marked (N. 2.); and that a list describing the districts named in such assignment, and naming the polling places to which such districts are respectively assigned, shall be lodged with the returning officer of the respective borough, who shall forthwith cause copies of such list to be printed, and to be fixed on the doors of the several churches and chapels within the borough for which such districts are assigned.

XXXIV. And be it enacted, That, if it shall seem fit to the Sheriff, the Court for the election of Knights of the Shire may be held, or the poll may be taken, at any place or spot in the neighbourhood of any place appointed by this Act for holding such Court or taking such poll respectively, at which such Court or poll may have heretofore been held or taken, or which may be convenient for either of those purposes; any thing herein contained notwithstanding. *Election or poll may take place at places in the neighbourhood of those named in this Act.*

XXXV. And whereas by the Act herein-before recited it is also provided that each of the places enumerated in the Schedules thereto annexed respectively marked (C.), (D.), and (E.), and that every city and borough in England which before the *Contents and boundaries shall be such as are set forth in Schedule (O.) to this Act.*

2 & 3 WILLIAM IV. CAP. 64.

passing of the said recited Act was entitled to return a member or members to serve in Parliament, (except the several boroughs enumerated in the Schedule thereto annexed, marked (A.), and except the several boroughs of New Shoreham, Cricklade, Aylesbury, and East Retford,) and that the borough of Brecon, and each of the towns of Swansea, Loughor, Neath, Aberavon, and Ken-fig, should, for the purposes of the said recited Act, include the place or places respectively which should be comprehended within such boundaries as should be settled and described by an Act to be passed for that purpose in this present Parliament, which Act when passed should be deemed and taken to be part of the said recited Act as fully and effectually as if incorporated therewith : (a) And whereas the Act so to be passed for settling and describing the boundaries of cities, boroughs, and places as in the said recited Act is mentioned in this present Act : And whereas the several cities, boroughs, and places whereof the boundaries were so to be settled and described as in the said recited Act is mentioned are the several cities, boroughs, and places which are specified in the Schedule to this Act annexed marked (O.); be it therefore further enacted and declared, That the several cities, boroughs, and places specified in the said Schedule to this Act annexed marked (O.) shall, as to the election of members or a member to serve in Parliament, respectively include the places and be comprised within the boundaries which in such Schedule are respectively specified and described in conjunction with the names of such cities, boroughs, and places respectively.

2 & 3 WILLIAM IV. CAP. 64.

XXXVI. And be it enacted, That, subject to any direction to the contrary, the following rules shall be observed in the construction of the several descriptions of boundaries contained in the said Schedule hereto annexed marked (O.); (that is to say,)

Rules for the construction of the descriptions contained in Schedule (O) to this Act.

1. That the words " Northward," " Southward," " Eastward," " Westward," shall respectively be understood to denote only the general direction in which any boundary proceeds from the point last described, and not that such boundary shall continue to proceed throughout in the same direction to the point next described :

2. That when any road is mentioned merely by the name of the place to which such road leads, the principal road thither from the city, borough, or place of which the boundary is in course of description shall be understood :

3. That whenever a line is said to be drawn from, to, or through an object, such line shall, in the absence of any direction to the contrary, be understood to be drawn from, to, or through the centre of such object, as nearly as the centre thereof can be ascertained :

4. That every building through which or through any part whereof any boundary hereby established shall pass shall be considered as within such boundary : provided always, that if the boundaries of any two or more of the cities, boroughs, and places whereof the contents and boundaries are hereby settled and described shall pass through the same building or any part thereof, such building shall be

considered as within that one of such two or more of the said cities, boroughs, and places which was before the passing of the herein-before recited Act entitled to return members or a member to serve in Parliament, or if neither or more than one of such two or more of the said cities, boroughs, and places shall have been so entitled, then within that one of them whereof the area as hereby established is the smallest:

5. That whenever any boundary by this Act established is said to pass along any other boundary, or along any road, lane, path, river, stream, canal, drain, brook, or ditch, the middle (as nearly as the same can be ascertained) of such other boundary, or of such road, lane, path, river, stream, canal, drain, brook, or ditch, shall be understood:

6. That the middle of any road or lane shall be understood as the middle of the carriageway along the same:

7. That when any boundary by this Act established is said to proceed along a road, lane, path, river, stream, canal, or drain, from or to an object, such boundary shall be understood to proceed from or to that point in the middle of such road, lane, path, river, stream, canal, or drain from which the shortest line would be drawn to the centre of such object, as nearly as the centre thereof can be ascertained:

8. That the point at which any fence, hedge, wall, boundary, road, lane, path, river, stream, canal, drain, brook, or ditch is said to cut,

2 & 3 WILLIAM IV. CAP. 64.

meet, join, cross, reach, or leave any fence, hedge, wall, boundary, road, lane, path, river, stream, canal, drain, brook, or ditch, shall be understood as that point at which a line passing along the middle of the fence, hedge, wall, boundary, road, lane, path, river, stream, canal, drain, brook, or ditch so cut, met, joined, crossed, reached, or left, would be intersected by a line drawn along the middle of the fence, hedge, wall, boundary, road, lane, path, river, stream, canal, drain, brook, or ditch so cutting, meeting, joining, crossing, reaching, or leaving, if such line were prolonged sufficiently far :

9. That when a line is said to be drawn to a road, lane, river, stream, or canal, such line shall be considered as prolonged to the middle of such road, lane, river, stream, or canal :

10. That by the words "sea" and "sea coast" shall be understood the low-water mark :

11. That if any deficiency shall be found to exist in the line of any boundary described in the said Schedule to this Act annexed marked (O.), by reason of the intervention of any space between any two immediately consecutive points, such deficiency shall be supplied by a straight line to be drawn from the one to the other of such two immediately consecutive points.

XXXVII. And be it further enacted, That, notwithstanding the generality of any description contained in the said Schedule to this Act annexed marked (O.), no city, borough, or place, the con-

Provision as to detached parts of parishes, &c. and for extra-parochial places.

40   2 & 3 WILLIAM IV. CAP. 64.

tents whereof are specified in such schedule, shall include any part of any parish, township, hamlet, chapelry, tithing, manor, or liberty which is detached from the main body of such parish, township, hamlet, chapelry, tithing, manor, or liberty, if, by reason of including such detached part, the boundary hereby established of such city, borough, or place would not be continuous, unless such detached part shall, before the passing of this Act, have formed part of such city, borough, or place for the purpose of the election of members to serve in Parliament; but that all places, parochial or extra-parochial, which are surrounded by the contents of which any city, borough, or place is said in such schedule marked (O.) to consist, but for which no provision is made in such Schedule (O.) shall be considered as included within such city, borough, or place, for the purpose of the election of members to serve in Parliament.

Misnomer not to vitiate, and the descriptions in Schedule (O.) to be considered as existing on the 1st Oct. 1831.

XXXVIII. Provided always, and be it enacted, That no misnomer or inaccurate description contained in this Act, or in any of the schedules hereto annexed, shall in anywise prevent or abridge the operation of this Act with respect to the subject of such description, provided the same shall be so designated as to be commonly understood; and that for the purpose of identifying the descriptions contained in the said schedule (O.) with the subjects of such descriptions respectively, such descriptions shall, if now inapplicable, be held to apply to such subjects as they existed on the first day of *October* One thousand eight hundred and thirty-one.

2 & 3 WILLIAM IV. CAP. 64.

XXXIX. Provided always, and be it enacted, That this Act may be amended or altered by any Act or Acts to be passed during this present Session of Parliament.

Act may be amended this Session.

D

SCHEDULES to which the foregoing Act refers.

SCHEDULE (M.)

Counties to which the isolated Parts belong.	Parishes, Townships, &c. of which, or of Parts of which, the isolated Parts consist.	Counties in which the isolated Parts are locally situate.	Counties and Divisions to which it is intended that the isolated Parts should be annexed.
England.			
Bedfordshire	Part of Studham Parish, partly in Beach-wood Park, in the County of Hertford	Hertfordshire	Hertfordshire.
Bedfordshire	Part of Ickleford Parish	Hertfordshire	Hertfordshire.
Berkshire	Part of Great Barrington Parish	Gloucestershire	Gloucestershire, Eastern Division.
Berkshire	Part of Inglesham Parish	Wiltshire	Wiltshire, Northern Division.
Berkshire	Part of Langford Parish	Oxfordshire	Oxfordshire.
Berkshire	Little Faringdon Tithing	Oxfordshire	Oxfordshire.
Berkshire	Part of Shilton Parish	Oxfordshire	Oxfordshire.
Buckinghamshire	Studley Parish, or Hamlet in the Parish of Beckley	Oxfordshire	Oxfordshire.
Buckinghamshire	Caversfield Parish	Oxfordshire	Oxfordshire.
Buckinghamshire	Part of Luffield Abbey, an Extra-parochial Place	Northamptonshire	Northamptonshire, Southern Division.

2 & 3 WILLIAM IV. CAP. 64.

Cheshire	Part of Disley Township, situate on the Derbyshire side of the River Goyt....	Derbyshire	Cheshire, Northern Division.
Cornwall	A small part of the Parish of St. Stephen by Saltash, on the Eastern Side of the River Tamar	Either in Devonshire or Cornwall	Devonshire, Southern Division.
Cornwall	Part of North Tamerton Parish, East of the Tamar	Either in Devonshire or Cornwall	Cornwall, Eastern Division.
Derbyshire	A portion of Derbyshire, consisting of the Parishes and Places following, i. e. Measham.................. Stretton-in-the-Fields .... Willesley............... Part of Appleby .... Oakthorpe .... Chilcote .... Part of Donisthorpe	Leicestershire	Derbyshire, Southern Division.
Derbyshire	Part of the Parish of Ravenstone	Leicestershire	Derbyshire, Southern Division.
Derbyshire	Part of the Township of Packington	Leicestershire	Derbyshire, Southern Division.
Derbyshire	Part of Scropton Township.............	Staffordshire	Staffordshire, Northern Division.
Derbyshire	Part of Beard Township, on the Cheshire side of the River Goyt..............	Derbyshire or Cheshire	Derbyshire, Northern Division.
Devonshire	Thorncombe Parish	Dorsetshire	Dorsetshire.
Devonshire	Part of Axminster Parish, namely, Burhall Downs and Easthay	Dorsetshire.......	Dorsetshire.

2 & 3 WILLILM IV. CAP. 64.

Counties to which the isolated Parts belong.	Parishes, Townships, &c. of which, or of Parts of which, the isolated Parts consist.	Counties in which the isolated Parts are locally situate.	Counties and Divisions to which it is intended that the isolated Parts should be annexed.
Devonshire..........	Part of the Parish of Saint John........	Cornwall	Cornwall, Eastern Division.
Devonshire..........	North Petherwin Parish...........	Cornwall	Devonshire, Northern Division.
Devonshire..........	Part of Wirrington Parish, West of the Tamar....................	Cornwall or Devonshire........	Devonshire, Northern Division.
Devonshire..........	Part of the Hamlet of Northcote, West of the Tamar.................	Cornwall or Devonshire........	Devonshire, Northern Division.
Devonshire..........	Part of Bridgerule Parish, West of the Tamar..................	Cornwall or Devon ..	Devonshire, Northern Division.
Devonshire..........	Part of Maker Parish in the Titling of Vaultersholme........	Cornwall	Cornwall, Eastern Division.
Dorsetshire..........	Stockland Parish...........	Devonshire	Devonshire, Southern Division.
Dorsetshire..........	Dallwood Township..........	Devonshire	Devonshire, Southern Division.
Durham	The District of Norhamshire	Northumberland ...	Northumberland, Northern Division.
Durham	The District of Islandshire, including the Farne Islands and Monkhouse	Northumberland ...	Northumberland, Northern Division.
Durham	The Parish of Bedlington or Bedlingtonshire	Northumberland ...	Northumberland, Northern Division.

2 & 3 WILLIAM IV. Cap. 64.

Durham · · · · · · · · · · ·	The Parish of Craike or Craikeshire · · · }	North Riding of York-shire · · · · · · · · · · · }	North Riding of York-shire.
Gloucestershire · · · · · ·	Minety Parish· · · · · · · · · · · · }	Wiltshire · · · · · · · · · · }	Wiltshire, Northern Division.
Gloucestershire · · · · · ·	Widford Parish · · · · · · · · · ·	Oxfordshire · · · · · · · · ·	Oxfordshire.
Gloucestershire · · · · · ·	Compton Parva Parish· · · · · · · · · · }	Warwickshire · · · · · · · · }	Warwickshire, Southern Division.
Gloucestershire· · · · · · ·	Sutton-under-Brails Parish. · · · · · · · · }	Warwickshire · · · · · · · · }	Warwickshire, Southern Division.
Gloucestershire · · · · · ·	Shennington Parish · · · · · · · · · · ·	Oxfordshire · · · · · · · · · ·	Oxfordshire.
Gloucestershire· · · · · · ·	Part of Lea Parish · · · · · · · · · · ·	Herefordshire· · · · · · · · ·	Herefordshire.
Herefordshire · · · · · · · ·	Farloe Chapelry · · · · · · · · · · · · ·	Shropshire · · · · · · · · · · }	Shropshire, Southern Division.
Herefordshire · · · · · · · ·	Rochford Parish · · · · · · · · · · · ·	Worcestershire · · · · · · · · }	Worcestershire, Western Division.
Herefordshire · · · · · · ·	Foothog Township · · · · · · · · · · · }	Between Monmouth-shire and Brecon-shire· · · · · · · · · · }	Herefordshire.
Herefordshire · · · · · · · ·	Litton and Cascob Township· · · · · ·	Radnorshire · · · · · · · · · ·	Radnorshire.
Herefordshire · · · · · · · ·	Bwlch Hamlet · · · · · · · · · · · · · ·	Monmouthshire · · · · · · · ·	Monmouthshire.
Herefordshire · · · · · · · ·	Part of the Parish of Trellick· · · · · · · ·	Monmouthshire · · · · · · · ·	Monmouthshire.
Hertfordshire· · · · · · · · ·	Part of Coleshill Hamlet · · · · · · · · ·	Buckinghamshire · · · · · ·	Buckinghamshire.
Hertfordshire· · · · · · · · ·	Part of Meppershall Parish. · · · · · · · ·	Bedfordshire· · · · · · · · · ·	Bedfordshire.
Huntingdonshire · · · · ·	Part of Catworth Township. · · · · · · · ·	Northamptonshire · · · }	Northamptonshire, Northern Division.
Huntingdonshire · · · ·	Swineshead Parish · · · · · · · · · · · ·	Bedfordshire· · · · · · · · · ·	Huntingdonshire.

45

Counties to which the isolated Parts belong,	Parishes, Townships, &c. of which, or of Parts of which, the isolated Parts consist.	Counties in which the isolated Parts are locally situate.	Counties and Divisions to which it is intended that the isolated Parts should be annexed.
Huntingdonshire	Part of Everton Parish	Between Bedfordshire and Cambridgeshire	Huntingdonshire.
Kent	Part of Woolwich Parish, North of the Thames	Kent or Essex	Kent, Western Division.
Monmouthshire	Welsh Bicknor Parish	Herefordshire	Herefordshire.
Oxfordshire	Boycot Township	Buckinghamshire	Buckinghamshire.
Oxfordshire	Lillingstone Lovell Parish	Buckinghamshire	Buckinghamshire.
Oxfordshire	Hackamstead Chapelry	Buckinghamshire	Buckinghamshire.
Oxfordshire	Great Lemhill Farm, Part of Broughton Poggs Parish	Gloucestershire	Gloucestershire, Eastern Division.
Shropshire	Part of Hales Owen Parish	Bounded by Worcestershire and Staffordshire	Worcestershire, Eastern Division.
Somersetshire	Holwell Parish, including Buckshall Tithing	Dorsetshire	Dorsetshire.
Hampshire	North Ambersham and South Ambersham Tithings in the Parish of Steep	Sussex	Sussex, Western Division.
Staffordshire	Broom Parish	Worcestershire	Worcestershire, Eastern Division.
Staffordshire	Clent Parish	Worcestershire	Worcestershire, Eastern Division.
Sussex	Part of Rogate Tithing, being a Farm called Rogate Bohunt Farm	Hampshire	Hampshire, Northern Division.
Warwickshire	Tutnal and Cobley Hamlet	Worcestershire	Worcestershire, Eastern Division.

2 & 3 WILLIAM IV. CAP. 64.

Warwickshire	Compton Scorpion Hamlet Whitchurch Parish Ditchforth Hamlet	cestershire and Gloucestershire	Warwickshire, Southern Division.
Wiltshire	Part of Wokingham Parish	Berkshire	Berkshire.
Wiltshire	Hinton Tithing in Hurst Parish	Berkshire	Berkshire.
Wiltshire	Didnam Tithing in Shinfield Parish	Berkshire	Berkshire.
Wiltshire	Swallowfield Parish	Berkshire	Berkshire.
Wiltshire	Kingswood Parish	Gloucestershire	Gloucestershire, Western Division.
Wiltshire	Poulton Parish	Gloucestershire	Gloucestershire, Eastern Division.

Worcestershire	Alderminster Parish
	Tredington Parish, including the following Hamlets:
	   Arinscot
	   Blackwell
	   Newbold and Tolton
	   Darlingscote and Longdon
	Shipston-on-Stour Parish
	Tidmington Chapelry
	Evenload Parish
	Blockley Parish, including the following Hamlets:
	   Northwich
	   Paxford
	   Draycott
	   Dorne
	   Ditchford
	   Aston Magna
	   Cutsdean or Cuddesden Chapelry
		Between Gloucestershire and Warwickshire	Worcestershire, Eastern Division.

Counties to which the isolated Parts belong.	Parishes, Townships, &c. of which, or of Parts of which, the isolated Parts consist.	Counties in which the isolated Parts are locally situate.	Counties and Divisions to which it is intended that the isolated Parts should be annexed.
Worcestershire	Iccomb Parish	Between Gloucestershire and Oxfordshire	Gloucestershire, Eastern Division.
Worcestershire	Dailsford Parish	Oxfordshire	Worcestershire, Eastern Division.
Worcestershire	Oldborough Parish	Warwickshire	Worcestershire, Eastern Division.
Worcestershire	Dudley Parish	Staffordshire	Worcestershire, Eastern Division.
Worcestershire	Edvin Loach Parish	Herefordshire	Worcestershire, Eastern Division.
Worcestershire	Warley Wigorn Township	Between Parts of Staffordshire and Shropshire	Worcestershire, Eastern Division.
Wales.			
Carnarvonshire	The Hundred of Creyddyn, Eirias Township or Hamlet	Denbighshire	Carnarvonshire.
Carnarvonshire	Maenan	Denbighshire	Carnarvonshire.
Denbighshire	Carreghovah Township	Between Shropshire & Montgomeryshire	Montgomeryshire.

2 & 3 WILLIAM IV. CAP. 64. 49

Flintshire	Part of the Hundred of Maylor, consisting of the following Parishes, Townships, or Places, or of Parts thereof respectively, namely, Overton Foreign and Overton Villa Knolton Bangor Erbistock Worthenbury Abenbury Vechan Hanmer Halghton Willington Iscoed Bettisfield Tybroughton Penley Bromington	Bounded by the Counties of Salop, Chester and Denbigh	Flintshire.
Flintshire	Sundry other small Plots of Land in the following Townships respectively, namely, Overton Villa Overton Foreign Bangor Worthenbury Sutton	Denbighshire	Flintshire.
Flintshire	Parts of Marford and Hoseley Townships	Denbighshire	Flintshire.
Flintshire	Part of Hawarden Township	Cheshire	Flintshire.
Glamorganshire	Flat Holmes	In the Bristol Channel	Glamorganshire.
Glamorganshire	Barry Island	In the Bristol Channel	Glamorganshire.
Brecknockshire	Part of Glasbury Parish	Brecknockshire or Radnorshire	Brecknockshire.

D 5

2 & 3 WILLIAM IV. CAP. 64.

SCHEDULE (N.)

Counties.	Divisions.	Polling Places.
ENGLAND.		
Bedfordshire		Bedford. Luton. Leighton. Ampthill. Biggleswade. Sharnbrooke.
Berkshire		Abingdon. Reading. Newbury. Wantage. Wokingham. Maidenhead. Great Faringdon. East Ilsley.
Buckinghamshire		Aylesbury. Buckingham. Newport Pagnel. Beaconsfield.
Cambridgeshire		Cambridge. Newmarket. Royston.
Isle of Ely		Ely. Wisbeach. Whittlesey.
Cheshire . . .	Northern Division	Knutsford. Stockport. Macclesfield. Runcorn.
Cheshire . . .	Southern Division	Chester. Nantwich. Northwich. Sandbach. Birkenhead.

2 & 3 WILLIAM IV. CAP. 64.

51

Counties.	Divisions.	Polling Places.
Cornwall . . .	Eastern Division	Bodmin. Launceston. Liskeard. Stratton. St. Austell.
Cornwall . . .	Western Division	Truro. Penzance. Helston. Redruth.
Cumberland . .	Eastern Division	Carlisle. Brampton. Wigton. Penrith. Aldstone.
Cumberland . .	Western Division	Cockermouth. Aspatria. Keswick. Bootle. Egremont.
Derbyshire . . .	Northern Division	Bakewell. Chesterfield. Chapel-en-le-Frith. Alfreton. Glossop.
Derbyshire . . .	Southern Division	Derby. Ashbourn. Wirksworth. Melbourn. Belper.
Devonshire . . .	Northern Division	South Molton. Collumpton. Barnstaple. Torrington. Holsworthy. Crediton.

2 & 3 WILLIAM IV. CAP. 64.

Counties.	Divisions.	Polling Places.
Devonshire . . .	Southern Division	Exeter. Honiton. Newton Abbot. Kingsbridge. Plymouth. Tavistock. Okehampton.
Dorsetshire		Dorchester. Wimborne. Wareham. Beaminster. Sherborne. Shaftesbury. Blandford. Chesilton.
Durham	Northern Division	Durham. Sunderland. Lanchester. Wickham. Chester-le-Street. South Shields.
Durham	Southern Division	Darlington. Stockton. Bishop's Auckland. Stanhope. Middleton Teesdale. Barnard Castle. Sedgefield.
Essex	Northern Division	Braintree. Colchester. Saffron Walden. Thorpe.
Essex	Southern Division	Chelmsford. Billericay. Romford. Epping. Rochford. Maldon.

2 & 3 WILLIAM IV. CAP. 64.   53

Counties.	Divisions.	Polling Places.
Gloucestershire	. Eastern Division	Gloucester. Stroud. Tewkesbury. Cirencester. Campden. Northleach. Cheltenham.
Gloucestershire .	. Western Division	Wotton-under-Edge. Newent. Newnham. Coleford. Sodbury. Thornbury. Dursley.
Hampshire . .	. Northern Division	Winchester. Alton. Andover. Basingstoke. Kingsclere. Odiham. Petersfield. Bishop's Waltham.
Hampshire . .	. Southern Division	Southampton. Fareham. Lymington. Portsmouth. Ringwood. Romsey.
Herefordshire		Hereford. Leominster. Bromyard. Ledbury. Ross. Kington.
Hertfordshire		Hertford. Stevenage. Buntingford. Bishop's Stortford. Hoddesdon. Hatfield. Hemel Hempstead

2 & 3 WILLIAM IV. CAP. 64.

Counties.	Divisions.	Polling Places.
Huntingdonshire		Huntingdon. Stilton.
Kent	Eastern Division	Canterbury. Sittingbourne. Ashford. New Romney. Ramsgate.
Kent	Western Division	Maidstone. Bromley. Blackheath. Gravesend. Tonbridge. Cranbrooke.
Lancashire . . .	Northern Division	Lancaster. Hawkeshead. Ulverston. Poulton. Preston. Burnley.
Lancashire . . .	Southern Division	Newton. Wigan. Manchester. Liverpool. Ormskirk. Rochdale.
Leicestershire . .	Northern Division	Loughborough. Melton Mowbray. Ashby-de-la-Zouch.
Leicestershire . .	Southern Division	Leicester. Hinckley. Market Harborough.
Lincolnshire . .	Parts of Lindsey	Lincoln. Gainsborough. Epworth. Barton. Brigg. Market Raisin. Great Grimsby. Louth. Spilsby. Horncastle.

2 & 3 WILLIAM IV. CAP. 64.

55

Counties.	Divisions.	Polling Places.
Lincolnshire .	Parts of Kesteven and Holland .	Sleaford. Boston. Holbeach. Bourn. Donington. Navenby. Spalding. Grantham.
Middlesex		Brentford. Enfield. King's Cross, or within half a mile thereof. Hammersmith. Bedfont. Edgware. Mile End. Uxbridge.
Monmouthshire		Monmouth. Abergavenny. Usk. Newport. The Rock Inn, in the parish of Bedwelty.
Norfolk	Eastern Division	Norwich. Yarmouth. Reepham. North Walsham. Long Stratton.
Norfolk	Western Division	Swaffham. Downham. Fakenham. Lynn Regis. Thetford. East Dereham.
Northamptonshire	Northern Division	Kettering. Peterborough. Oundle. Wellingborough. Clipston.

2 & 3 WILLIAM IV. CAP. 64.

Counties.	Divisions.	Polling Places.
Northamptonshire	Southern Division	Northampton. Daventry. Towcester. Brackley.
Northumberland	Northern Division	Alnwick. Berwick. Wooler. Elsdon. Morpeth.
Northumberland	Southern Division	Hexham. Newcastle uponTyne Haltwhistle. Bellingham. Stamfordham.
Nottinghamshire	Northern Division	Nottingham. Mansfield. East Retford.
Nottinghamshire	Southern Division	Newark upon Trent. Bingham. Southwell.
Oxfordshire		Oxford. Deddington. Witney. Nettlebed.
Rutlandshire		Oakham.
Shropshire . . .	Northern Division	Shrewsbury. Oswestry. Whitchurch. Wellington.
Shropshire . . .	Southern Division	Church Stretton. Bridgnorth. Ludlow. Bishop's Castle. Wenlock.

2 & 3 William IV. Cap. 64.

Counties.	Divisions.	Polling Places.
Somersetshire . .	Eastern Division	Wells. Bath. Shepton Mallet. Bedminster. Axbridge. Wincanton.
Somersetshire . .	Western Division	Taunton. Bridgwater. Ilchester. Williton.
Staffordshire . .	Northern Division	Stafford. Leek. Newcastle-under-Lyme. Cheadle. Abbots Bromley.
Staffordshire . .	Southern Division	Walsall. Lichfield. Wolverhampton. Penkridge. King's Swinford.
Suffolk	Eastern Division	Ipswich. Needham. Woodbridge. Framlingham. Saxmundham. Halesworth. Beccles.
Suffolk	Western Division	Bury St. Edmund's. Wickham Brook. Lavenham. Stowmarket. Botesdale. Mildenhall. Hadleigh.
Surrey	Eastern Division	Croydon. Reigate. Camberwell. Kingston.

2 & 3 WILLIAM IV. CAP. 64.

Counties.	Divisions.	Polling Places.
Surrey	Western Division	Guildford. Dorking. Chertsey.
Sussex	Eastern Division	Lewes. East Grinstead. Battle. Mayfield.
Sussex	Western Division	Chichester. Steyning. Petworth. Horsham. Arundell.
Warwickshire	Northern Division	Coleshill. Nuneaton. Coventry. Birmingham. Dunchurch.
Warwickshire	Southern Division	Warwick. Kineton. Stratford. Henley. Southam.
Westmoreland		Appleby. Kirkby-Stephen. Shap. Ambleside. Kendal. Kirkby-Lonsdale.
Isle of Wight		Newport. West Cowes.
Wiltshire	Northern Division	Devizes. Melksham. Malmsbury. Swindon.
Wiltshire	Southern Division	Salisbury. Warminster. East Everley. Hindon.

2 & 3 WILLIAM IV. CAP. 64.

Counties.	Divisions.	Polling Places.
Worcestershire	. Eastern Division	Droitwich. Pershore. Shipston. Stourbridge.
Worcestershire	. Western Division	Worcester. Upton. Stourport. Tenbury.
Yorkshire . . .	North Riding .	York. Malton. Scarborough. Whitby. Stokesley. Guisborough. Romaldkirk. Richmond. Askrigg. Thirsk. Northallerton. Kirby Moor Side.
Yorkshire . . .	East Riding . .	Beverley. Hull. Driffield. Pocklington. Bridlington. Howden. Hedon. Settrington.
Yorkshire . . .	West Riding . .	Wakefield. Sheffield. Doncaster. Snaith. Huddersfield. Halifax. Bradford. Barnsley. Leeds. Keighley. Settle. Knaresborough. Skipton. Pately Bridge. Dent.

60   2 & 3 WILLIAM IV. CAP. 64.

WALES.

Counties.	*Divisions.*	*Polling Places.*
Anglesea		{ Beaumaris. Holyhead. Llangefni.
Breeknockshire		Brecon.
Caermarthenshire		{ Llandilo Vawr. Caermarthen. Llandovery. Newcastle Emlyn. Saint Clears. Llanelly. Llansawel.
Cardiganshire		{ Cardigan. Aberystwith. Lampeter. Tregaron.
Carnarvonshire		{ Carnarvon. Conway. Capel Cerrig. Pwllheli.
Denbighshire		{ Denbigh. Wrexham. Llanrwst. Llangollen. Ruthin.
Flintshire		{ Flint. Rhuddlan. Overton.
Glamorganshire		{ Bridgend. Cardiff. Swansea. Neath. Merthyr-Tydvil.
Merionethshire		{ Harlech. Bala. Dolgelly. Towyn. Corwen.

2 & 3 WILLIAM IV. CAP. 64.

Counties.	Divisions.	Polling Places.
Montgomeryshire		Montgomery. Llanidloes. Machynlleth. Llanfyllin. Llanvair.
Pembrokeshire		Haverfordwest. Pembroke. Narberth. Fishguard. Newport. Tenby. Mathry.
Radnorshire		New Radnor. Presteign. Rhaydr. Painscastle. Colwyn. Knighton. Pen-y-bont.

SCHEDULE (N. 2.)

Boroughs.	Polling Places.
New Shoreham	New Shoreham. Cowfold.
Cricklade	Cricklade. Brickworth. Swindon.
Aylesbury	Aylesbury.
East Retford	East Retford. Ollerton. Worksop. Gringley-on-the-Hill.

SCHEDULE (O.)

1.—COUNTY OF BEDFORD.

BEDFORD.—The old borough of Bedford.

2.—COUNTY OF BERKS.

ABINGDON.—The old borough of Abingdon.

READING.—The old borough of Reading.

WALLINGFORD.—The old borough of Wallingford; the several parishes of Brightwell, Sotwell, North Moreton. South Moreton, Bensington, Crowmarsh, and Newnham Murren ; the liberty of Clapcot, and the extra-parochial precinct of the castle ; and also all such parts of the several parishes of Cholsey, Aston Tirrel, and Aston Upthorpe as are situate on that side of the line next herein-after described. on which the town of Wallingford lies ; (that is to say,)

From Blewberry, along the road called "The Icknield Way," to the point on King's Standing Hill at which the same meets the boundary of the parish of Cholsey ; thence, eastward. along the boundary of the parish of Cholsey to the point at which the same reaches the River Thames.

NEW WINDSOR.—The old borough of New Windsor, the lower ward of the Castle, and so much of the parish of Clewer as is situated to the east of the following boundary ; (that is to say,)

2 & 3 WILLIAM IV. CAP. 64. 63

From the point at which the Goswell Ditch joins the River Thames, along the Goswell Ditch to the point at which the same meets Clewer Lane; thence, westward, along Clewer Lane to a point twenty-five yards distant from the point last described ; thence in a straight line to the north-western corner of the enclosure wall of the Cavalry Barracks; thence along the Western Enclosure Wall of the Cavalry Barracks to the point at which the same cuts the boundary of the parish of New Windsor.

3.—COUNTY OF BUCKINGHAM.

BUCKINGHAM. — The several Parishes of Buckingham, Maidsmorton, Thornborough, Padbury, Hillesden, Preston Bissett, Tingewick, and Radclive-cum-Chackmore.

GREAT MARLOW.—The several Parishes of Great Marlow, Little Marlow, Medmenham, and Bisham.

CHIPPING WYCOMBE.—The Parish of Chipping Wycombe.

4.—COUNTY OF CAMBRIDGE.

CAMBRIDGE.—The old borough of Cambridge.

5.—COUNTY OF CHESTER.

NORTHERN DIVISION.

MACCLESFIELD.—From the point at which the boundary of the borough of Macclesfield meets the Leek Road near Moss Pool, southward, along the Leek Road to the bridge over the Macclesfield canal; thence, eastward, along the Macclesfield Canal to the point at which the same meets the boundary of the Borough; thence, eastward, along the boundary of the Borough to the point at which the same is again met by the Macclesfield Canal; thence, northward, along the Macclesfield Canal to the point at which the same crosses Shore's Clough Brook; thence, westward, along Shore's Clough Brook to the point at which the same meets the boundary of the township of Hurdsfield; thence, southward,

64   2 & 3 WILLIAM IV. CAP. 64.

along the boundary of the township of Hurdsfield to the point at which the same meets the boundary of the Borough of Macclesfield; thence, westward, along the boundary of the borough of Macclesfield to the point first described.

STOCKPORT.—The township of Stockport, and the respective hamlets of Brinksway and Edgeley, together with those parts of the respective townships of Brinnington and Heaton Norris which are included within the following boundaries respectively (that is to say,)

Brinnington.—From the point at which the boundary of the township of Stockport would be cut by a straight line to be drawn from the bridge over the River Mersey on the Bredbury and Hyde Road to the Corn Mill on the township of Heaton Norris, between the Manchester and Stockport Canal and the Reddish Road, and now in the occupation of Mr. Walmsley, along such straight line to the point at which the same cuts the River Tame; thence along the River Tame to the point at which the same meets the boundary of the township of Stockport; thence, eastward, along the boundary of the township of Stockport to the point first described.

Heaton Norris.—From the point at which the boundary of the township of Heaton Norris meets the Manchester Road, between a public house called the Ash, and Danby Lane, along the Manchester Road to the point at which the same meets Danby Lane; thence along Danby Lane to the point at which the same is cut by a straight line drawn thereto from the first mile stone on the Altringham Road through the western angle of the public house called the Heaton Norris Club House; thence along the said straight line to the point at which the same meets the Southern Boundary of the township of Heaton Norris; thence, eastward, along the boundary of the township of Heaton Norris to the point first described.

SOUTHERN DIVISION.

CHESTER.—The old city of Chester, and also the space included within the following boundary; (that is to say,)

From the second city boundary stone in Boughton Ford Mead, and on the eastern bank of the River Dee, in a straight line to the western extremity of a lane which leads from Stock Lane to Boughton Heath; thence in a straight line to the southern extremity of Heath Lane; thence along Heath Lane to the point at which the same joins the Christleton Road; thence along the Christleton Road to the point at which the same is joined by New Lane; thence along New Lane to the point at which the same meets Filkin Lane; thence along Filkin Lane to the point at which the same joins, at Asp Tree Turnpike Gate, the Tarvin Road; thence along the Tarvin Road to Tarvin Bridge; thence along the Nantwich Canal to the point at which the same meets the old City Boundary; thence, Southward, along the old City Boundary to the Second City Boundary Stone aforesaid.

6.—COUNTY OF CORNWALL.

EASTERN DIVISION.

BODMIN. — The several parishes of Bodmin, Lanivet, Lanhydrock, and Helland.

LAUNCESTON.—The old borough of Launceston and the parish of St. Stephen, and all such parts of the several parishes of Lawhitton, St. Thomas the Apostle, and South Petherwin as are without the old borough of Launceston.

LISKEARD.——The parish of Liskeard, and also all such parts of the old borough of Liskeard as are without the parish of Liskeard.

WESTERN DIVISION.

HELSTONE.—The old borough of Helstone, the parish of Sithney, and also the space included within the following boundary; that is to say,

From Coverack Bridge, over the River Loo, in a straight line across the Wendron Road to the western extremity of a lane leading by Wheal Ann to Graham Mine; thence along the said lane to the point at which the same meets a small stream; thence, southward, along the said stream to the point at which the same meets a lane leading from Wendron to Trecoose and Constantine: thence, eastward, along the said lane to Trecoose and Constantine, to the point at which the same meets the boundary of the parish of Wendron; thence, southward, along the boundary of the parish of Wendron to Coverack Bridge.

E

66   2 & 3 WILLIAM IV. CAP. 64.

ST. IVES.—The old borough of St. Ives, and the respective parishes of Lelant and Towednack.

PENRYN AND FALMOUTH.—From the point, on the north of Penryn, at which the boundary of the old borough leaves the boundary of the parish of Mylor, westward, along the boundary of the old borough to the point at which the same meets the road from Penryn to Helstone; thence in a straight line to the point, called Hill Head, at which the road to Penryn from Budock joins the road to Penryn from Constantine; thence in a straight line to the nearest point of the boundary of the parish of Falmouth; thence, southward, along the boundary of the parish of Falmouth to the point at which the same meets the boundary of the detached portion of the parish of Budock; thence in a straight line to the northern point at which the boundary of the detached portion of the parish of Budock leaves the boundary of the parish of Falmouth; thence, westward, along the sea coast to the point at which the same is met by the boundary of the parish of St. Gluvias; thence, eastward, along the boundary of the parish of St. Gluvias to the point first described.

From Bosvigo Bridge over the Kenwyn River, and on the boundary of the old borough, along Bosvigo Lane, to the point at which the same joins the Redruth Road; thence along the Redruth Road to the point at which the same is joined, near Chapel-Hill Gate, by Green Lane; thence along Green Lane to the point at which the same joins the Falmouth road; thence along an occupation road leading through Newham-Farm Land to the point at which such occupation road meets Newham-Farm Lane; thence along a fence which proceeds from Newham-Farm Lane, and is the south-western boundary of two fields respectively called Great Beef Close and Little Beef Close, to the point at which such fence meets the north-western fence of a field called Bramble Close; thence, eastward, along the fence of Bramble Close to the point at which the same reaches the shore of Calenick Creek; thence along the shore of Calenick Creek to Lower Newham Wharf; thence in a straight line across the Truro and Falmouth River to the south-eastern extremity of Sunny-Corner Wharf; thence in a straight line to Sunny Corner; thence in a straight line to the point at which Trenack Lane would be cut by a straight line to be drawn from the eastern extremity of Newham-Farm Lane to the point called Hill Head, at which St. Clement's Lane meets the St. Austell old

2 & 3 WILLIAM IV. CAP. 64.

turnpike road; thence in a straight line to Mitchell-Hill Gate, on the old London Road; thence in a straight line to the point at which the boundary of the old borough would be cut by a straight line to be drawn from Mitchell-Hill Gate to Kenwyn Church; thence, northward, along the boundary of the old borough to Bosvigo Bridge.

7.—COUNTY OF CUMBERLAND.

EASTERN DIVISION.

CARLISLE.—The ancient city of Carlisle, and the respective townships of Botchergate and Rickergate, and also all such part of the township of Caldewgate as is comprised within the boundary hereafter described; (that is to say,)

From the bridge over the River Caldew uniting the township of Caldewgate with the old city of Carlisle, southward, along the River Caldew to the point at which the same leaves the boundary of the township of Caldewgate; thence, westward, along the boundary of the township of Caldewgate to the point at which the road from the Kell Houses to Carlisle joins the Wigton Road; thence in a straight line to the point at which the bye road from Stainton, over the Summer House Ford in the River Eden, and across the canal from the Solway to Carlisle, meets the road from Great and Little Orton to Carlisle at a place called New Town; thence along the said road from Stainton to the point at which the same reaches the Summer House Ford; thence along the boundary of the township of Caldewgate to the bridge first described.

WESTERN DIVISION.

COCKERMOUTH.—The several townships of Cockermouth, Eaglesfield, Brigham, Papcastle, and Bridekirk; and also that detached portion of the township of Dovenby which lies between the respective townships of Papcastle, Bridekirk, and Cockermouth.

WHITEHAVEN.—From the point on the sea coast, north of Whitehaven, at which the boundary of the township of Preston Quarter meets the boundary of the township of Moresby, eastward, along the boundary of the township of Preston Quarter, to the point at which the stream which flows through the village of Hensingham falls into the Poc

68   2 & 3 WILLIAM IV. CAP. 64.

Beck; thence in a straight line to the point on the sea coast at which the boundary of the township of Preston meets the boundary of the township of Sandwich; thence along the sea coast to the point first described.

8.—COUNTY OF DERBY.

SOUTHERN DIVISION.

DERBY.—The old borough of Derby.

9.—COUNTY OF DEVON.

NORTHERN DIVISION.

BARNSTAPLE.—From the new bridge over Braddiford Water, on the new Braunton Road, along the hedge which is the eastern boundary of the East Pillow March Field, to the point at which the same cuts Poleshill Lane; thence along Poleshill Lane to the point at which the same meets Hall's Mill Lane; thence along Hall's Mill Lane to the point at which the same meets the Mill Leat; thence along the Mill Leat to the point at which the same meets Shearford Lane; thence along Shearford Lane to the point at which the same joins the Roborough Road; thence along the Roborough Road to the point at which the same is met by Smoky House Lane; thence along Smoky House Lane to the point at which the same is cut by a hedge which divides the field called Great Mill Close from the field called Little Mill Close; thence along the last-mentioned hedge and in a line in continuation of the direction thereof, to the point at which such line cuts the River Yeo; thence, eastward, along the boundary of the old borough of Barnstaple to the point at which the same meets, in Cooney Cut, the south-eastern fence of a field called " Ham ;" thence along the last-mentioned fence to the point at which the same cuts Land Key Road; thence in a straight Line to the point on Rumson Hill at which Windy Ash Lane meets the Brindon Cross Road; thence along Windy Ash Lane to the point at which Wood Street Water crosses the same; thence along Wood Street Water to the point at which the same joins the River Taw; thence along the River Taw to the point at which the same is joined by the River Yeo; thence along the River Yeo to the Swing Bridge on the new Braunton Road;

2 & 3 WILLIAM IV. CAP. 64.

thence along the new Braunton Road to the new bridge first described.

TIVERTON.—The parish of Tiverton.

SOUTHERN DIVISION.

ASHBURTON.—The parish of Ashburton.

DARTMOUTH.—From the point on the sea coast at which the boundary of the parish of Townstall meets the boundary of the parish of Stoke Fleming, northward, along the boundary of the parish of Townstall, to the point at which the same meets the Stoke Road; thence along the Stoke Road, passing Swallaton Cross and Swallaton Gate, to the point at which the Stoke Road meets the Milton Road; thence along the Milton Road to the point at which the same is met by the boundary of the parish of Townstall; thence, westward, along the boundary of the parish of Townstall to the point at which the same reaches Old Mill Creek; thence along the low-water mark to the point first described.

DEVONPORT.—The parish of Stoke Damerill, and the township of Stonehouse.

EXETER.—From the turnpike gate on the Morton Road, southward, along Cowick Lane to the point at which the same meets Stone Lane; thence along Stone Lane to the point at which the same meets the road from Exeter to Alphington; thence, southward, along the road from Exeter to Alphington to the point at which the same is joined by Marsh Barton Lane; thence along Marsh Barton Lane to the point at which the same reaches the western branch of the River Exe; thence in a straight line to the point at which Abbey Lane meets the Eastern Branch of the River Exe; thence, southward, along the Leat to the point at which the same is joined by the brook which runs down through East Wonford; thence along the said brook to the point at which the same crosses the old Stoke and Tiverton Road near the road to Mincing Lake Farm; thence along the old Stoke and Tiverton Road to the point at which the same meets the boundary of the County of the City; thence, northward, along the boundary of the County of the City to the point near Foxhays at which a branch of the River Exe, flowing through Exwick, joins the main stream thereof; thence in a straight line to the point at which the road from Exwick to the turnpike gate on the Morton Road is joined

70   2 & 3 WILLIAM IV. CAP. 64.

by a road leading from Foxhays to Cleave; thence along the said road from Exwick to the turnpike gate on the Morton Road to the point at which the same reaches such turnpike gate.

HONITON.—The parish of Honiton.

PLYMOUTH.—From the north-eastern boundary stone in a straight line to the nearest point of the line of the Embankment; thence, southward, along the line of the Embankment to the point at which the same meets the boundary of the old borough; thence, southward, along the boundary of the old borough to the point first described.

TAVISTOCK.—The parish of Tavistock, except the Manor of Cudliptown.

TOTNES. — The parish of Totnes, and the Manor of Bridgetown.

10—COUNTY OF DORSET.

BRIDPORT.—From the Toll Bar on the Exeter Road in a straight line to the northern extremity of the fence which separates the field called " Marland Five Acres" from the field called " Higher Girtups and Dogholes;" thence along the western Fence of the Field Higher Girtups and Dogholes to the point at which the same reaches a lane leading into Mead Lane; thence along the said lane leading into Mead Lane to the point at which the same reaches Mead Lane; thence along Mead Lane to the point at which the same joins the Chard Road; thence, northward, along the Chard Road to the point at which the same is joined by the first lane on the right called " Green Lane;" thence in a straight line to Allington Mill; thence in a straight line to the point at which Coneygere Lane joins the Pymore Road; thence along Coneygere Lane to the point at which the same joins the Beaminster Road; thence in a straight line to the Bridge over the River Asher close by the Flood Houses; thence along the River Asher to the point at which the same would be cut by a straight line to be drawn from the eastern extremity of Coneygere Lane to the Turnpike Gate on the Dorchester Road; thence along the said straight line to the Turnpike Gate on the Dorchester Road; thence, southward, along the Dorchester Road to the point at which the same is joined by Bothenhampton Lane; thence along Bothenhampton Lane

2 & 3 WILLIAM IV. CAP. 64.   71

to the point at which the same is met by the stream which forms the boundary between the respective parishes of Walditch and Bothenhampton; thence along the said stream to the point at which the same falls into the River Asher; thence down the River Asher (following the easternmost branch thereof at the points at which the same divides into two branches) to Squib's Bridge; thence in a straight line to the south-eastern corner of Keemy Cottage on the Bothenhampton Road; thence in a straight line to the eastern extremity of Wonderwell Lane; thence, westward, along Wonderwell Lane to the point at which the same joins the Burton Bradstock Road; thence, southward, along the Burton Bradstock Road to Wich Gate; thence in a straight line through the Bombardier's House to the Sea Coast; thence along the Sea Coast to the eastern extremity of West Cliff; thence, northward, along West Cliff, and along the western boundary of the Ship Yard of Messieurs Matthews and Company, to the point at which the same meets the boundary of the field called Pitfield Marsh; thence, northward, along the boundary of Pitfield Marsh to the points at which the same meets the River Brit at Ire Pool; thence up the River Brit to the point at which the same is joined by the stream which forms the boundary between the respective parishes of Symondsbury and Allington; thence along the last-mentioned stream to the point at which the same meets the fence which runs down thereto from the Toll Bar at the Exeter Road; thence along the last-mentioned fence to the Toll Bar on the Exeter Road.

DORCHESTER.—From the second or middle Bridge on the Sherborne Road, along the northern branch of the River Frome, passing under Grey's Bridge, to the point at which such northern branch is met, near Stanton's Cloth Factory, by the boundary of the parish of Fordington; thence, southward, along the boundary of the parish of Fordington to the point at which the same meets the Wareham Road; thence, westward, along the Wareham Road to the Turnpike Gate; thence in a straight line to the centre of the barrow called " Two Barrows;" thence in a straight line to the centre of the amphitheatre called Maumbury Ring; thence in a straight line to the centre of the barrow called Lawrence Barrow, near the Exeter Road; thence in a straight line to the south-western corner of the Barrack Wall; thence northward, along the Barrack Wall and Palisade to the point at which such Palisade meets the southern branch of the River Frome; thence

72   2 & 3 WILLIAM IV. CAP. 64.

in a straight line to the second or middle bridge on the Sherborne Road.

LYME REGIS.—The respective parishes of Lyme Regis and Charmouth.

POOLE.—The county and town of Poole, the parish of Hamworthy, and the respective tithings of Parkstone and Longfleet.

SHAFTESBURY. — The old borough of Shaftesbury; the several out-parishes of Holy Trinity, St. James, and St. Peter ; the several parishes of Cann, St. Rombald, Motcomb, East Stower, Stower Provost, Todbere, Melbury Abbas, Compton Abbas, Dowhead St. Mary, and St. Margaret's Marsh and the chapelry of Hartgrove.

WAREHAM.—The old borough of Wareham; the parishes of Corfe Castle and Bere Regis ; the several out-parishes of Lady Saint Mary, Holy Trinity, and St. Martin; and the chapelry of Arne ; that part of the parish of East Stoke which adjoins the eastern boundary of the old borough of Wareham; and also such part of the parish of East Morden as is comprised within the following boundary ; (that is to say,)
From the point at which the boundary of the parish of East Morden meets the southern boundary of Morden Park Wood, southward, along the boundary of Morden Park Wood, to the point at which the same meets the Sherford Lake ; thence, eastward, along the Sherford Lake to the point at which the same meets the boundary of the parish of East Morden ; thence, southward, along the boundary of the parish of East Morden to the point first described.

WEYMOUTH AND MELCOMBE REGIS.—From the old Sluice on the Wareham Road in a straight line to the point at which the northern wall of the old Barrack Field meets the Dorchester Road ; thence along the said northern wall, and in a line in the direction thereof, to the point at which such line meets the boundary of the old borough ; thence, northward, along the boundary of the old borough to the point at which the same meets the Upper Wyke Road, thence, westward, along the Upper Wyke Road to the point at which the same is joined by a cross road leading to the Lower Wyke Road, otherwise called Buxton's Lane ; thence along the said cross road to the point at which the same joins the said Lower Wyke Road; thence along the said Lower Wyke Road to the point at which the same joins the Sandsfoot Castle Road; thence, northward, along the Sandsfoot Castle Road to the point at which the same is met by the Footpath leading by Lovel's Farm to Bincleves; thence along the said Footpath to the point at which the same reaches the edge of the Cliff at Bincleves; thence along the Sea Coast to the old sluice aforesaid.

11.—COUNTY OF DURHAM.

NORTHERN DIVISION.

DURHAM.—From Shincliffe Bridge over the River Wear, on the Stockton Road, along the Stockton Road, to the point at which the same is met by a lane leading into the Darlington Road; thence along the said lane to the point at which the same joins the Darlington Road; thence along the Darlington Road to the point at which the same is met by Potter's Lane; thence along Potter's Lane to the point at which the same meets Quarry Head Lane; thence along Quarry Head Lane to the point at which the same meets Margery Lane; thence along Margery Lane to the point at which the same meets Flass Lane; thence along Flass Lane to the point at which the same meets a lane leading into the newly cut Turnpike Road which forms the commencement of the Newcastle Road; thence along the last mentioned lane to the point at which the same joins the said newly cut road; thence, northward, along the said newly cut road to the point at which the same joins the old line of the Newcastle Road; thence in a straight line through the northernmost of the two outbuildings attached to Kepier's Hospital to the River Wear; thence along the River Wear to the point at which the same meets Kepier Lane; thence along Kepier Lane, passing under the old arches of the hospital, to the point at which the same lane is joined, on the south-west of High Grange Farm, by a lane leading into the Loaning Head Road; thence along the last mentioned lane, crossing the Sunderland Road, to the point at which the same lane joins the Loaning Head Road; thence along the Loaning Head Road to the point at which the same is met by a Beck running close to the north of Pellaw Wood and to the south of Gilesgate Church; thence along the said Beck to the point at which the same falls into the River Wear; thence along the River Wear to Shincliffe Bridge.

E 5

74   2 & 3 WILLIAM IV. CAP. 64.

GATESHEAD.—The parish of Gateshead, and also all such part of the chapelry of Heworth in the parish of Jarrow as is situated to the west of a straight line to be drawn from Kirton Toll Gate House to Blue Quarry Mill, and prolonged each way to the boundary of the parish of Gateshead.

SOUTH SHIELDS. — The respective townships of South Shields and Westoe.

SUNDERLAND.—The parish of Sunderland, and the several townships of Bishop Wearmouth, Bishop Wearmouth Panns, Monk Wearmouth, Monk Wearmouth Shore, and Southwick.

12.—COUNTY OF ESSEX.

NORTHERN DIVISION.

COLCHESTER.—The old borough of Colchester.

HARWICH.—The old borough of Harwich.

SOUTHERN DIVISION.

MALDON.—The old borough of Maldon, and the parish of Heybridge.

13.—COUNTY OF GLOUCESTER.

EASTERN DIVISION.

CHELTENHAM.—The parish of Cheltenham.

CIRENCESTER.—The parish of Cirencester.

GLOUCESTER.—From the old City Boundary Stone on the western side of the lane called Castle Lane, leading from Westgate Street to the County Gaol, northward, along the old City Boundary to the Boundary Stone, south of the London Road, which marks the easternmost point of the old City Boundary; thence in a straight line through the eastern corner of the Mill upon the River Twiver, between the old City Boundary and the Tramroad from the Gloucester and Berkeley Canal to Cheltenham, to the said Tramroad; thence along the said Tramroad to the point at which the same is met by Barton Lane; thence along Barton Lane to the point

2 & 3 WILLIAM IV. CAP. 64.

at which the same crosses the Sud Brook; thence along the Sud Brook to the point at which the same falls into the Gloucester and Berkeley Canal; thence along the Gloucester and Berkeley Canal to the point at which the same is met by the old City Boundary; thence, westward, along the old City Boundary to the point first described.

STROUD.—The several parishes of Stroud, Bisley, Painswick, Pitchcomb, Randwick, Stonehouse, Leonard-Stanley, King's-Stanley, Rodborough, Minchinhampton, Woodchester, Avening, and Horseley, except that part of the parish of Leonard-Stanley which is called Lorridge's Farm, and is surrounded by the parish of Berkley.

TEWKESBURY.—The parish of Tewkesbury.

14.— COUNTY OF HANTS.

NORTHERN DIVISION.

ANDOVER. — The respective parishes of Andover and Knights Enham, and the tithing of Foxcot.

PETERSFIELD.—The old borough of Petersfield, and the tithing of Sheet; the several parishes of Buriton, Lyss, and Froxfield; the several tithings of Ramsden, Langrish, and Oxenbourn, in the parish of East Meon; and also the parish of Steep, except the respective tithings of North and South Ambersham.

WINCHESTER.—From St. Winnal's Church in a straight line to the Cottage on the new Alresford Road, which is north-west of the White House on St. Giles's Hill; thence in a straight line to the Turnpike Gate at Barr End; thence in a straight line to the point at which the Gosport Road joins the Southampton Road; thence in a straight line to the point at which an angle is made in the northern bank of the lane leading from St. Cross to Compton Down, perpendicularly above the deep hollow in the said lane; thence in a straight line to the Cock Lane Turnpike Gate; thence in a straight line to the Three Horse Shoes public house on the Week Road; thence in a straight line to the house on the Andover Road which is immediately north-west of the point at which the boundary of the City of Winchester crosses the same road; thence in a straight line to the south-eastern

76 2 & 3 WILLIAM IV. CAP. 64.

corner of the Fir Plantation on the western side of the Basingstoke Road; thence in a straight line to St. Winnal's Church.

SOUTHERN DIVISION.

CHRISTCHURCH.—The parish of Christchurch, and the chapelry of Holdenhurst, except such part of the tithing of Hurn in the parish of Christchurch as is situated to the north of the following boundary; (that is to say,)

From the point at which the western boundary of the parish of Christchurch crosses the road from Dudsbury to Hurnbridge, in a straight line to the south-western corner of Merritown Common; thence along the southern boundary of Merritown Common and of Hurn Common to the point at which the southern boundary of Hurn Common reaches the Moor's River; thence in a straight line to the southern boundary post of the parish of Christchurch on the Ringwood Road, close by Fillybrook Plantation.

LYMINGTON.—The parish of Lymington, and also such part of the parish of Boldre as is comprised in the following boundary; (that is to say,)

From East-end Bridge, on the eastern boundary of the parish of Boldre, in a straight line through Boldre Church to the western bank of Lymington River; thence, southward, along the western bank of Lymington River to the point at which the same meets the boundary of the parish of Boldre; thence, southward, along the boundary of the parish of Boldre to East-end Bridge aforesaid.

PORTSMOUTH.—The old borough of Portsmouth, and the parish of Portsea.

SOUTHAMPTON.—The town and county of the town of Southampton.

15.—COUNTY OF HEREFORD.

HEREFORD.—The whole space contained within the boundary of the liberties of the City of Hereford, including Castle Green.

LEOMINSTER.—The parish of Leominster.

16.—COUNTY OF HERTFORD.

St. Alban's.—From the Turnpike Gate on the London Road east of St. Alban's, called St. Alban's Gate, in a straight line to the point at which the boundary of the old borough crosses the river at the bottom of the Cotton Mill Lane ; thence, southward, along the boundary of the old borough to the point at which the western boundary of the parish of St. Alban leaves the river ; thence in a straight line, through the south-eastern corner of St. Michael's Churchyard, to the Hempstead Road ; thence, northward, along the Hempstead Road to the point at which the same meets the road leading to Gorehambury, formerly the Redbourn Road ; thence in a straight line to the western extremity of the tongue of land in the river just above Kingsbury Fishpond ; thence in a straight line to the side bar belonging to Kingsbury Turnpike Gate, by the side of the new Redbourn Road ; thence eastward, in a straight line to the point at which the boundary of the old borough meets Luton Lane ; thence, eastward, along the boundary of the old borough to the point at which the same crosses Sweetbriar Lane ; thence in a straight line to St. Alban's Turnpike Gate aforesaid.

Hertford.—From the Corporation Post at the bottom of Port Hill, along the Bengeo Road to the point at which the same is cut by the northern fence of Port Hill Field ; thence along the northern and western fences of Port Hill Field to the point at which such western fence cuts the Mole Wood Mill Road ; thence in a straight line through Sele Farm Bridge to the Stevenage Road ; thence in a straight line to the point at which the Hertingfordbury Road is crossed by the boundary of the Out-borough of Hertford ; thence, southward, along the boundary of the Out-borough of Hertford to the corporation post at the bottom of Port Hill.

17.—COUNTY OF HUNTINGDON.

Huntingdon.—The old borough of Huntingdon, and the parish of Godmanchester.

18.—COUNTY OF KENT.

EASTERN DIVISION.

Canterbury. — From the westernmost point, near St. Jacob's, at which the boundary of the City Liberties meets

78 2 & 3 WILLIAM IV. CAP. 64.

the Ashford Road, in a straight line to the point at which the respective boundaries of the parishes of Harbledown, St. Dunstan, and Holy Cross Westgate meet; thence, northward, along the eastern boundary of the parish of Harbledown to the point at which the same turns north-westward near the Whitstable Road, thence, in a straight line, in the direction of St. Stephen's Church, to the point at which such straight line cuts the boundary of the parish of St. Stephen; thence, eastward along the boundary of the parish of St. Stephen to the point at which the same meets the boundary of the parish of Holy Cross Westgate; thence in a straight line, through the point at which the road to St. Stephen's Church meets the road to Sturry, to the nearest branch of the River Stour; thence along the said branch of the River Stour to the Corporation Stone, Number 5; thence, eastward, along the boundary of the City Liberties, including the whole of the borough of Longport, to the point first described.

Dovor.—From the Jetty, along the boundary of the Liberties of the Town and Port of Dovor, on the eastern side of the Castle, and through the parish of Charlton to the Boundary Stone at which the boundary of the said liberties meets the boundary of the parish of Buckland in Back Lane; thence along Back Lane to the point at which the same meets the road leading down to Crabbe Turnpike Gate on the London Road; thence in a straight line, in a westerly direction, to the point at which the boundary of the parish of Buckland crosses the London Road; thence along the boundary of the parish of Buckland to the point at which the same crosses the river; thence in a straight line to the point at which the boundary of the parish of Buckland meets the road leading to Combe Farm; thence along the boundary of the parish of Buckland to the point at which the boundary of the parish of Hougham is intersected by the boundary of the liberties aforesaid; thence along the boundary of the said Liberties to the Sea Coast; thence along the Sea Coast to the Jetty.

Hythe.—The old borough of Hythe; the liberties of the town of Folkstone; and the several parishes of West Hythe, Saltwood, Cheriton, Folkstone, and Newington, except that detached part of the parish of Newington called Marwood Land.

Sandwich.—The several parishes of St. Mary, St. Peter. and St. Clement; and the extra-parochial precinct of St. Bartholomew, Sandwich; the parish of Deal; and the parish of Walmer.

2 & 3 WILLIAM IV. CAP. 64.

79

WESTERN DIVISION.

CHATHAM.—From the easternmost point at which the boundary of the city of Rochester meets the right bank of the River Medway, southward, along the boundary of the city of Rochester to the boundary stone of the said city marked 5; thence in a straight line to the Windmill in the parish of Chatham on the top of Chatham Hill; thence in a straight line to the Oil Windmill in the parish of Gillingham, between the village of Gillingham and the Fortifications; thence in a straight line through Gillingham Fort to the right bank of the River Medway; thence along the right bank of the River Medway to the point first described.

GREENWICH.—From the point at which the Royal Arsenal Canal at Woolwich joins the River Thames, along the said canal to the southern extremity thereof; thence in a straight line to the south-western corner of the Ordnance Store-keeper's house; thence in a straight line, in the direction of a stile in the Footpath from Woolwich to Plumstead Common, over Sand Hill, to the boundary of the parish of Woolwich; thence, southward, along the boundary of the parish of Woolwich to the point at which the same meets the boundary of the parish of Charlton; thence, westward, along the boundary of the parish of Charlton to the point at which the same turns southward near the Dovor Road; thence along the Dovor Road to the nearest point of the boundary of the parish of Greenwich; thence, westward, along the boundary of the parish of Greenwich to the point at which the same turns abruptly to the south, close by the Dovor Road; thence in a straight line, in a westerly direction, to the nearest point of the boundary of the parish of Greenwich; thence, westward, along the boundary of the parish of Greenwich to the point at which the same meets the boundary of the parish of Saint Paul, Deptford; thence, southward, along the boundary of the parish of Saint Paul, Deptford, to the point at which the same meets the River Thames; thence along the River Thames to the point first described.

MAIDSTONE.—The old borough of Maidstone.

ROCHESTER.—The whole space comprised within the boundaries of the liberties of the old City of Rochester, and also such parts of the respective parishes of Strood and Frindsbury as are situated between the left bank of the River Medway and the boundary hereafter described; (that is to say,)

2 & 3 WILLIAM IV. CAP. 64.

From the entrance from the River Medway of the Thames and Medway Canal, along a footpath which leads up the hill towards Upnor, to the point (on the top of the hill) at which the same is met by a road or path leading towards Frindsbury Church; thence along such road or path to the point at which the same joins Parsonage Lane; thence along Parsonage Lane to the point at which the same joins the road from Frindsbury to Hoo; thence in a straight line to the northernmost angle of the boundary of the parish of Strood; thence, westward, along the boundary of the parish of Strood to the point at which the same meets the London Road; thence towards Rochester along the London Road to the point at which the same is joined by the road from the Three Crouches; thence in a straight line to the point at which the left bank of the River Medway would be cut by a straight line to be drawn from the point last described to Fort Clarence.

19.—COUNTY OF LANCASTER.

NORTHERN DIVISION.

BLACKBURN.—The township of Blackburn.

CLITHEROE.—The respective Chapelries of Downham and Clitheroe; and the Four townships of Whally, Wiswall, Pendleton, and Hensborn, and Little Mitton and Colcoats.

LANCASTER.—From the point on the River Lune at which the respective boundaries of the townships of Lancaster, Skerton, and Heaton-with-Oxcliffe meet, westward, along the boundary of the township of Lancaster to the point at which the respective boundaries of the townships of Lancaster, Bulk, and Quernmore meet; thence in a straight line to the Aqueduct Bridge over the Caton Road; thence, northward, along the Canal from Preston to Kendal to the Fourth Bridge over the same from the Aqueduct; thence in a straight line to the point at which Bracken Lane meets Scale Lane; thence along Scale Lane to the point at which the same reaches the River Lune; thence along the River Lune to the point first described.

PRESTON.—The old borough of Preston, and the township of Fishwick.

2 & 3 WILLIAM IV. CAP. 64.

81

SOUTHERN DIVISION.

ASHTON-UNDER-LYNE.—The whole space over which the provisions of an Act passed in the seventh and eighth years of the reign of his late Majesty King George the Fourth, and intituled " An Act for lighting, cleansing, watching, and " otherwise improving the Town of Ashton-under-Lyne in " the County Palatine of Lancaster, and for regulating the " Police thereof," at present extend.

BOLTON-LE-MOORS. — The several townships of Great Bolton, Little Bolton, and Haulgh, except that detached part of the township of Little Bolton which is situate to the north of the town of Bolton.

BURY.—From the point in the Hamlet of Starling at which a boundary stone marks the boundary of the respective townships of Elton and Ainsworth, along the lane from Starling to Walshaw Lane, to the point in the hamlet of Walshaw Lane at which a Boundary Stone marks the boundary of the respective townships of Elton and Tottington Lower End; thence, eastward, along the boundary of the township of Elton to the point at which the same meets the Woodill Brook: thence in a straight line to the point at which the Pigs Lea Brook falls into the River Irwell; thence, eastward, along the boundary of the township of Bury to the point at which the same meets the boundary of the township of Elton; thence, westward, along the boundary of the township of Elton to the point first described.

LIVERPOOL.—From the western extremity of Dingle Lane, on the south of the town, along Dingle Lane, to the point at which the same meets Ullet Lane ; thence along Ullet Lane to the point at which the same meets Lodge Lane ; thence along Lodge Lane to the point at which the same meets Smithdown Lane; thence along Smithdown Lane to the point at which the same is met by the boundary of the township of Wavertree ; thence, northward, along the boundary of the township of Wavertree to that point thereof which is nearest to the south-eastern corner of the wall of the new Botanic Gardens ; thence in a straight line to the said south-eastern corner; thence along the eastern wall of the new Botanic Gardens to the point at which such wall reaches Edge Lane ; thence, eastward, along Edge Lane to a point seventy-four yards distant from the point last described; thence in a line parallel to

82   2 & 3 WILLIAM IV. CAP. 64.

the new street called Grove Street to the point at which such parallel line reaches the London Road; thence along the London Road to the point at which the same is joined by Deane Street; thence in a straight line to the boundary stone in Rake Lane, near the southern extremity of Whitefield Lane; thence, northward, along the boundary of the township of Everton to the point at which the same joins the boundary of the township of Kirkdale; thence, northward, along the boundary of the township of Kirkdale to the point at which the same reaches the High-water Mark of the River Mersey; thence along the High-water Mark of the River Mersey to that point thereof which is nearest to the point first described; thence in a straight line to the point first described.

MANCHESTER.—The several townships of Manchester, Chorlton Row otherwise Chorlton-upon-Medlock, Ardwick, Beswick, Hulme, Cheetham, Bradford, Newton, and Harpur Hey.

OLDHAM.—The several townships of Oldham, Chadderton, Crompton, and Royton.

ROCHDALE.—The space defined in the 101st Section of an Act passed in the sixth year of the reign of his late Majesty King George the Fourth, and intituled " An Act for lighting, " cleansing, watching, and regulating the town of Rochdale " in the County Palatine of Lancaster."

SALFORD.—From the northernmost point at which the boundary of the township of Salford meets the boundary of the township of Broughton, northward, along the boundary of the township of Broughton, to the point at which the same meets the boundary of the township of Pendleton; thence, westward, along the boundary of the township of Pendleton to the point at which the same meets the boundary of the detached portion of the township of Pendlebury; thence, southward, along the boundary of the detached portion of the township of Pendlebury to the point at which the same meets the boundary of the township of Salford; thence, westward, along the boundary of the township of Salford to the point first described.

WARRINGTON.—The respective townships of Warrington and Latchford; and also those two detached portions of the township of Thelwall which lie between the boundary of the township of Latchford and the River Mersey.

WIGAN.—The township of Wigan.

20.—COUNTY OF LEICESTER.

SOUTHERN DIVISION.

LEICESTER.—The old borough of Leicester, and the space over which the magistrates of the old borough of Leicester at present exercise a jurisdiction concurrently with the magistrates of the county of Leicester, including the Castle View.

21.—COUNTY OF LINCOLN.

PARTS OF LINDSEY.

LINCOLN.—The old city of Lincoln, the Bail and Close, and a certain common, belonging to the Freemen of Lincoln, called Canwick Common, together with all extra-parochial places, if any, which are surrounded by the old city of Lincoln the Bail and Close, and the said Common, or any or either of them, or by the boundaries or boundary of any or either of them.

GREAT GRIMSBY.—The several parishes of Great Grimsby, Great Coates, Little Coates, Bradley, Laceby, Waltham, Scartho, Clee, Weelsby, and Cleethorpes.

PARTS OF KESTEVEN AND HOLLAND.

BOSTON.—The old borough of Boston, the parish of Skirbeck, and the Hamlet of Skirbeck Quarter, including the Fen Allotment of the Hamlet of Skirbeck Quarter, but not the Fen Allotment of the parish of Skirbeck.

GRANTHAM.—The parish of Grantham, (including the several townships of Spittlegate, Manthorpe with Little Gonerby, and Harrowby,) and that part of the parish of Somerby which is contained between the boundary of the parish of Grantham and High Dyke.

STAMFORD.—The old borough of Stamford, and such part of the parish of Saint Martin Stamford Baron as lies between

84   2 & 3 WILLIAM IV. CAP. 64.

the boundary of the old borough and the following boundary; (that is to say,)

From the westernmost point at which the boundary of the parish of Saint Martin meets the boundary of the old borough, southward, along the boundary of the parish of Saint Martin, to the northernmost point at which the same meets the Woothorpe Road; thence in a straight line to the southern Tower, on the London Road, of the Gateway to Burghley House; thence, northward, along the Wall of Burghley Park to the point at which the same meets an occupation road called the "New Road," which runs from the Barnack and Pilsgate Road to the River Welland; thence along the said occupation road, and in a line in continuation of the direction thereof, to the point at which such line cuts the boundary of the old borough.

22.—COUNTY OF MIDDLESEX.

FINSBURY.—The several parishes of Saint Luke, Saint George the Martyr, Saint Giles-in-the-Fields, Saint George Bloomsbury, Saint Mary Stoke Newington, and Saint Mary Islington; the several Liberties or Places of Saffron Hill, Hatton Garden, Ely Rents, Ely Place, the Rolls, Glass House Yard, and the Charter House; Lincoln's Inn and Gray's Inn; the parish of Saint James and Saint John Clerkenwell, except that part thereof which is situate to the north of the parish of Islington; those parts of the respective parishes of Saint Sepulchre and Saint Andrew, Holborn, and of Furnival's Inn and Staple Inn respectively, which are situated without the Liberty of the City of London.

LONDON.—The whole space contained within the exterior boundaries of the Liberties of the City of London, including the Inner Temple and the Middle Temple.

MARY-LE-BONE.—The several parishes of Saint Mary-le-bone, Saint Pancras, and Paddington.

TOWER HAMLETS.—The several divisions of the Liberty of the Tower, and the Tower Division of Ossulston Hundred.

WESTMINSTER.—The old City and Liberties of Westminster, and the Duchy Liberty.

2 & 3 WILLIAM IV. CAP. 64.

85

23.—COUNTY OF MONMOUTH.

MONMOUTH DISTRICT.

MONMOUTH.—The parish of Monmouth, and all such parts of the old borough of Monmouth as lie without the parish of Monmouth.

NEWPORT.—From the point, on the south of the town, at which the Mendle Gief Road is joined by a husbandry road leading to Hundred Acres Gout, along the Mendle Gief Road, to the point at which the same meets the Cardiff Road; thence, westward, along the Cardiff Road to the point at which the same meets the streamlet from Cwrty-bella Well; thence along the said streamlet to the Pool on the western side of Friar's Garden Wall; thence along the Watercourse up from the said Pool to another Pool on the western side of Bull Field; thence along the western fence of Bull Field to the point at which the same fence cuts the road from Stow to Risca; thence, westward, along the road from Stow to Risca to the point at which the same is cut by the fence which runs northward from the east end of the cottages belonging to John Ricketts; thence along the last mentioned fence to the north-western corner of the field of which it is the western boundary; thence, eastward, along the northern fence of the last mentioned field to the point at which the same is intersected by the fence of the adjoining field; thence, northward, along the last mentioned fence to a well head; thence along the stream leading therefrom to the point at which the same meets the boundary of the old borough; thence, northward, along the boundary of the old borough to the point at which the same meets the River Usk at the mouth of Cridan Pill; thence along the River Usk to the point at which the same is joined by a Pill opposite the castle; thence along the said Pill to the Gout; thence along the watercourse, in a direction nearly due east, to the point at which the same meets the new road to Caerleon; thence along the new road to Caerleon to the point at which the same joins the old road to Christ Church; thence along the New Reen to the point at which the same meets Liswerry Pill; thence along Liswerry Pill to the point at which the same joins the River Usk; thence along the River Usk to the point at which the same is joined by Hundred Acres Gout; thence along Hundred Acres Gout to the point at which the same is met by the said husbandry road leading thereto from the Mendle Gief Road;

thence along the said husbandry road to the point first described.

Usk.—From the Bridge on the north of the town, called "Cym-cayo Bridge," along the brook over which the said bridge is built, to the point at which the same falls into the River Usk; thence down the River Usk, and along the boundary of the old borough, to the point at which the same cuts the mill stream; thence in a straight line to the Farm House of Little Castle Farm; thence along the eastern side of the fence of the farmyard of Little Castle Farm to the north eastern corner of such farmyard; thence in a straight line to the Oak Tree in the wood hedge on the summit of Lady Hill; thence in a straight line to the point at which Cwm-cayo Brook would be cut by a straight line to be drawn from the Tree last described to Cwm-cayo Bridge; thence along Cwm-cayo Brook to Cwm-cayo Bridge.

24.—COUNTY OF NORFOLK.

EASTERN DIVISION.

Norwich.—The city and county of the city of Norwich, together with all such extra-parochial places as are contained within the outer boundary of the city and county of the city of Norwich.

Great Yarmouth.—The old borough of Great Yarmouth and the parish of Gorlestone.

WESTERN DIVISION.

King's Lynn.—The old borough of King's Lynn.

Thetford.—The old borough of Thetford.

25.—COUNTY OF NORTHAMPTON.

NORTHERN DIVISION.

Peterborough.—The parish of St. John Baptist, Peterborough, together with the extra-parochial district known by the name of "The Minster Precincts."

SOUTHERN DIVISION.

Northampton.—The old borough of Northampton.

2 & 3 WILLIAM IV. CAP. 64.

87

26.—COUNTY OF NORTHUMBERLAND.

NORTHERN DIVISION.

BERWICK-UPON-TWEED.—The parish of Berwick, and the respective townships of Tweedmouth and Spital.

MORPETH.—The several townships of Morpeth, Buller's Green, Newminster Abbey, Catchburn with Morpeth Castle and Stobhill, Hepscott, and Tramwell with High Church, and the parish of Bedlington.

SOUTHERN DIVISION.

NEWCASTLE-UPON-TYNE.—The town and county of the town of Newcastle, and the several townships of Byker, Heaton, Jesmond, Westgate, and Elswic.

TYNEMOUTH and NORTH SHIELDS.—The several townships of Tynemouth, North Shields, Chirton, Preston, and Cullercoats.

27.—COUNTY OF NOTTINGHAM.

NORTHERN DIVISION.

NOTTINGHAM.—The county of the town of Nottingham.

SOUTHERN DIVISION.

NEWARK-UPON-TRENT.—The old borough of Newark.

28.—COUNTY OF OXFORD.

BANBURY.—The parish of Banbury.

OXFORD.—From the tree on the east of the city called 'Joe Pullen's Tree," in a straight line to the boundary stone n the lane called " Mrs. Knapp's Free Board ;" thence along he said lane to the western extremity thereof; thence in a straight line to the centre of the island situate at the junction of the stream called " Harson's Heat" with the River Charwell; thence, westward, along the River Charwell to the point at which the same joins the old city boundary; thence, westward, along the old city boundary to the point at which the

88   2 & 3 WILLIAM IV. CAP. 64.

River Charwell divides into two streams; thence along the easternmost of such two streams to King's Mill; thence in a straight line to the easternmost part of King's Mill; thence in a straight line to " Joe Pullen's Tree."

NEW WOODSTOCK.—The old borough of New Woodstock; the several parishes of Bladon, Begbrook, Shipton-on-Cherwell, Hampton Gay, Tackley, Wootton, Stonesfield, Coombe, and Handborough; the parish of Kidlington, except the respective Hamlets of Gosford and Water Eaton; the hamlet of Old Woodstock and Blenheim Park.

29.—COUNTY OF SALOP.

NORTHERN DIVISION.

SHREWSBURY.—From the point at which the River Severn is joined by a stream or watercourse which flows by the Dog Kennel, and under Bow Bridge, along the said stream or watercourse to the point at which the same reaches the road leading from Old Heath into the Chester Road ; thence along the said road from Old Heath to the point at which the same joins the Chester Road; thence along the Chester Road to the point at which the same is met by a watercourse which runs round the Corporation Gardens and Round Hill, and joins the River Severn near the house called " The Flash;" thence along the last-mentioned watercourse to the point at which the same reaches the old Baschurch Road; thence along the old Baschurch Road to the point at which the same is met by a footpath leading along the wall of Flash House towards the River Severn; thence along the said footpath to the point at which the same meets again the last-mentioned watercourse; thence along the last-mentioned watercourse to the point at which the same joins the River Severn; thence along the River Severn to the point at which the same is met by the common boundary of the respective parishes of Saint Chad and Saint Julian; thence, eastward, along the boundary of the parish of Saint Chad to the point at which the same reaches a lane or road which leads from the Montgomery Road into lands belonging to Mrs. Cartwright ; thence along such lane or road to the point at which the same joins the Montgomery Road; thence in a straight line to the point at which the stream from the Conduit Head joins the Radbrook Stream; thence along the Radbrook Stream to the point at which the

2 & 3 WILLIAM IV. CAP. 64.

89

same reaches Kingsland Lane; thence along Kingsland Lane to the point at which the same joins the Bishop's Castle Road; thence along the Bishop's Castle Road to the point at which the same is met by the boundary of the parish of Saint Julian; thence, eastward, along the boundary of the parish of Saint Julian to the point at which the same meets the boundary of the parish of Holy Cross; thence, eastward, along the boundary of the parish of Holy Cross to the point first described.

SOUTHERN DIVISION.

BRIDGENORTH.—The old borough of Bridgenorth, and the several parishes of Quatford, Oldbury, Tasley, and Astley Abbotts.

LUDLOW.—From the point on the south of the town at which Dirty Brook joins the River Teme, north-eastward, along the boundary of the township of Ludford to that point thereof which is nearest to the south-western corner of the piece of land called " Rock Close ;" thence in a straight line to the said south-western corner; thence along the western fence of Rock Close to the point at which the same cuts the road to the Sheet; thence towards Ludlow along the road to the Sheet to the point at which the same is joined by a road leading by Gallows Bank into Rock Lane; thence along the last-mentioned road to the point at which the same reaches Rock Lane; thence along Rock Lane to the point at which the same is joined by a road to the Sandpits Turnpike; thence along the said road to the Sandpits Turnipike to the point at which the same is met by the eastern fence of the garden of the public house called the " Cross Keys;" thence in a straight line to the point at which Fishmore Brook would be cut by a straight line to be drawn from the point last described to Stanton Lacy House; thence along the Fishmore Brook to the point at which the same joins the River Corve; thence up the River Corve to the point at which the same meets the fence which separates the lands occupied by Mr. William Russell from the lands occupied by Mr. Henry Lloyd; thence along the last-mentioned fence to the point at which the same meets the Shrewsbury Road; thence along the fence which separates the two fields respectively called " The Lease Piece" and " Pike Field" to the point at which such fence meets the Burway Road; thence, northward, along the Burway Road to the point at which the same is met by the fence which separates the two fields respectively called " The

F

2 & 3 WILLIAM IV. CAP. 64.

Marshes" and "The Ox Pasture;" thence along the last-mentioned fence to the point at which the same meets the River Teme; thence in a straight line to the point at which the fence which divides the lands of the Honourable Robert Henry Clive from lands of the corporation of Ludlow, in the occupation of Mr. William Smith, meets the Prior Halton Road; thence towards Ludlow along the Prior Halton Road to the point at which the same is met by the fence which divides the lands of the corporation of Ludlow, occupied by the late Mr. Johnnes and Mr. George Anderson, from the lands of the said corporation occupied by the late Mr. Anthony Jones and Mr. Robert Meyrick; thence along the last-mentioned fence to the point at which the same meets the Brick House Road; thence in a straight line to the eastern corner of Whitecliff Coppice; thence, southward, along the north-eastern fence of Whitecliff Coppice to the point at which the same meets the boundary of the township of Ludford; thence, southward, along the boundary of the township of Ludford to the point first described.

WENLOCK.—The old borough of Wenlock.

30.—COUNTY OF SOMERSET.

EASTERN DIVISION.

BATH.—The old city of Bath, the respective parishes of Bathwick and Lyncomb and Wyncomb, and also that part of the parish of Walcot which lies without the old city of Bath and adjoins the boundary of the old city of Bath.

BRISTOL.—From the point on the north-east of the city at which the eastern boundary of the out-parish of Saint Paul meets the north-western boundary of the out-parish of St. Philip and Jacob, eastward, along the boundary of the parish of Saint Philip and Jacob to that point thereof which is nearest to the point at which the Wells Road leaves the Bath Road; thence in a straight line to the said point at which the Wells Road leaves the Bath Road; thence along the Wells Road to the Knowle Turnpike Gate; thence along the road which leads from the Knowle Turnpike Gate to Bedminster Church to the point at which the same is crossed by Bedminster Brook; thence along Bedminster Brook to the point at which the same crosses the road from Locks Mill to Bedminster;

2 & 3 WILLIAM IV. CAP. 64. 91

thence along the last-mentioned road, passing the southern extremity of the village of Bedminster, to the point at which the same meets the brook at Marsh Pit; thence along the last-mentioned brook to the point at which the same meets the boundary of the parish of Clifton; thence, northward, along the boundary of the parish of Clifton to the boundary stone marked (C. P) and (W P) 12), marking the north-eastern angle of the boundary of the parish of Clifton, and situate on Durdham Down, east of the Shirehampton Road; thence in a straight line to the southernmost point at which the boundary of the tithing of Stoke Bishop meets Parry's Lane; thence, eastward, along the boundary of the tithing of Stoke Bishop to the point at which the same joins the boundary of the out-parish of St. Paul; thence, northward, along the boundary of the out-parish of St. Paul to the point first described.

FROME.—From Cottle's Oak Turnpike Gate, along Barton Lane, to the point at which the same meets Green Lane; thence along Green Lane to the point at which the same meets the lane to Hellicar's Grave; thence along the lane to Hellicar's Grave to the southern extremity thereof; thence in a straight line through Plaguy House into Grove Lane; thence in a straight line to the point at which the road from Tytherington is met by the Lane to Adderwell at a place called the Mount; thence along the lane to Adderwell to the eastern extremity thereof near Bellows Hole; thence in a straight line to the point at which Frome River would be cut by a straight line to be drawn from the point last described to the house called " Mrs. White's" or "Southfield Farm House;" thence, northward, along Frome River to the point at which the same is joined by Rodden Lake Streamlet; thence along Rodden Lake Streamlet to Rodden Bridge at the end of Rodden Lane; thence along Rodden Lane to the point called Clink Crossways; thence in a straight line to the Twelfth Mile Stone on the Bath Road; thence in a straight line to the north-eastern corner of Mr. Shepherd's Garden Wall; thence in a straight line, through the house of Thomas Ball and Mrs. Slade, to Frome River; thence along Frome River to the northernmost part of the buildings of the Dye House, late the property of Samuel Button; thence in a straight line to the centre of Kissing Batch Pond; thence in a straight line to Cottle's Oak Turnpike Gate.

WELLS.—From the point on the north-east of the city at

92 2 & 3 WILLIAM IV. CAP. 64.

which the old city boundary meets Back Lane, along Back Lane to the point at which the same joins the Bath Road; thence in a straight line across the Bath Road to the northern extremity of Drang Lane; thence along Drang Lane, and along the footpath across Drang Meadow, to the point at which such footpath joins the road which leads to the turnpike on the Shepton Mallett Road; thence, westward, along the road so joined to the next city boundary stone; thence, southward, along the old city boundary to the point first described.

WESTERN DIVISION.

BRIDGEWATER.—From the easternmost point at which the boundary of Three Elm Field meets the River Parret, westward, along the boundary of Three Elm Field to the point at which the same meets Reed Moor Pill; thence, westward, along Reed Moor Pill to the point at which the same reaches the southern boundary of the two fields respectively called the " Pasture Ground;" thence in a straight line to the point at which the boundary of the parish of Wembdon would be cut by a straight line to be drawn from the point last described to the spire of Bridgewater Church; thence, southward, along the boundary of the parish of Wembdon to the point at which the same meets the Cannington Road; thence, westward, along the Cannington Road to the point at which the same is met by the boundary of the field called " Six Acres;" thence, westward, along the boundary of the field called " Six Acres" to the point at which the same meets, near the Horse and Jockey Inn, the road from West Street; thence, westward, along the road from West Street to the point at which the same is met by the western boundary of Matthew's Field; thence along the western boundary of Matthew's Field to the point at which the same meets the Town Mill Leat; thence along the Town Mill Leat to the point at which the same reaches the south-eastern corner of Matthew's Field; thence in a straight line to the point at which Hamp Brook meets Hamp Lane; thence along Hamp Lane to the point at which the same joins West Road; thence along West Road to the point at which the same is joined by Row's Lane; thence along Row's Lane to the point at which the same meets the fence which incloses the grounds of the house called " Hamp," belonging to John Chapman, Esquire; thence, southward, along the last-mentioned fence to the point at which the same meets a stream at Barland Lane Bridge; thence along the said stream to the point at which the same falls into the River Parret at Barland

Clize; thence, westward, along the River Parret to the point at which the same is joined by the boundary of the northernmost of the two contiguous fields respectively called " Five Acres;" thence, eastward, along the boundary of the last-mentioned field to the point at which the same meets the boundary of the field called " Four Acres;" thence, northward, along the boundary of the field called " Four Acres" to the point at which the same meets the boundary of a field called " Five Acres;" thence, eastward, along the boundary of the last-mentioned field called " Five Acres " to the point at which the same meets the Weston Zoyland Road; thence, eastward, along the Weston Zoyland Road to the point at which the same is met by an occupation road leading towards the North; thence along the said occupation road to the northern extremity thereof; thence along the fence which is the western boundary of the fields respectively called " Ten Acres," " Seven Acres," and " Five Acres," formerly belonging to Alexander Popham, Esquire, to the point at which such fence meets the fence of a field called " The Hundred Acres;" thence in a straight line to the southern extremity, close by a penfold, of the fence which divides the two fields respectively called " Part of the Hundred Acres;" thence, eastward, along the boundary of the easternmost of the two last-mentioned fields to the point at which such boundary meets the Bath Road; thence, northward, along the boundary of the field called "Small Croft" to the point at which the same meets the Bristol Road; thence, westward, along the boundary of Great Castle Field to the point at which the same meets the River Parret; thence along the River Parret to the point first described.

Taunton.—From the point on the north-west of the town at which Mill Lease Stream crosses Greenway Lane, along Greenway Lane to the point at which the same joins the Kingston Road; thence along the Kingston Road to the point at which the same is joined by the Cheddon Road; thence along the Cheddon Road to the point at which the same is joined by Priors Wood Lane; thence along Priors Wood Lane to the point at which the same is met by the Obridge Stream; thence along the Obridge Stream to the point at which the same falls into the River Tone; thence, Southward, along the River Tone to the point at which the same is met by Mill Lane; thence along Mill Lane to the point at which the same joins the Bridgewater Road; thence along the Bridgewater Road to the point at which the same is joined

94   2 & 3 WILLIAM IV. CAP. 64.

by Bath Pool Lane; thence in a straight line to Stream Plat Bridge; thence along the stream over which Stream Plat Bridge is built, through Holway Bridge, to the point at which the same stream meets the boundary of the parish of Wilton at Cuckoo Corner; thence, westward, along the boundary of the parish of Wilton to the point at which the same meets Sherford Stream; thence along Sherford Stream to the point at which the same meets Sherford Lane; thence along Sherford Lane to the point at which the same joins the Honiton Road; thence along the Honiton Road to the point at which the same is joined by Hoverland Lane; thence along Hoverland Lane to the point at which the same meets Ganton Stream; thence along Ganton Stream to the point at which the same meets the boundary of the parish of Wilton; thence, northward, along the boundary of the parish of Wilton to the point at which the same meets the Bishops Hull Road; thence, northward, along the Bishops Hull Road to the point at which the same is joined by Long Run Lane; thence in a straight line to the Turnpike House on the Staplegrove Road; thence along the Staplegrove Road to the point at which the same is crossed by Mill Lease Stream; thence along Mill Lease Stream to the point first described.

31.—COUNTY OF STAFFORD.

NORTHERN DIVISION.

NEWCASTLE-UNDER-LYME.—The old borough of New-castle-under-Lyme, and the portion of the parish of Stoke-upon-Trent which is surrounded partly by the boundary of the old borough of Newcastle-under-Lyme and partly by the boundary of the Township of Knutton.

STAFFORD.—From the point at which the boundary of the old borough is cut by a straight line drawn from the windmill near the bridge on the Doxey Road to the stile at the southern end of the footpath from the Newport Road into the Penkridge Road, along the said straight line to the point at which the same meets the Penkridge Road; thence, south-ward, along the Penkridge Road to the point at which a stream of water running along the eastern side of that road turns eastward therefrom; thence along the said stream to the point at which the same meets Spittal Brook; thence along Spittal Brook to the point at which the same meets the River Sow; thence along the River Sow to the point at which the same meets the boundary of the old borough; thence, northward, along the boundary of the old borough to the point first described.

STOKE-UPON-TRENT.—The several townships of Penkhull with Boothen, Tunstall, Burslem, Hanley, Shetlon, Fenton Vivian, Lane End, Fenton Culvert, and Longton, the vill of Rushton Grange, and the hamlet of Sneyd.

SOUTHERN DIVISION.

LICHFIELD.—The county of the city of Lichfield, and the place called The Close, which is encompassed by the said county.

TAMWORTH.—The parish of Tamworth.

WALSALL.—The parish of Walsall, except that detached part thereof which is surrounded by the respective parishes of Aldridge and Rushall, and the chapelry of Pelshall.

WOLVERHAMPTON. —The several townships of Wolverhampton, Bilston, Willenhall, and Wednesfield, and the parish of Sedgeley.

32. COUNTY OF SUFFOLK.

EASTERN DIVISION.

IPSWICH.—The old borough of Ipswich.

WESTERN DIVISION.

BURY ST. EDMUND'S.—The old borough of Bury St. Edmund's.

EYE.—The several parishes of Eye, Hoxne, Denham, Redlingfield, Occold, Thorndon, Braisworth, Yaxley, Thrandiston, Broome, and Oakley.

SUDBURY.—The old borough of Sudbury, and the township or hamlet of Ballingdon cum Brunden; together with all or any extra-parochial places or place surrounded by the boundaries either of the old borough of Sudbury, or of the township or hamlet of Ballingdon cum Brunden.

96

2 & 3 WILLIAM IV. CAP. 64.

33.—COUNTY OF SURREY.

EASTERN DIVISION.

LAMBETH.—The Parish of Saint Mary Newington, the parish of Saint Giles Camberwell, except the manor and hamlet of Dulwich, and also such part of the parish of Lambeth as is situate to the north of the line herein-after described, including the extra-parochial space encompassed by such part :

From the point at which the road from London to Dulwich by Red Post Hill leaves the road from London over Herne Hill in a straight line to Saint Matthew's Church at Brixton ; thence in a straight line to a point in the boundary between the respective parishes of Lambeth and Clapham, one hundred and fifty yards south of the middle of the carriageway along Acre Lane.

REIGATE.—The parish of Reigate.

SOUTHWARK.—The old borough of Southwark, including the Mint and manor of Suffolk ; the several parishes of Rotherhithe, Bermondsey, and Christ Church ; and the Clink liberty of the parish of Saint Saviour.

WESTERN DIVISION.

GUILDFORD.—From the point on the north of the town at which a creek leading from Dapdune House joins the River Wey, in a straight line to the point at which the road called the New Road joins the Stoke Road ; thence along the New Road to the point at which the same joins the Kingston Road ; thence along the Kingston Road to the point at which the same joins Cross Lane ; thence along Cross Lane to the point at which the same joins the Epsom Road ; thence in a straight line to the point in Chalky Lane at which the boundary of Trinity Parish leaves the same ; thence along the southern boundary of Trinity Parish to the point at which such boundary enters Gaol Lane ; thence in a straight line to the point at which the River Wey turns abruptly to the north at a wharf close by the Horsham Road ; thence in a straight line to the point at which the path from Guildford across Bury Fields abuts on the Portsmouth Road ; thence in a straight line to the south-western corner of Cradle Field ; thence along the western hedge of Cradle Field to the point at which

2 & 3 William IV. Cap. 64. 97

the same cuts the old Farnham Road ; thence in a straight line towards Worplesdon Semaphore to the point at which such line cuts the new Farnham Road; thence in a straight line to the point first described.

34.—COUNTY OF SUSSEX.

EASTERN DIVISION.

Brighthelmstone.—The respective parishes of Brighthelmstone and Hove.

Hastings.—The town and port of Hastings and its liberties, including that detached part of the parish of Saint Leonard which lies near the town of Winchelsea, and including also the liberty of the Sluice, but excluding all such other parts of the old borough of Hastings as are detached from the main body thereof.

Lewes.—From the Town Mill on the north-western side of the town in a straight line to the Smock Windmill, which is the most southerly of the two windmills called " The Kingstone Mills;" thence in a straight line to the point at which the boundary of the parish of Southover crosses the Cockshut Stream ; thence along the Cockshut Stream to the point at which the same joins the River Ouse ; thence along the River Ouse to the point at which the same would be cut by a straight line to be drawn from the point last described to the point on the Eastern Cliff known as the site of an old windmill ; thence in a straight line to the said point on the Eastern Cliff; thence in a straight line to the windmill called " Malling Mill ;" thence in a straight line to the point at which the stream which turns the paper mill falls into the River Ouse ; thence in a straight line to the Town Mill.

Rye.—The ancient towns of Rye and Winchelsea, the several parishes of Rye, Peasemarsh, Iden, Playden, Winchelsea, East Guildford, Icklesham, and Udimer, and also that part of the parish of Brede which lies between the parishes of Udimer and Icklesham.

WESTERN DIVISION.

Arundel.—The parish of Arundel.

F 5

98   2 & 3 WILLIAM IV, CAP. 64.

CHICHESTER.—From the eastern extremity of the boundary of the old city liberty at St. James's Post, northward, along the said boundary to the point at which the same meets the old Broill Road : thence in a straight line to the westernmost point at which the boundary of the parish of Saint Peter the Great meets the boundary of the parish of Saint Bartholomew; thence, southward, along the boundary of the parish of Saint Bartholomew to the point at which the same crosses the new road to Fishbourn ; thence in a straight line to the turnpike gate on the Stockbridge Road ; thence in a straight line to the canal bridge adjoining the basin ; thence in a straight line to the southern extremity of Snag Lane ; thence in a straight line to the southern extremity of Cherry Orchard Lane ; thence in a straight line to the point at which the Rumboldsweek Road meets the Oving Road ; thence in a straight line to the point first described.

HORSHAM.—The parish of Horsham.

MIDHURST. — The several parishes of Midhurst, Easebourn, Heyshot, Chithurst, Graffham, Didling, and Cocking ; and the tithing of South Ambersham in the parish of Steep ; that part of the parish of Bignor which is surrounded by the parish of Easebourn ; those parts of the several parishes of Wool Lavington, Bepton, and Woolbeding which adjoin the parish of Midhurst ; that part of the parish of Lynch which adjoins the said part of the parish of Bepton ; and also that part of the parish of Lynch in which Woodman's Green is situate ; all such parts of the respective parishes of Stedham and Iping as are not situated to the north of the cross road which runs from Woodman's Green, between North End Farm and Hobbert's Farm, to Milland Marsh ; the parish of Trotton, except that part thereof which lies to the north of the cross road from Vining Common to Home Hill and Cobed Hall called Lonebecch Lane ; and all such parts of the respective parishes of Sellham and Lodsworth, and of the tithing of North Ambersham, as are not situated to the north of the brook which runs from Cook's Bridge on the London Road to Lickfold Bridge.

2 & 3 William IV. Cap. 64. 99

35.—COUNTY OF WARWICK.

NORTHERN DIVISION.

Birmingham.—The respective parishes of Birmingham and Edgebaston, and the several townships of Bordesley, Duddeston and Nechels, and Deritend.

Coventry.—The city of Coventry and the suburbs thereof.

SOUTHERN DIVISION.
Warwick.—The old borough of Warwick.

36.—COUNTY OF WESTMORLAND.

Kendal.—The respective townships of Kendal and Kirkland, and all such parts of the township of Nether Graveship as adjoin the township of Kendal.

37.—ISLE OF WIGHT.

Newport.—From the point on the south of the town at which the footpath to Shide joins the Niton Road at Trattles Butt, in a straight line to the house in the parishes of Carisbrooke which belongs to Joshua Spickernell, and is now in the occupation of Mrs. Stanborough; thence in a straight line across the Gatcombe Road to the house which belongs to James Barlow Hoy, Esquire, and is now in the occupation of James Dennett; thence in a straight line in the direction of West Mill to the point at which such straight line cuts the Lukeley or Carisbrook Stream; thence, northward, along the Lukeley or Carisbrook Stream to the point at which the same meets the boundary of the old borough; thence, northward, along the boundary of the old borough to Pan Bridge: thence in a straight line to the point at which the footpath to Shide meets Church Litton Lane; thence along the said footpath to the point first described.

38.—COUNTY OF WILTS.

NORTHERN DIVISION.
Calne.—The parish of Calne, and also those parts of the respective parishes of Blackland and Calstone Willington

100   2 & 3 WILLIAM IV. CAP. 64.

which are surrounded by the parish of Calne, including all such parts, if any, of the old borough of Calne as are without the parish of Calne.

CHIPPENHAM.—The several parishes of Chippenham, Hardenhuish, and Langley Burrell, and the extra-parochial space called Pewisham.

DEVIZES.—The borough of Devizes, including the respective parishes of St. John the Baptist and the Blessed Virgin Mary, and also so much of the chapelry of St. James and of the parish of Rowde as lies between the boundary of the old borough and the following boundary; (that is to say,)

From the point at which the boundary of the parish of St. John the Baptist would be cut by a straight line to be drawn from the Dairy Farm House on the Chippenham Road called Ox House, to the Round Tower of the new County Bridewell, in a straight line to Ox House; thence in a straight line to a house occupied by Mr. Mayo, called Brow Cottage; thence in a straight line to the point at which the towing path of the Kennet Canal meets Dye House Lane; thence, eastward, along the Kennet Canal to the point at which the same turns northward near London Bridge; thence in a straight line drawn due east to a point one hundred yards distant; thence in a straight line to Mr. Gundry's house on the Salisbury Road; thence in a straight line to a house called Southgate, occupied by Mr. Slade; thence in a straight line to the southernmost point at which Gallows Acre Lane is met by the boundary of the parish of St. John the Baptist.

MALMSBURY.—The old borough of Malmsbury, the respective out-parishes of St. Paul Malmsbury and St. Mary Westport, and the several parishes of Brokenborough, Charlton, Garsdon, Lea, Great Somerford, Little Somerford, Foxley, and Bremhilham.

MARLBOROUGH.—The old borough of Marlborough and the parish of Preshute.

———

SOUTHERN DIVISION.

SALISBURY.—From the south-western extremity of the wall of the Poorhouse at Fisherton Anger, in a straight line to a point in the Wilton Road which is three hundred and

2 & 3 WILLIAM IV. CAP. 64.

101

thirty yards distant from the point at which the Wilton Road joins the Devizes Road; thence in a straight line to a point in the Devizes Road which is six hundred and forty yards distant from the point at which the Wilton Road joins the Devizes Road; thence in a straight line to the point at which the Stratford Road joins the Marlborough Road; thence in a straight line to the point called Whipping Cross Tree; thence in a straight line to the point at which the road from Salisbury to Laverstock joins the road from Salisbury to Clarendon; thence in a straight line to the point at which the eastern boundary of the city meets the River Avon; thence along the River Avon to the point at which the same joins the River Nadder; thence along the River Nadder to the point first described.

WESTBURY.—The parish of Westbury.

WILTON.—The several parishes of Wilton, Fugglestone, Stratford-under-the-Castle, Great Durnford, Woodford, South Newton, Wishford, Barford, Burcombe, Netherhampton, West Harnham, and Britford; such part of the parish of Fisherton Anger as will not by the provisions of this Act be included within the boundary of the city of Salisbury; and also all such parts of the several parishes of Bishopston, Toney Stratford, Combe Bisset, and Humington, as are situated to the north of a straight line to be drawn from Odstock Church to the point on Combe Hill at which a fence dividing the Down from the cultivated land meets the old road from Salisbury to Blandford, and thence through the centre of the clump of trees called Fallstone Middle Nursery to the western boundary of the parishes of Bishopston; together with all such part of the extra-parochial place called Grovely Wood as is situate to the east of a straight line to be drawn from the point at which the western boundary of the parish of Wishford meets the northern boundary of Grovely Wood, to the point at which the western boundary of the parish of Barford meets the southern boundary of Grovely Wood.

39.—COUNTY OF WORCESTER.

EASTERN DIVISION.

DROITWICH.—The old borough of Droitwich; the several parishes of Dodderhill, Hampton Lovett, Doverdale, Salwarp,

102　2 & 3 WILLIAM IV. CAP. 64.

Martin Hussingtree, Oddingley, Hadsor, Hindlip, Himble-ton, and Elmbridge; the Moreway-end Division and the Broughton Division of the parish of Hanbury; the extra-parochial places called Crutch and Westwood Park; together with the two parts of the respective parishes of Claines and Warndon which are surrounded by the respective parishes of Hindlip and Martin Hussingtree; and also the extra-parochial place called Shell, and the detached part of the parish of Inkberrow, which are respectively contained between the parish of Himbleton and the Broughton Division of the parish of Hanbury.

DUDLEY.—The parish of Dudley.

EVESHAM.—The old borough of Evesham.

WESTERN DIVISION.

BEWDLEY.—The parish of Ribbesford, and the several hamlets of Wribbenhall, Hoarstone, Blackstone, Netherton, and Lower Mitton with Lickhill.

KIDDERMINSTER.—From the point at or near Proud Cross at which the boundary of the old borough meets the Broom-field Road, along the boundary of the old borough, to the point at which the Abberley Road meets the Black Brook; thence, westward, along the Abberley Road to the first point at which the same is met by a hedge running due south there-from; thence along the said hedge to its southern extre-mity near a stone quarry; thence in a straight line to the said stone quarry; thence in a straight line to the first mile stone on the Bewdley Road; thence, westward, along the Bewdley Road to the point at which the same is joined by a footpath leading to the Stourport Road; thence along the said footpath to the point at which the same meets the boundary of the old borough; thence, southward, along the boundary of the old borough to the point at which the same meets the south-eastern fence of a wood called "The Copse," situated on the eastern bank of the River Stour; thence along the said fence to the point at which the same meets Hoo Lane; thence across Hoo Lane, over a stile called "Gallows Stile," along a footpath leading from the said stile to the lane from Hoo Brook to Comberton Hill, to the point at which the last mentioned footpath meets the lane from Hoo Brook to Comberton Hill; thence, northward,

2 & 3 William IV. Cap. 64. 103

along the lane from Hoo-Brook to Comberton Hill to the point at which the same meets the boundary of the old borough; thence, northward, along the boundary of the old borough to the point first described.

Worcester.—From the Liberty Post on the Tewkesbury Road, southward, along the Tewkesbury Road, to the point beyond the turnpike at which the same road is met by Duck Brook; thence along Duck Brook to the point at which the same crosses the London Road; thence in a straight line to the western extremity of the road which leads out of the London Road to Lark Hill; thence along the said road to Lark Hill to the eastern extremity thereof; thence along a footpath leading to the New Town Road to the point at which the same reaches the New Town Road; thence, westward, along the New Town Road to the point at which the same is crossed by the footpath leading from the House of Industry to the Porte Fields Road; thence along the last-mentioned footpath to the point at which the same joins the Porte Fields Road; thence along a footpath which leads from the Porte Fields Road, past Rainbow Villa, into the Astwood Road, to the point at which such footpath joins the Astwood Road; thence along a road which leads from the Astwood Road to the Whey Tavern to the point at which such road crosses the Worcester and Birmingham Canal; thence along the Worcester and Birmingham Canal to the bridge which is nearest to Gregory's Mill; thence along the road leading from the said bridge to the Birmingham Road to the point at which the same is crossed by the Barborne Brook; thence along the Barborne Brook to the point at which the same falls into the River Severn; thence along the River Severn to the point at which the same is met by the boundary of the parish of St. Clement; thence, westward, along the boundary of the parish of St. Clement to the point at which the same meets the boundary of the township of St. John; thence, westward, along the boundary of the township of St. John to the point at which the same meets the Hereford Road; thence along the Hereford Road to the point at which the same is met by Powick Lane, leading to Powick Bridge; thence, southward, along Powick Lane to the point at which the same terminates in a footpath; thence in a straight line to the point at which Cut Throat Lane is met by a footpath leading from Boughton Fields to the Malvern Road; thence along the last-mentioned footpath to the point at which the same joins the Malvern Road; thence, northward, along the Malvern Road to the

104   2 & 3 WILLIAM IV. CAP. 64.

point at which the same meets the boundary of the township of St. John ; thence, eastward, along the boundary of the township of St. John to the point at which the same meets the boundary of the parish of St. Clement; thence, eastward, along the boundary of the parish of St. Clement to the point at which the same meets the River Severn; thence, southward, along the River Severn to the point at which the same is met by the old city boundary ; thence, southward, along the old city boundary to the Liberty Post aforesaid.

40.—COUNTY OF YORK.

NORTH RIDING.

MALTON.—The respective parishes of St. Leonard and St. Michael, New Malton, the parish of Old Malton, and the parish of Norton.

NORTHALLERTON.—The respective townships of Northallerton and Romanby, and the chapelry of Brompton.

RICHMOND.—The respective parishes of Richmond and Easby.

SCARBOROUGH.—The parish of Scarborough, together with the Extra-parochial Precinct of Scarborough Castle.

THIRSK.—The several townships of Thirsk, Sowerby, Carlton Miniott, Sand Hutton, Bagby, and South Kilvington.

WHITBY.—The several townships of Whitby, Ruswarp, and Hawsker-cum-Stainsacre.

YORK.—From the ancient barn on the Easingwold Road, two hundred yards beyond the first mile stone on that road, in a straight line to the Lady or Clifton Mill ; thence in a straight line to the Pepper or Stray Mill ; thence in a straight line to the point at which the Stockton Road would be cut by a straight line to be drawn thereto from the Pepper or Stray Mill through the New Manor House ; thence along the Stockton Road to the point at which the same is joined by a lane leading from the eastern extremity of the village of Heworth towards the north ; thence in a straight line to the point at which the Tang Hall Beck would be cut by a

2 & 3 WILLIAM IV. CAP. 64. 105

straight line to be drawn from the point last described to Heslington Mill; thence along Tang Hall Beck to the point at which the same crosses the boundary of the county of the City of York; thence, southward, along the boundary of the county of the City of York to the point at which the same would be cut by a straight line to be drawn thereto from the south-eastern corner of the barracks through Lamel Mill; thence in a straight line to the south-eastern corner of the barracks; thence along the southern wall of the barracks to the point at which the same cuts the Selby Road; thence along the Selby Road to the point at which the same is joined by Fulford Church Lane; thence along the northern hedge of Fulford Church Lane to the point at which the same ceases to be continuous, close by a farm building belonging to Mr. Ellis; thence in a straight line, in the direction of the said hedge, to the River Ouse; thence along the River Ouse to the southernmost point at which the same is met by the boundary of the City Liberty; thence, westward, along the boundary of the City Liberty to the point at which the same again meets the River Ouse; thence along the River Ouse to the point at which the same would be cut by a straight line to be drawn from the barn first described to Acomb Church; thence in a straight line to the barn first described.

EAST RIDING.

BEVERLEY.—The several parishes of St. Mary, St. Martin, and St. Nicholas, and also such part of the parish of St. John as is comprised within the liberties of Beverley.

KINGSTON UPON HULL.—The several parishes of St. Mary, the Holy Trinity, Sculcoates, and Drypool; together with the extra-parochial space called Garrisonside, and all other extra-parochial places, if any, which are surrounded by the boundaries of the said parishes of St. Mary, the Holy Trinity, Sculcoates, and Drypool, or any or either of them; and also all such part of the parish of Sutton as is situated to the south of a straight line to be drawn from Sculcoates Church to the point at which the Sutton Drain meets the Summergangs Drain.

WEST RIDING.

BRADFORD.—The several townships of Bradford and Manningham and Bowling, and the township of Horton, including the hamlets of Great and Little Horton.

106   2 & 3 WILLIAM IV. CAP. 64.

HALIFAX.—From the point on the north of the town at which the respective boundaries of the several townships of Halifax, North Owram, and Ovenden meet, westward, along the boundary of the township of Halifax, to the point at which the same meets the road leading from a house called Shay to Bank Top; thence along the said road from Shay to Bank Top to the point at which the same meets the road leading from South Owram to North Owram; thence along the said road from South Owram to North Owram to God Lane Bridge; thence in a straight line to the south-eastern corner of New Town on the Bradford Road; thence in a straight line to the point first described.

HUDDERSFIELD.—The township of Huddersfield.

KNARESBOROUGH.—The boundary described in the second section of an Act passed in the Fourth Year of the Reign of His late Majesty King George the Fourth, and intituled " An Act for paving, lighting, watching, cleansing, and " improving the town of Knaresborough in the west riding " of the county of York, and that part of the township of " Scriven-with-Tentergate which adjoins the said town, and " is called Tentergate."

LEEDS.—The parish of Leeds.

PONTEFRACT.—The old borough and township of Ponte-fract, and the extra-parochial space called the Pontefract Park District, the Castle Precincts, and also the several townships of Tanshelf, Monkhill, Knottingley, Ferrybridge, and Carleton.

RIPON.—The township of Ripon; and also such part of the township of Aismunderby-cum-Bondgate as is situate to the north of the point on the south of the town of Ripon at which the Ripley Road meets the Littlethorpe Road, and which is the southern extremity of the nearly disjointed portion of the township of Aismunderby-cum-Bondgate.

SHEFFIELD.—The parish of Sheffield.

WAKEFIELD.—From the southernmost point at which the boundary of the township of Wakefield leaves the River Calder, along the boundary of the township of Wakefield, to the point at which the same is intersected by a hedge running

2 & 3 WILLIAM IV. CAP. 64. 107

nearly north close by the western side of Park Gate Farm; thence in a straight line to the point at which the footpath leading to St. Swithin's Well joins the footpath from East Moor to Old Park; thence in a straight line to the point at which the Stanley Road would be cut by a straight line to be drawn from the point last described to the cupola of the Lunatic Asylum; thence along the Stanley Road to the point at which the same is met by the East Moor Road; thence along the East Moor Road to the point at which the same meets the boundary of the township of Wakefield; thence, westward, along the boundary of the township of Wakefield to the point at which the same meets the boundary of the detached portion of the township of Alverthorp which lies north of the township of Wakefield; thence, westward, along the boundary of the said detached portion of the township of Alverthorp to the point at which the same joins again the boundary of the township of Wakefield; thence, southward, along the boundary of the township of Wakefield to the point at which the same meets Balne Lane; thence along Balne Lane to the point at which the same is met by Humble Jumble Lane; thence along Humble Jumble Lane to the point at which the same meets the footpath to Flanshaw Lane; thence along the footpath to Flanshaw Lane to the point at which the same meets Smithson's Railroad; thence along Smithson's Railroad to the point at which the same meets the Dewsbury Road; thence along the Dewsbury Road to the point at which the same meets the new or occupation road which unites the Dewsbury and Horbury Roads; thence along the said New Road to the point at which the same meets the Park Wall of Thorne's House; thence, northward, along the said wall to the point at which the same meets the Road from Thorne's to Horbury; thence along the road from Thorne's to Horbury to the point at which the same meets the stream called " The Gilsike ;" thence along the said stream to the point at which the same falls into the River Calder; thence along the River Calder to the point first described.

WALES.

41.—COUNTY OF ANGLESEA.

BEAUMARIS DISTRICT.

AMLWCH.—From the point on the north-east of the town at which Rhyd Talog Brook falls into the sea at Porth Aber Cawell, southward, along the boundary of the parish of Almwch to the point called Croes Eilian ; thence along the Plas Dulas Road to the point called Penllaethdy Mawr; thence along the road leading to Pentre Felin, across the Llanerchy-y-medd Road, to the point called Pentre Felin Adda Cross Roads; thence along a road towards Pary's Farm to the point at which the same is met by the first bye road on the right leading to Bod-gadfa Farm; thence along the said bye road, passing Bod-gadfa Farm, to the point at which the same bye road is crossed (between Bod-gadfa Farm and a Cottage called Yr-hen Odyn) by the Lastre Brook ; thence along the Lastre Brook, crossing the Holyhead Road, to the point at which the same brook falls into the river called Afon Park Llechog ; thence along the Afon Park Llechog to a Ford in the Cemmaes Road called Rhyd-carreg-cath ; thence along the Cemmaes Road to the Cottage called Bryn-y-Cyll, at which the same road is met by the church pathway ; thence along the church pathway to the stile over a brook which divides the land of the Marquis of Anglesea from the Coed Helen and Lysdulas property, and which stile is close by a spring called Ffynnon Casyris ; thence along the last-mentioned brook to the point at which the same is met by a boundary fence (a few yards north of a cottage called Cae-bach) running in the direction of Mona Mill ; thence along the said fence to the point at which the same cuts the Porth Llechog Road ; thence, towards Amlwch, along the Porth Llechog Road to the point at which the same is met by the Ffynnon-y-Garreg-fawr Pathway ; thence along the Ffynnon-y-Garreg-fawr pathway to the spring called Ffynnon-y-Garreg-fawr ; thence along the stream which proceeds from the said spring to the point at which the same stream falls into the sea ; thence along the sea to the point first described.

2 & 3 WILLIAM IV. CAP. 64. 109

BEAUMARIS.—The old borough of Beaumaris.

HOLYHEAD.—From that part of the common called " The Towyn," on the southeast of the town, which is nearest to Holyhead Common, along the road leading to Penrhos which adjoins the Towyn, (and is to the east of a cottage called " Pen-Towyn," occupied by John Davis,) to the point at which the said road to Penrhos is met by another road leading to a piece of waste land called " The Cyttir ;" thence along the said road to the Cyttir to the point at which the same meets the road which leads across the Cyttir ; thence along the said road across the Cyttir to the point at which the same meets the old Post Road to Bangor ; thence along the old Post Road to Bangor to Pentraeth ; thence along the road which leads from Pentraeth in a westerly direction, and south of the new brewery, to the point at which the same joins another road ; thence, northward, along the road so joined to the point at which the same meets the Penrhos foila Road ; thence along the Penrhos foila road to the point at which the same meets the road which leads by the Ucheldre Windmill to the South Stack ; thence along the said road to the South Stack, including the messuage, with the offices and garden thereunto belonging, now in the occupation of Captain Colin Jones, to the westernmost point (near a cottage called " Cerrig-y-lloi") at which the same is crossed by a stream running from the Holyhead Mountain; thence along the said stream to the point at which the same falls into the sea ; thence along the sea coast to that point thereof which is nearest to the point first described ; thence in a straight line to the point first described.

LLANGEFNI.—From the point at which the boundary wall between the property of Admiral Lloyd and the property of Owen Williams, Esquire, meets the old Bangor Road, east of a cottage called Min'fford, along the said boundary wall to the point at which the same reaches a spring and a footpath called Llwybyr Tregarnedd-bach ; thence along a hedge which, running from the said spring and footpath, forms a continuation of the line of the said boundary wall, and runs through the land of John Hampton Lewis, Esquire, to the point at which such hedge meets the River Cefni ; thence, southward, along the River Cefni to the point at which the same is met by the boundary of the parish of Llangefni ; thence, westward, along the boundary of the parish of Llangefni to the point at which the same meets the bye road

110   2 & 3 WILLIAM IV. CAP. 64.

called Llidiart-y-Pandy; thence along the said bye road Llidiart-y-Pandy to the spot called Croes-lon-pen-y-Nant; thence, southward, along the market road to the point at which the same joins the Rhos-y-meirch road ; thence along the Rhos-y-meirch road to the first point at which the same is cut (beyond the road leading to Clai) by hedges running from each side of the road at right angles ; thence along the hedge which runs from the last-mentioned point towards Pencraig to the point at which the same reaches an old quarry ; thence along a hedge which proceeds from the said old quarry, and forms a continuation of the hedge last described, passing Tyn-y-coed Farm, to the point at which the same hedge cuts the Llanddyfnan Road ; thence along the Llanddyfnan Road, towards Llanddyfnan, to the point at which the same meets the boundary of the Pencraig-fawr Farm ; thence, southward, along the boundary of the Pen-craig-fawr Farm to the point at which the same meets the old Bangor Road ; thence along the old Bangor Road to the point first described.

42.—COUNTY OF BRECON.

BRECON.—The old borough of Brecon, and the extra-parochial districts of the castle and Christ's College.

43.—COUNTY OF CAERMARTHEN.

CAERMARTHEN DISTRICT.

CAERMARTHEN.—The old borough of Caermarthen.

LLANELLY.—From the point in Wern-y-Goosy Meadow on the north-west of the town at which the old course of the stream, which is the old borough boundary, makes a sharp turn, in a straight line to the southern extremity of the western fence of Cae Mawr Issa Field ; thence, northward, along the fence of the Cae Mawr Issa Field to the point at which the same meets the wall which is the western boundary of Furnace Garden ; thence along the said wall to the point at which the same meets Pen-y-Fai Lane ; thence along Pen-y-Fai Lane to the point at which the same meets the Caermarthen Road ; thence in a straight line to the north-

2 & 3 WILLIAM IV. CAP. 64.

western corner of the garden of Cae Mawr Cottage, lately burnt down ; thence along the fence which divides the garden of Cae Mawr Cottage and the field Cae Isha from the field Cae-ycha to the point at which the same meets the fence which divides the field Cae-ycha from the field Cae-bank ; thence along the last-mentioned fence to the northern corner of the field Cae-bank ; thence in a straight line through the southern extremity of the north-eastern boundary of the field Cae-bank, across the tram-road, to the old borough boundary ; thence, eastward, along the old borough boundary to the point first described.

44.—COUNTY OF CARDIGAN.

CARDIGAN DISTRICT.

ABERYSTWITH.—From the outermost point of the rock Graig-lias on the sea coast visible from the point described, in a straight line to the northern extremity of the stone wall which divides the land called Pant-y-gyrn from the land called Frôn ; thence along the said wall to the point at which the same meets the wall which divides the land Pant-y-gyrn from the land Frôn-uchaf; thence, eastward, along the boundary of Frôn-uchaf to the turnstile at the south-eastern corner thereof ; thence in a straight line to the mill in the Tanyard near the road leading to Llanbadarn-fawr ; thence in a straight line to the wooden dam just above Plas-greig ; thence, southward, along the boundary of the old borough to the sea coast ; thence along the sea coast to the point first described.

ADPAR.—The old borough of Adpar and the hamlet of Emlyn in the parish of Cennarth.

CARDIGAN.—The old borough of Cardigan, and also Bridgend Hamlet and Abbey Hamlet in the parish of Saint Dogmel in the county of Pembroke.

LAMPETER.—From the point on the Creithin Brook at which the northern boundary of the Glebe meets the boundary of the old borough, along the northern boundary of the Glebe to the point at which the same meets again the boundary of the old borough ; thence, northward, along the boundary of the old borough to the point first described.

112   2 & 3 William IV. Cap. 64.

45.—COUNTY OF CARNARVON.

CARNARVON DISTRICT.

Bangor.—From the point on the north-east of the town at which the road from the park wall of Penrhyn Castle to the Menai Straits joins the Menai Straits at the high-water mark, along the said road to the point at which the same meets the said park wall; thence, westward, along the said park wall to the entrance gate to Lime Grove; thence in a straight line across the road to the nearest point in the boundary wall immediately opposite, which bounds a field belonging to Lime Grove; thence along the said boundary wall to the point at which the River Cegin enters the grounds of ———— Pennant, Esquire; thence along the River Cegin to the bridge across the Shrewsbury Road; thence in a straight line to a square brick seat or monument situate on a knoll in a field called Cae Pant; thence in a straight line to the nearest point of the road to Felin Esgob; thence in a straight line to the nearest point of the road to Brynniau; thence in a straight line to the point at which the road from Bangor to the Menai Bridge leaves the road from Bangor to Carnarvon; thence along the said road to the Menai Bridge, in the direction of such bridge, to the gate on the right hand side which opens into an occupation road leading to Penrallt; thence in a straight line to the point at which the low-water mark in the straights of Menai would be cut by a straight line to be drawn from the gate last described to the windmil called Llandegfan Mill, which is on the opposite side of the Straits; thence along the said low-water mark to the point thereof which is nearest to the point first described; thence in a straight line to the point first described.

Carnarvon.—The old borough of Carnarvon.

Conway.—The old borough of Conway.

Cricceith—The old old borough of Cricceith.

Nevin.—The old borough of Nevin.

Pwllheli. — From the south-western extremity of the boundary of the old borough on the sea coast, along the boundary of the old borough (leaving the sea coast) to the point at which the same is met by a small stream called

2 & 3 WILLIAM IV. CAP. 64.

113

"Afongoegen;" thence along the said stream to the bridge called "Sarn, or Pont-penmaen;" thence along the southern branch of the said stream to the point at which the same meets the boundary of the old borough; thence, northward, along the boundary of the old borough to the point at which the same meets a road leading from Deneio Church into the Carnarvon Road; thence along the said road from Deneio Church to the point at which the same is cut by the fence of a field called "Cae Fynnow," in the occupation of Hugh Williams of Bryn Crin; thence along the last mentioned fence to the point at which the same cuts an occupation road leading from Bryn Crin farmhouse into the Carnarvon Road; thence along the said occupation road to the point at which the same joins the Carnarvon Road; thence, northward, along the Carnarvon road to the point at which the same is met by a road on the right leading to Abereirch; thence along the said road to Abereirch to the point at which the same meets a road leading from Pwllheli to Tremadoc; thence in a straight line to the sea, at the nearest point: thence, westward, along the sea coast to the point first described.

46.—COUNTY OF DENBIGH.

DENBIGH DISTRICT.

DENBIGH.—The old borough of Denbigh.

HOLT.—The old borough of Holt.

RUTHIN.—The old borough of Ruthin.

WREXHAM.—The respective townships of Wrexham Abbot and Wrexham Regis; and also such part of the township of Esclusam-below as is surrounded by the townships of Wrexham Abbot and Wrexham Regis, or one of them.

47.—COUNTY OF FLINT.

FLINT DISTRICT.

ST. ASAPH.—From the point on the north-west of the town at which the boundary of the township of Talar meets the River Elwy, westward, along the boundary of the township of

G

2 & 3 WILLIAM IV. CAP. 64.

Talar, to the Green Gate Bridge over the brook Nant-y-franol; thence along the brook Nant-y-franol to the point at which the same meets the Holyhead Road; thence, eastward, along the Holyhead Road to the point at which the same is met by the boundary of the township of Talar : thence eastward, along the boundary of the township of Talar to the point at which the same meets the boundary of the township of Bryn Polin; thence, southward, along the boundary of the township of Bryn Polin to the point at which the same meets the Upper Denbigh Road; thence, northward, along the Upper Denbigh Road to the point at which the same is met by a road or lane leading to Ysguborgoed; thence along such road or lane leading to Ysguborgoed to the point at which the same meets the River Clwyd; thence along the River Clwyd to the point at which the same is met by the southern boundary of the township of Cyrchynan ; thence in a straight line to the point first described.

CAERGWYLE.—The old borough of Caergwyle.

CAERWYS.—The old borough of Caerwys.

FLINT.—The old borough of Flint.

HOLYWELL.—From the boundary stone on the hill Pen-y-bryn, and on the western side of the hedge (which is between the cottage occupied by William Williams and the south-eastern corner of the plantation of Richard Sankey, Esquire), in a straight line to the boundary stone of the township of Holywell which is on the eastern side of the St. Asaph Road ; thence in a straight line to a bridge (in the lane leading to and past Greenfield Hall) over a watercourse running into the River Dee ; thence, eastward, along the said watercourse to the point at which the same meets the boundary of the township of Greenfield ; thence, southward, along the boundary of the township of Greenfield to the point at which the same meets the boundary of the township of Holywell ; thence along the eastern and southern or exterior boundary of the township of Holywell to the boundary stone first described.

MOLD.—The township of Mold.

OVERTON.—The old borough of Overton.

RHUDDLAN.—The old borough of Rhuddlan.

2 & 3 WILLIAM IV. CAP. 64. 115

48.—COUNTY OF GLAMORGAN.

MERTHYR TYDVIL.—From the point on the north of Merthyr Tydvil at which the northern boundary of the hamlet of Gellydeg meets the river called the Great Taff, northward, along the Great Taff, to the point at which the same is cut by the southern fence of Cilsanos Common ; thence, eastward, along the fence of Cilsanos Common to the point at which the same cuts the Brecon Road ; thence, southward, along the Brecon Road to the point at which the same meets the Vainor Road ; thence, eastward, along the Vainor Road to the point at which the same meets a bye road leading to Cefn-coed-y-Cwymner ; thence in a straight line to the point at which the Little Taff would be cut by a straight line to be drawn from the point last described to the southern mouth of a culvert on the eastern side of the Little Taff; thence, up the Little Taff, along the boundary of the parish of Merthyr Tydvil to the point at which the Cwm Bargoed stream is joined by a little brook from the Coli ravine ; thence in a straight line to the north-eastern corner of the stone fence of Pen-dwy-cae Vawr Farm ; thence along the road which passes Pen-dwy-cae Vawr Farmhouse to the point at which the same meets the mountain track from Dowlais to Quaker's Yard ; thence, southward, along the said track, between the farms of Pen-dwy-cae Vach and Pen-dwy-cae Vawr, to the point at which such track meets a road running nearly due west, by a stone quarry, to Pen-y-rhw Gymra Cottage ; thence along the last-mentioned road to the point at which the same reaches the southern side of Pen-y-rhw Gymra Cottage ; thence in a straight line to the point at which the southern boundary of Troed-y-rhw Farm meets the Cardiff Road ; thence along the southern boundary of Troed-y-rhw Farm to the point at which the same meets the Great Taff; thence in a straight line to the bridge over the Cardiff Canal called Pont-y-nant Maen ; thence, northward, along the Cardiff Canal to the point at which the same is intersected by the Cwmdu Brook ; thence along the Cwmdu Brook to its source ; thence in a straight line drawn due west to the boundary of the parish of Aberdare ; thence, southward, along the boundary of the parish of Aberdare to the point at which the same meets the boundary of the hamlet of Gellydeg ; thence, eastward, along the boundary of the hamlet of Gellydeg to the point first described.

G 2

116   2 & 3 WILLIAM IV. CAP. 64.

CARDIFF DISTRICT.

CARDIFF.—The old borough of Cardiff; and so much, if any, of either or both of the respective parishes of St. John and St. Mary as lies without the old borough.

COWBRIDGE.—The old borough of Cowbridge.

LLANTRISSENT.—The old borough of Llantrissent.

SWANSEA DISTRICT.

ABERAVON.—From the point on the south of the town at which the River Avon falls into the sea, northward, along the eastern boundary of the hamlet of Havod-y-Porth, to that point in a stone fence which is immediately opposite a small round pool; thence along the said stone fence to the point at which the same meets a lane or path leading to a small cottage; thence along such lane or path to the ford across a brook immediately opposite Margam Chapel; thence along the road to Dyffrynucha to the point at which the same meets the railroad from the Tai-bach copper works to Michalston; thence, northward, along the said railroad to the point at which the same crosses a small stream running into the River Avon; thence along the said stream to the point at which the same falls into the River Avon; thence in a straight line to the point at which a stream which runs through the Cwm Bychan ravine falls into the River Avon; thence along the last-mentioned stream to the point at which the same meets the boundary of the parish of Baglan; thence, southward, along the boundary of the parish of Baglan to the point at which the same meets the boundary of the parish of Aberavon; thence, westward, along the boundary of the parish of Aberavon to the point at which the boundary of the old borough leaves the same; thence along the boundary of the old borough to the point at which the same meets the boundary of the hamlet of Havod-y-Porth; thence, southward, along the boundary of the hamlet of Havod-y-Porth to the point first described.

KENFIG.—The old borough of Kenfig.

LOUGHOR.—The old borough of Loughor.

NEATH.—From the point lowest down the River Neath at which the boundary of the old borough leaves the River

2 & 3 WILLIAM IV. CAP. 64. 117

Neath, along the boundary of the old borough, leaving the River Neath, to the point at which Caerfwell Ditch joins the River Neath; thence along Caerfwell Ditch to the point at which the same meets the lane called Heol-morfa; thence along the lane Heol-morfa to the point at which the same joins the high road to Merthyr; thence along the high road to Merthyr to the point at which the road to Pontardawey leaves the same; thence along the road to Pontardawey to the point at which the same is joined by a lane called Rheol-y-glow; thence along the lane Rheol-y-glow to the point at which the same meets a brook; thence along such brook to the point at which the same meets Rheol-wern-fraith Lane; thence along Rheol-wern-fraith Lane to the point at which the same is cut by a fence forming the north-western boundary of Cae-canddaw Field; thence along the last-mentioned fence to the point at which the same meets the brook running to Nantlyros; thence along the brook running to Nantlyros to the point at which the same joins the canal; thence along the canal to the point at which the same crosses the stream Clydach; thence along the stream Clydach to the point at which the same joins the River Neath; thence along the River Neath to the point first described.

SWANSEA.—From the point at which the northern boundary of the parish of St John is crossed by the road to Llangefelach Church, northward, along the road to Llangefelach Church, to the point at which the same is joined by a lane called Rheol-y-cnap; thence along the lane Rheol-y-cnap, and along a lane which is a continuation thereof, and which joins the turnpike road to Neath opposite the Llandwr Engine, to the point at which such last-mentioned lane joins the turnpike road to Neath; thence, northward, along the turnpike road to Neath to the point at which the same is joined, between the Duke's Arms public house and a blacksmith's shop, by a road leading towards Clâs Mont Farm; thence along the last-mentioned road to the point at which the same is met, opposite the lane from Pen-lan commonly called Pen-lan Road, by a track leading to a well head: thence along the said track to the point at which the same reaches the said well head; thence along the stream which flows from the said well head to the point at which the said stream falls into the stream called Nant Velin; thence along the stream Nant Velin to the point at which the same crosses the road which leads from Morriston into the road from Llangefelach Church to the bridge over the River Tawey;

G 3

118 2 & 3 WILLIAM IV. CAP. 64.

thence along the said road from Morriston to the point at which the same joins the road from Llangefelach Church to the bridge over the River Tawey; thence along the last-mentioned road to the point at which the same reaches the said bridge over the River Tawey; thence, eastward, along the turnpike road to Neath to the point at which the same is met near the Star public house by a lane which leads from the southern extremity of the parish of Llansamlet, over Cilfay Hill and by Bon-y-maen, to Llansamlet Church; thence along the last-mentioned lane to the point at which the same meets the boundary of the hamlet of St. Thomas near Tregwl; thence, eastward, along the boundary of the hamlet of St. Thomas to the point at which the same meets the boundary of the town and franchise; thence, westward, along the boundary of the town and franchise to the point at which the same meets the boundary of the parish of St. John; thence, westward, along the boundary of the parish of St. John to the point first described.

49.—COUNTY OF MONTGOMERY.

MONTGOMERY DISTRICT.

LLANFYLLIN.—From the southern extremity, on the north-west of the town, of the private road which leads from the Llangynog turnpike road to Bodfach Hall, along the said private road to the point at which the same is met by the boundary of the field Cae Evan Griffith; thence, northward, along the boundary of the field Cae Evan Griffith to the point at which the same meets the boundary of the field Maes Ucha; thence, eastward, along the boundary of the field Maes Ucha to the point at which the same meets the boundary of the field Cae-pella Bwlch-y-llan; thence, north-ward, along the boundary of the field Cae-pella Bwlch-y-llan to the point at which the same meets the Llangedwyn Road; thence along the northern fences of the respective fields Cae Dû, Cae Main, and Cae Dû Mawr, and along the eastern fence of the field Cae Dû Mawr, to the point at which the last-mentioned fence reaches the Derwlwyn Wood; thence in a straight line across the Derwlwyn Wood to the northern extremity of the eastern fence of Glynie Isá tenement; thence along the eastern fence of Glynie Isá tenement to the point at which the same meets the Brynelldyn Road; thence along the Brynelldyn Road to the point at which the same

2 & 3 WILLIAM IV. CAP. 64. 119

reaches Green Hall Park; thence, southward, along the boundary of the field Caer Frôn to the point at which the same meets the boundary of the field Caer Gwenithdir; thence, southward, along the boundary of the field Caer Gwenithdir to the point at which the same meets the River Cain; thence along the River Cain to the bridge called Pont-y-Derwlwyn; thence along Pont-y-Derwlwyn Lane to the point at which the same meets the Bachie Road; thence along the Bachie Road to the eastern corner of Garth Wood; thence along the south-western fences of the fields Caer Garth and Cyfie Ucha, and of the wood Coed Pen-y-Garth, and, westward, along the southern fence of the field Cae Gwenith, to the point at which such southern fence cuts the occupation road to Pen-y-Garth Farm; thence in a straight line to the eastern extremity of the southern fence of the field Llwyn Bricks; thence, westward, along the boundary of the field Llwyn Bricks to the point at which the same meets the fence of the field Cae Bath; thence, westward, along the fence of the field Cae Bath to the point at which the same meets the Brook Abel; thence along the Brook Abel to the point at which the same is met by the western fence of the easternmost of the fields respectively called Lower Meadow; thence along the western fence of the last-mentioned field to the point at which the same cuts the lane to Tynewydd; thence, northward, along the boundary of the field Llwyn Hir to the point at which the same meets the boundary of the field Cae Mawr; thence, northward, along the boundary of the field Cae Mawr to the point at which the same meets the boundary of the field Cae Bach; thence, eastward, along the boundary of the field Cae Bach to the point at which the same meets the boundary of the field Upper Coed Llan; thence, eastward, along the boundary of the field Uppe Coed Llan to the point at which the same meets the boundary of the field Lower Coed Llan; thence, northward, along the boundary of the field Lower Coed Llan to the point at which the same meets the occupation road to Pen Coed Llan; thence in a straight line to the point first described.

LLANIDLOES.—From the point on the south-east of the town at which Cwm Jonathan rill crosses the Rhaydr Road, southward, along Cwm Jonathan rill, to the point at which the same is met by the hedge on the right hand which is nearest to the point at which Cwm Jonathan rill crosses the cart lane from Ty-coch to Llanidloes; thence along the said hedge to the point at which the same meets the Ty-coch

120   2 & 3 WILLIAM IV. CAP. 64.

stream; thence along the Ty-coch stream to the point at which the same reaches the Llangurig Road; thence, northward, along the Llangurig Road to the point at which the same is cut by the nearest hedge on the left hand; thence along the last-mentioned hedge to the point at which the same reaches a water-cut bank; thence, southward, along the said water-cut bank to the point at which the same reaches a hedge running in the direction of the turnpike on the Pymlymon Road; thence along the last-mentioned hedge to the point at which the same reaches the River Severn; thence along the River Severn to the point at which the same is cut by a line drawn thereto in continuation of the direction of the hedge on the northern end of Pen-y-Green; thence along the last-mentioned line, and along the hedge in continuation whereof it is drawn, to the point at which such hedge reaches the hedge of Mr. Price's wood; thence in a straight line to the point at which the stream called Cefn Cummere Dingle meets the Pen-y-bank Road; thence along the Cefn Cummere Dingle to the point at which the same joins the Clywedog River; thence, westward, along the boundary of the township of Cilmachallt, to the point at which the same meets a small watercourse which runs along the western hedge of Berth Lloyd coppice; thence along the said watercourse to the point at which the same reaches the lane from Llanidloes to Gorn; thence, westward, along the lane from Llanidloes to Gorn to the point at which the same reaches the hedge which runs along the eastern side of the Chapel House; thence along the last-mentioned hedge to the point at which the same reaches Lletty-coch-y-nant brook; thence, westward, along Lletty-coch-y-nant brook to the point at which the same is met on the left hand by a small stream; thence along the last-mentioned stream to the spring from which the same proceeds; thence in a straight line to the nearest point in the road from Llanidloes to the barn Leasow; thence, westward, along the road from Llanidloes to the barn Leasow to the point at which the same meets the boundary of the borough of Llanidloes; thence, southward, along the borough of Llanidloes to the point at which the same meets Cwm Jonathan rill; thence along Cwm Jonathan rill to the point first described.

MACHYNLLETH.—The township and liberties of Machynlleth; and also that detached part of the township of Isygarreg which adjoins the north-eastern boundary of the township and liberties of Machynlleth.

2 & 3 William IV. Cap. 64. 121

Montgomery.—The old borough of Montgomery.

Newtown.—The parish of Newtown, and the respective townships of Hendidley and Gwestydd.

Welshpool.—The parish of Pool, and the township of Gungrog Fechan in the parish of Guilsfield, except that part of the township of Cyfronnydd in the parish of Pool which is detached from the main body of such parish.

50.—COUNTY OF PEMBROKE.

HAVERFORDWEST DISTRICT.

Fishguard.—From the point at which the low-water mark would be cut by a straight line to be drawn thereto from the gate of the fort, through the eastern extremity of the southern wall of the fort, in a straight line to the gate of the fort; thence in a straight line to the north-western corner of Parc-y-Morfa meadow; thence along the western fence of Parc-y-Morfa meadow to the south-western corner thereof; thence in a straight line to the highest point of Parc-y-Morfa rock; thence in a straight line to the north-western corner of the fence which divides the Glyn Amel property from the property of Mr. Vaughan; thence, southward, along the said fence of the Glyn Amel property to the point at which the same meets the northern stream of the River Gwaine; thence up the said stream to the point at which the same meets the boundary of the old borough: thence, eastward, along the boundary of the old borough to the point at which the same meets the low-water mark; thence, eastward, along the low-water mark to the point first described.

Haverfordwest.—From the point at which a straight line drawn from St. Thomas's Church to the gate at the north-eastern corner of the field called Hill Park cuts the boundary of the old borough, along such straight line to the said gate; thence in a straight line to the gate which crosses the road leading to Scotch Well House; thence along the last-mentioned road to the point at which the same reaches Scotch Well House; thence along the road which leads by Sandpool into the Cardigan Road to the north-eastern corner of Sandpool; thence in a straight line to the cottage of Philip White; thence in a straight line to the left pier of the Weir on the River Cleddy; thence along the River Cleddy to the point

122   2 & 3 WILLIAM IV. CAP. 64.

at which the same would be cut by a straight line to be drawn
from Prendergast Church to the gate leading from the lane
on the north-east of Little Slade Farm into the paddock of
Little Slade Farm; thence in a straight line to the last-mentioned gate; thence in a straight line to the point at which
the boundary of the old borough would be cut by a straight
line to be drawn from the last-mentioned gate to the point at
which the Poorfield Road (otherwise called Jury Lane) leaves
the St. David's Road; thence, westward, along the boundary
of the old borough to the point first described.

NARBERTH.—From the southern end of the Turnpike Gate
House on the Redstone Road, westward, along the fence
which abuts on the said house and is the northern boundary
of a field of which George Harris is tenant and Mr. Thomas
Eaton landlord, to the north-western corner of the said field;
thence in a straight line to the north-eastern corner of a field
belonging to George Devonald, Esquire, and bounded on the
south by the turnpike road to Haverfordwest; thence along
the private road which runs from the last-mentioned field to
the point at which the said private road meets the said road
to Haverfordwest; thence in a straight line across the said
road to Haverfordwest to the point at which the same is met
by the western boundary of the Town Moor; thence, southward, along the western and southern boundary of the Town
Moor to the gate of a lane at the south-eastern corner
thereof; thence along the said lane to the point at which the
same meets the boundary of Narberth Churchyard; thence,
westward, along the boundary of Narberth Churchyard to
the south-western corner thereof; thence in a straight line
to the point at which the stream from Narberth Bridge would
be cut by a straight line to be drawn from the point last described to the point at which the road from the parsonage
meets the road from Pembroke; thence up the said stream
to the point at which the same is joined by the stream from
Narberth Mill; thence up the stream flowing from Narberth
Mill to the south-western corner of the field of which Lewis
Watkins is tenant and Baron Retzen is landlord; thence,
eastward, along the boundary of the last mentioned field to
the point at which the same meets the southern boundary of
the field belong to Mr. Henry Davies, in which there is a
turnstile; thence, eastward, along the southern boundary of
the said field of Mr. Henry Davies, and the southern and
eastern boundary of the adjoining field belonging to George
Phillips, Esquire, to the point at which the eastern boundary

2 & 3 WILLIAM IV. CAP. 64. 123

of the said field of George Phillips, Esquire, meets the occupation road leading to Blackalder; thence, eastward, along the occupation road to Blackalder to the point at which the same meets the south-eastern boundary of the easternmost of two contiguous fields of which Mrs. Evans is tenant and Daniel Thomas landlord; thence along the boundary of the last-mentioned field to the point at which the same meets the Carmarthen Road; thence in a straight line across the Carmarthen Road to the south-eastern corner of the field belonging to John Lewis; thence along the eastern boundary of John Lewis's field to the point at which the same cuts the Cardigan Road; thence in a straight line across the Cardigan Road to the south-western corner of Jesse's Well House; thence in a straight line to the point at which the fence of the grounds attached to the house called Bloomfield's would be cut by a straight line to be drawn from the point last decribed to the house called Bloomfield's; thence, westward, along the last-mentioned fence to the point at which the same cuts the Redstone Road; thence along the Redstone Road to the point first described.

PEMBROKE DISTRICT.

MILFORD.—From the point at which Prix Pill falls into the sea, along Prix Pill, to the point at which the same is met by the lane coming down by Cwm, and sometimes called Cwm Lane: thence along Cwm Lane to the point at which the same meets the road from Haverfordwest; thence along the road from Haverfordwest to the point at which the same is met by Priory Lane; thence along Priory Lane to the point at which the same meets, on the left, a road sometimes called the New Road; thence along the New Road to the point at which the same meets a lane sometimes called White Lady's Lane, leading to a field north of the brewery, sometimes called Haggard Field; thence along White Lady's Lane to the point at which the same is cut by the fence of Haggard Field; thence, northward, along the fence of Haggard Field to the north-western corner thereof; thence in a straight line in the direction of the northern fence of Haggard field to Priory Pill; thence in a straight line to the White Warehouse standing at the head of the Rope Walk in Hubberstone Parish; thence along Spike Lane which proceeds from the said White Warehouse to the point at which the same meets Conjwick Lane; thence along Conjwick Lane to the point at which the same meets the lane which was lately

124   2 & 3 WILLIAM IV. CAP. 64.

part of Point Field; thence along the lane lately part of Point Field to the point at which the same ends on the common; thence in a straight line through the westernmost point of the fort to the sea coast; thence along the sea coast to the point first described.

PEMBROKE.—The respective parishes of St. Mary and St. Michael, and also the space comprised within the boundary hereafter described (together with all such parts, if any, of the old borough of Pembroke as lie without the said boundary):

From the point on the south-west of the town at which the brook called the Taylor's Lake meets the boundary of the parish of St. Mary, northward, along the said brook, to the point at which the same joins the Pill near Quoit's Mill; thence along the said Pill to the point at which the same meets the boundary of the parish of St. Mary; thence, eastward, along the boundary of the parish of St. Mary to the point first described.

TENBY.—The In-Liberty of Tenby.

WISTON.—The old borough of Wiston.

51.—COUNTY OF RADNOR.

RADNOR DISTRICT.

CEFN LLYS.—The old borough of Cefn Llys.

KNIGHTON.—The old borough of Knighton.

KNUCKLAS.—The old borough of Knucklas.

PRESTEIGN.—The ancient lordship, manor, and borough of Presteign, together with such parts, if any, of the township of Presteign, and of the chapelry of Discoyd, as are without the ancient lordship, manor, and borough of Presteign; and also the space included within the following boundary; (that is to say,)

From the point on the north of the town at which Norton Brook falls into the River Lug, in a straight line to the point at which the road to Wigmore and Ludlow is met by the road to Kinsham Village; thence in a straight line to the point at

2 & 3 William IV. Cap. 64. 125

which the right-hand branch of the Clatter Brook falls into the River Lug ; thence along the River Lug to the point first described.

New Radnor.—The old borough of New Radnor.

Rhaydrgwy.—From the point at which the boundary of the old borough would be cut by a straight line to be drawn from Rhadyr Church to the bridge over the Gwynllin Brook on the new road to Aberystwith, in a straight line to the said bridge ; thence along the Gwynllin Brook to the Weir or dam head ; thence along the southern bank of the mill dam to the point at which the same is cut by the eastern fence of Gwynllin lain Field ; thence, southward, along the eastern fence of Gwynllin lain Field to the gate leading into the yard of the Grist Mill and woollen manufactory belonging to David Evans ; thence along the road which crosses the said yard to another gate at the south-eastern corner thereof; thence in a straight line to the north-eastern corner of the farmhouse called Ty-Newidd or New House ; thence in a straight line to the point at which the boundary of the old borough would be cut by a straight line to be drawn from the New House to the bridge over the River Wye ; thence, southward, along the boundary of the old borough to the point first described.

INDEX

TO

THE TREATISE.

A.

ABERAVON,
Will share in Election with Swansea, &c. *page* 13, 43.
Polling at, 106.

ABODE,
Place of, must be stated, in what cases, 57, 76, 77, 94, 101.
omission as to, may be supplied, when, 67, 88.

ACTION against Sheriffs, Returning Officers, and others, for neglect of Duties under the Act, 116.

ADJOURNMENT,
of Poll in cases of Riot, 112.
of Barrister's Court, 64, 88.

ADMISSION, or Title to Admission, of Freemen previous to what day will entitle to Vote, 43.

APPOINTMENT by Sheriff of Returning Officer for New Boroughs, 101.

ABJURATION, Supremacy and, Oath of, 109.

AFFIRMATION, to be administered to Quakers, &c. by Barrister when Revising Lists, 64, 88.

ADVERTISEMENT,
to be Published by Barrister, for Counties, 63.
Expenses of, 113.

AINSTY of YORK, to be included in North Riding of Yorkshire, 2.

ALLEGIANCE, Oath of, 109.

H 2

INDEX.

ALMS,
Disqualification by receipt of, 51.
not ground of permanent forfeiture of reserved right, 48.

ANCIENT DEMESNE, Tenants in, Right of, for Counties, 22, 23, 24.

ANNUITIES, Freehold, Registration of, not dispensed with, 16.

APPEAL,
Barrister's Court, Court of, from Overseers, 70.
Committee, Select, Court of, from Barrister's Decision, 111.

ASSESSOR, same mode of Proceeding before Revising Barrister as used to be had before Assessor, 65.

ASSESSED TAXES, what must have been paid to give Right of Voting for Borough, 31 to 35.

AYLESBURY,
Borough of, to include certain adjacent Districts, 11.
Provision as to Rights Reserved in, 50.
Polling Districts for, 98.

B.

BARRISTERS,
Appointment of, 61, 82.
Revision of Lists by, how to be conducted in Counties, 63 to 70.
in Boroughs, 83 to 89.
Remuneration of, 113.
Expenses of, ib.

BENEFICE, Title by promotion to, 16, 17, 21, 26.

BIRTH, Freemen by, rights of, 43.

BOOKS,
containing Lists of Voters for Counties, 71.
for Boroughs, 89.
Poll-Books, custody of, at County Elections, 95.
at Borough Elections, 101.

BOOTHS,
Provisions as to, for Counties, 92.
for Boroughs, 97.

INDEX.

BOROUGHS,
 Meaning of that Word, 45.
 Classification of Members for, 6.
 what will return Two Members, 7, 8, 9.
 what will return One, 9, 10.
 Division of Rights of Voting for, 30.
  1stly. New Rights defined, 30 to 39.
  2dly. Old Rights reserved in perpetuity, what they are, 39 to 44.
  3dly. Old Rights reserved for a time, 45 to 50.
 Registration of Voters for, 72 to 89.
 Proceedings preparatory to Elections at, 97.
      during Elections at, 98 to 101.
 Welsh, Elections at, 104.
 Boundaries of, how settled, 14.
 Contributory, enumeration of, 12, 13.
  Polling at, 104.
  Qualification arising in, 30.

BOUNDARIES,
 of Divided Counties, how settled, 3.
 of all Cities and Boroughs, how settled, 14.
 to what Boundaries Rights reserved in perpetuity apply, 50.
 to what those reserved for a time, 49.

BRECON, Borough of, commencement and duration of Poll at, 106.

BRIBERY OATH, when to be administered, 109.

BRISTOL, Reserved Rights in, 5, 41.

BUILDING, will give Vote for Borough to Occupier, when, 30, 163.

BURGAGE TENANTS, Rights of, reserved in perpetuity, when, 39 to 42.

BURGESSES, Rights of, reserved in perpetuity, when, 42.

C.

CAMBRIDGE UNIVERSITY,
 Exempted from operation of the Act, 39.
 Premises in Colleges of, will not qualify for Town, 167.

CANDIDATES,
 may Contract for Booths at County Elections, 93.
        at Borough Elections, 99.

INDEX.

CANDIDATES—*continued.*
 to bear Expenses of Booths, &c. in equal proportions, 93, 99.
 Persons proposing Candidate without his consent to be liable to
  Expenses as if they were Candidates, *ib.*
 may require Questions and Oaths to be put at Elections, 108.

CARDIFF, what Boroughs will share in Election with, 13, 14.

CERTIFICATE of Elector's having taken Oath required, 110.

" CHARGES," meaning of word, 18.

CHURCHWARDENS,
 included in words " Overseers of the Poor," 144, note.
 disqualified from being Returning Officers for New Boroughs,
  102.

CHEQUE CLERK at Elections, appointment of, 93.

CIRCUIT, Revising Barrister's, 63, 84.

" CITIES and BOROUGHS," meaning of words, 45.

CITIES being Counties of themselves,
 New Rights of Voting for Boroughs will extend to, 39.
 Classification of, as regards Right of Voting, 5.
 included in words " Cities and Boroughs," 45.

CITY of LONDON, Freemen and Liverymen of, Rights of, Reserved in perpetuity, 42.

CLAIMS,
 Notice of, for Counties, 56.
   for Boroughs, 78.
   for City of London, by Liverymen, 81.
 Decision on, by Barrister for Boroughs, 86.

CLERK, TOWN, Duty of, as to Lists of Freemen, 168 to 176.

CLERK of the PEACE,
 Duty of, as to Lists of Voters, 61, 70, 71.
 Expenses of, 115.

COMMISSIONERS to administer Oaths at Elections, 109, 110.

COMMISSIONERS, Lords of Treasury, to make Order for Payment of Barristers, 113.

COMMITTEE for TRIAL of PETITIONS, what they can take
  cognizance of, 111.

INDEX.

CONTRIBUTORY BOROUGHS,
Enumeration of, 13.
Qualification arising in, as to, 30.
Polling at, 104.

COPIES of LISTS to be printed for Sale, 113.

COPYHOLDERS, Rights of, for Counties defined, 20, 21, 22.

COPY of COURT ROLL, Tenants by, 23.

CORRECTION OF MISTAKES, by Revising Barrister, 67, 83.

COUNCIL, Order in, as to Year 1832, 121.

COUNSEL, not to attend Barrister's Court, 65, 88.

COUNTING-HOUSE, will give Vote for Borough to Occupier,
when, 30, 163.

COUNTIES,
Classification of, 1.
Division of, 3.
what to return Four Knights, 3.
what to return Three, 4.
what to return Two, 4.
what Welsh Counties to return One Knight, 4.
what Counties of Cities and Towns incorporated with Counties
at large, 5.
New Rights of Voting for Boroughs extended to, 39.
included in words " Cities and Boroughs," 45.
Electors for, Classification of, 15.
1st. Freeholders, Qualification of, 15 to 17.
Existing Freeholders for Life, rights of, 18.
what Property will not give Vote for, if it would for
Borough, 18, 19.
2dly. Copyholders, Right of, defined, 20 to 22.
3dly. Tenants in Ancient Demesne, Right of, defined, 22,
23, 24.
4thly. Leaseholders, Right of, defined, 24, 25, 26.
5thly. Occupying Tenants, (without reference to length of
terms,) Right of, defined, 27, 28.
Registration of Voters for, 54 to 71.
Expenses incident to, 113.
Elections for, Notice of, 91.
Proceedings before and at, 90 to 96.
Expenses of, 95.
Proceedings common to, with Borough Elections,
107.

INDEX.

CUSTOMARY TENANT, Rights of, for Counties, 23.

D.

DATES, of Registration for 1832, altered by Order in Council, 118.

DEMAND, not necessary to make Rates " payable" within meaning of the Act, 32.

DEPUTY,
    to be appointed by Sheriff, for Counties, 92.
        Duty of, at Elections, *ib.* 95.
        Payment of, 93.
    of Returning Officer, for Boroughs, Payment of, 99.
    of any Returning Officer, may appoint Commissioners to administer Oaths, 110.
        may adjourn Poll for Riot, 112.
    of Returning Officer for Welsh Boroughs, to take Poll at Contributory Boroughs, 104, 105.

DESCENT, Title by, 16, 21.

DEVISE, Title by, 16, 17, 21, 26.

DISTANCE, how measured, 35.

DISTRICTS,
    Polling, in Elections for Counties, 91, 94.
                 for Boroughs, 98, 99, 100.

DISSOLUTION OF PARLIAMENT, in the year 1832, before First Registration is completed, 119.

DISQUALIFICATION,
    from Voting for Borough by Receipt of Alms, 51.
        when not permanent, 48.
    of Revising Barrister to serve in Parliament, 62, 83.
    from being Returning Officers for New Boroughs, what, 102.

DIVISIONS OF COUNTIES,
    how settled, 3.
    each Division to be as a separate County, *ib.*

DIVISION, by Returning Officer of Borough into Polling Districts, 98.

INDEX.

E.

EAST RETFORD,
Borough of, to include certain adjacent Districts, 11.
Provision as to Rights Reserved in, 50.
Polling Districts for, 98.

ELECTIONS,
Proceedings before and at, in Counties, 90 to 96.
in Boroughs in England, 97 to 103.
in Welsh Boroughs, 104, 105, 106.
Notice of, for Counties, 91.
for Boroughs, 97.

ELECTION LAWS, what to remain in force, 90.

ELECTORS,
for Counties, 15 to 29.
for Boroughs, 30 to 53.

EQUITABLE ESTATES, Provisions as to, 29.

ERRORS, in Register, not to be fatal, when, 110.

EXETER, Reserved Rights in, 5, 41.

EXCLUSION of certain Rights acquired since 1st March, 1831, 48.

EXCLUSIVE JURISDICTIONS, Sheriffs may act within, 92.

EXPENSES,
of Overseers, &c. 114.
of Barristers, 113.
of Booths, &c. 93, 99.

EXTRA-PAROCHIAL PLACES,
Provisions as to, in Counties, 59.
in Boroughs, 76.

F.

FRANCHISE,
Elective, for Counties, 15 to 29.
for Boroughs, 30 to 53.

FREEHOLD,
Qualifying, Value of, in Counties, 17.
which would confer Right for Borough, not to give Vote for County, 18.

INDEX.

FREEHOLDER,
    Right of, for Counties, 15 to 20.
    for Life, in Counties, Provisions as to, **17, 18.**
    in Counties of Cities and Towns, Rights of, reserved in Perpe-
        tuity, when, 39 to 42.
        need not be assessed to Land Tax, 42.

FREEMEN,
    Rights of, reserved in Perpetuity, when, **39 to 43.**
    in respect of Birth, 43.
             of Servitude, *ib.*
             of Marriage, *ib.*
             Honorary, *ib.*
    of *Swansea, Loughor, Neath, Aberavon,* and *Ken-fig,* Provision
        as to, 44.
    Qualification of, to be perfect on Last Day of July, 44.
    Lists of, how to be made out, 74.
    Duty of Town Clerks with regard to, 168 to 176.

FREEMEN AND LIVERYMEN,
    of the City of London, Rights of, reserved in Perpetuity, 42.
    Registration of, 74, 80, 81, 82.
    Polling by, 100.

G.

GUILDHALL, Freemen and Liverymen of London to Poll in, 100.

GLAMORGANSHIRE, to return Two Knights of the Shire, 4.

H.

HAVERFORDWEST, Reserved Rights in, 5, 41.

HIGH CONSTABLE, List of Voters to be transmitted to, by Over-
    seers, and then by High Constable to Clerk of the Peace, 61.

HORSHAM,
    Provision as to Freeholds in, which give Right of Voting for
        Shoreham, 155.
    those parts of the Rape of Bramber, which are included in
        the Borough of Horsham by Boundary Act, will give no
        Right for Shoreham, 11.

HOUSE, will give Qualification for Borough to Occupier, when, 30,
    163.

HULL. See KINGSTON-UPON-HULL.

INDEX.

I.

INTERPRETATION OF ACT, Rules for, contained in the 79th Section, 143.

ISLE OF WIGHT,
to be a County returning One Knight, 5.
Returning Officer for, ix.
Elections for, to be holden at Newport, ix.

J.

JOINT TENANTS, Right of, for Counties, 25, 26.

JOINT OCCUPIERS, when they will be entitled to vote for Boroughs, 37, 164.

JUDGES,
Appointment of Revising Barristers by, for Counties, 61, 65.
for Cities and Boroughs, 82.

JUSTICES OF THE PEACE,
Meaning of Word explained by Interpretation Clause, lxi.
may act within Places of Exclusive Jurisdiction, *ib.*

JURISDICTIONS, EXCLUSIVE,
Sheriffs may act within, 92.
Justices of the Peace, &c. may act within, lxi.

K.

KENFIG,
to share in Election with Swansea, &c. 13, 43.
Polling at, 106.

KESTEVEN and HOLLAND,
Parts of, to be as a separate County, 2.
Sleaford to be principal Place of Election for, 91.
Polling Places in, appointed by Boundary Act, *ib.*

KINGSTON-UPON-HULL, County of Town of, to be included in East Riding of Yorkshire, 2.

KNIGHTS of the SHIRE,
Total number of, 1.
Classification of Counties, as to number of for each, *ib.*

INDEX.

L.

LAND will give Vote for Borough to Occupier, when, 30, 162.

LAND-TAX, Assessment to, dispensed with, 16, 22, 27, 28.

LEASEHOLDERS, Right of for Counties, 24 to 27.

LINCOLNSHIRE to return Four Knights, 2.

LINDSEY.
Parts of, to be as a separate County, 2.
Lincoln to be Principal Place of Election for, 91.
Polling Places in appointed by Boundary Act, *ib.*

LISTS,
of Voters for Counties, 54.
for Boroughs, 75.
of Freemen, 77.
of Claimants, 79.
of Persons objected to, 58, 79.
Duties of Overseers as to making out Lists of Voters,
for Counties, 132 to 145.
for Boroughs, 146 to 167.
of Town Clerks as to making out Lists of Freemen, 168 to 176.

LIVERYMEN,
of City of London, Rights of Reserved, 39, 42.
Lists of, to be made out by Clerks of Livery Companies, 80.
Registration of, 80, 81, 82.
Polling by, 100.

LITCHFIELD, Reserved Rights in, 5, 41.

LONDON,
City of, Lists of Voters for, 80.
Polling of Liverymen in, 100.
See FREEMEN and LIVERYMEN.

LOUGHOR,
will share in Election with Swansea, &c, 13, 43.
Polling at, 106.

M.

MALMSBURY,
Hundred of, what part will confer no Right for Cricklade, 11.
Provision as to Freeholds in, which give Right of Voting for Cricklade, 155.

MARRIAGE, Title by, 16, 17, 21, 26.

INDEX.

MAYOR of Contributory Borough to be Deputy for taking the Poll, 105.

MEMBERS,
  for Counties, 1—5.
  for Boroughs, 6—14.
  of Parliament cannot be Revising Barristers, 62, 83.
    Persons qualified to be, exempt from serving as Returning Officer for New Boroughs, 102.

MILES, how to be measured, 35.

MISNOMERS in Register not to be fatal, when, 110.

MISTAKES in Register, 110.
  Correction of, by Barrister, 67, 88.

MONMOUTH,
  Mode of Polling at, 104.
  Newport and Usk to share with, ib.

MORAVIANS, Affirmations to be administered to, 64, 88.

MORTGAGOR and MORTGAGEE, Rights of for Counties, 28.

MUNICIPAL OFFICER, Chief, of any Contributory Borough to be Deputy of Returning Officer, 105.

N.

NAMES,
  Mistake in, when not fatal, 110.
    may be corrected by Barrister, 67, 88.
  of Parishes and Townships in Counties to be fixed on Booths, 92.
  of Districts in Boroughs, 98.

NEATH,
  will share in Election with Swansea, &c. 13, 43.
  Polling at, 106.

NEWPORT in Monmouthshire,
  will share in Election with Monmouth, 104.
  Polling at, ib.

NEWPORT, Isle of Wight,
  Clerk of the Peace of, to be Clerk of the Peace for Isle of Wight for purposes of the Act, lxi.
  Elections for Isle of Wight to be holden at, ix.

INDEX.

NORWICH, Reserved Rights in, 5, 41.

NOTICES,
    In Counties,
        by Overseers to Persons claiming to Vote, 56.
        by Claimants to Overseers, 56.
        by Objectors to Overseers, 59.
        by Objectors to Parties objected to, 66.
        by Barrister of time of holding his Court, 63.
    In Boroughs,
        by Claimants to Overseers, 78.
                  to Town Clerk, 78.
        by Objectors to Overseers, 78.
                  to Town Clerk, 79.
        by Barrister of time of holding his Court, 84.
        by Liverymen claiming to be on the Lists for City of London, to Returning Officer, 81.
        by Persons objecting to Liverymen, to Returning Officer, 82.
    of Election for Counties, 91.
              for Boroughs, 97.
              for Counties ot Cities of Towns, *ib.*
              for Welsh Boroughs, 104.
    by Returning Officer in Borough of his Regulations as to Booths, &c. 98.

NOTTINGHAM, Reserved Right in, 5, 41.

O.

OATHS,
    to be administered by Barrister, 64, 88.
    what to be taken at Elections, how and when to be administered, 108, 109.
    Penalties for false Oaths, 109.

OBJECTIONS, notices of. See Notices.

"OBJECTED TO,"
    Overseers to put opposite to Names of Persons whose Qualification for Counties is doubtful, 58.
    Course to be pursued by Barrister as to such Names, 66.

OCCUPATION
    of Lands or Tenements (without reference to length of time) will give Vote for Counties, when, 27, 28, 29.
    of what Property in Boroughs will give Vote for, 30.

INDEX.

OCCUPIERS in Boroughs may demand to be rated, when, 37.

OCCUPIERS, JOINT, what Value will give them a Right of Voting for Borough, 37, 164.

OFFICE,
Title by promotion to, 16, 17, 21, 26.
under the Crown disqualifies from being Revising Barrister, 62, 83.

OFFICER, Chief Municipal of any Contributory Borough to be Deputy of Returning Officer, 105.

OMISSIONS in Lists, Barristers may supply, 67, 88.

ORDER IN COUNCIL for altering Dates in 1832, 121.

OVERSEERS,
meaning of Word, 144.
duty of, for Counties, 132 to 145.
    for Boroughs, 146 to 167.
expenses of, 113, 114, 115.
disqualified from being Returning Officers for New Boroughs, 102.

OWNER, what Property occupied by Party as, will give Right for Borough, 30.

OXFORD UNIVERSITY,
not affected by the Act, 39.
Chambers or Premises in Halls and Colleges of, will not give Right of Voting for City, 167.

P.

" PARISH," meaning of Word, 143.

PARLIAMENT,
Members of, disqualified from acting as Revising Barrister, 62, 83.
    Persons qualified, to be exempt from serving as Returning Officer for New Boroughs, 102.

PAROCHIAL RELIEF,
Disqualification by receipt of, 51.
not ground of permanent forfeiture of Reserved Right, 48.

PARTNERS, joint occupation of Premises by, 154.

INDEX.

PAYABLE, meaning of that Word, 32.

PENALTIES
for False Swearing, 109.
for Wilful Neglect of Duties under the Act, 116.

PENRYN, Borough of, to include Falmouth, 11.

PERJURY, Penalties for, 109.

PERPETUITY, Old Rights reserved in, 39 to 45.

PETITION to House of Commons, how far Register may be questioned on, 111.

POLL CLERKS,
Duties of, for Counties, 94.
for Boroughs, 98, 101.
payment of, 93, 99.

POLL
may be adjourned in case of Riot, 112.
when it may be closed before the time fixed by the Act, 112.

POLLING
for Counties, how to be conducted, 91 to 96.
for Boroughs, 97 to 102.
for Welsh Boroughs, 104.
for Shoreham, Cricklade, Aylesbury, and East Retford, 98.
of Liverymen for City of London, 100.

POOR RATES. See RATES.

PORT-REEVE
of Swansea to be the Returning Officer, 106.
of any Contributory Borough, to be Deputy of Returning Officer, 105.

POT-WALLOPERS, Right of reserved, how, 47.

PRECEPTS, all to be expressed so as may be necessary to carry the Provisions of the Act into effect, 90.

PRECINCT,
having no Overseers of its own, Provision as to, for Counties, 59.
for Boroughs, 76.

PREMISES, change of, when it will deprive Party of Right of Voting for Borough, 32.

INDEX.

Q.

QUAKERS, Affirmations to be administered to, 64, 88.

QUALIFICATIONS,
for Counties, 16 to 29.
for Boroughs, 30 to 53.
how far Register conclusive as to, 107.

QUESTIONS AT POLL, what, 108.

R.

RATES, POOR, what must have been paid to give new Right of Voting for Boroughs, 31 to 35.

REGISTER
of County Voters, how constituted, 71.
of Borough Voters, how, 89.
custody of, 71, 89.
how far conclusive, 107.
mistakes in, 110.
may be corrected by order of Select Committee, 111.

REGISTRATION,
of County Voters, 54 to 71.
of Borough Voters, 72 to 89.
event of first not being complete before Dissolution of Parliament, how provided for, 118.

RENT. Occupying Tenants, at what rent to Vote for Counties, 27.

RENT CHARGE, freehold, Registration of, not dispensed with, 16.

RESERVATION of Old Rights of Voting for Boroughs,
first, in Perpetuity, 39.
secondly, for a Time, 45.

RESIDENCE,
within Borough, what necessary, 31.
limits of, how to be measured, 35.
definition of, 52.

RETFORD. See EAST RETFORD.

RETURNING OFFICER,
duty of, for Counties, 90.
for Boroughs, 97.
for City of London, as to Lists of Liverymen, 80, 81.

I

INDEX.

REVISION OF LISTS
for Counties, 63.
for Boroughs, 86.

RIDINGS OF YORKSHIRE
to be as separate Counties, 1, 2.
North Riding, principal place of Election for, at York, 91.
West Riding, at Wakefield, *ib.*
East Riding, at Beverley, *ib.*

RIOTS, adjournment of Poll in case of, 112.

ROMAN CATHOLICS, Oath of, at Elections, 109.

S.

SANDWICH, Borough of, to include Deal and Walmer, 11.

SCOT and LOT Right Reserved, how, 47.

SCRUTINY, before Returning Officer abolished, 111.

SEAMEN Absent on his Majesty's Service not to forfeit Reserved Right for Borough, 48.

SERVITUDE, Freemen in respect of, Right reserved, when, 42.

" SEVEN MILES," how to be Measured, 35.

SHERIFF,
Duty of, as to County Elections, 90.
Of Yorkshire—his Duty as to Proclaiming Day of Election, 91.

SHOP will give Vote for Borough to Occupier, when, 30, 162.

SHOREHAM,
Borough of, to include certain adjacent Districts, 10, 11.
Provision as to Rights Reserved in, 50.
List of Persons entitled to Vote for, in respect of Freeholds in Horsham, 155.

SLEAFORD, Principal Place of Election for parts of Kesteven and Holland, 91.

SOLDIERS Absent on Service not to forfeit Reserved Right for Borough, 48.

SUCCESSION,
Title by, 16, 26.
Premises occupied in, in order to give Vote for Borough, may be different, 31.

INDEX.

SUCCESSIVE OCCUPATION of Premises in a Borough, when
 it will entitle to Vote, 31, 161.

SWANSEA,
 New Borough of, how constituted, 13, 14, 43.
 Freemen of, Provision as to, 168.

T.

TAXES, Assessed, what must have been Paid to give New Right of
 Voting for Borough, 31 to 35.

TENANT, what Property occupied by Party as will give Right of
 Voting for Borough, 30.

TENANTS Occupying, (without reference to length of Term,)
 may Vote for County, when, 27.

TENANTS in Ancient Demesne, Right of, for Counties, 22, 3, 4.

TENDER of VOTES at Election, 110.

TOWN CLERKS,
 Duty of, as to Making out Lists of Freemen, 168 to 176.
  to be Discharged by Person executing duties similar
   to those of Town Clerk where there is no Town
   Clerk, 168.

" TOWNSHIP," Meaning of Word, 143.

TREASURERS for COUNTIES, Payments to be made to and by,
 in respect of Expense of Registration, 116.

TRUSTEES, Provision as to, 28.

U.

UNDER LESSEE, in Occupation, Right of, to vote for Counties, 26.

UNIVERSITIES,
 not affected by the Reform Act, 39.
 Chambers or Premises in Colleges or Halls of, not to give Right
  of Voting for City of Oxford or Town of Cambridge, 167.

USK,
 to share in Election with Monmouth, 104.
 Polling at, ib.

INDEX.

V.

VALUE,
    of Qualifying Freehold in Counties, 17, 18.
    of Qualifying Property in Boroughs, 31.
    how to be ascertained, 162, 163.

VOTERS,
    for Counties, 15 to 29.
    for Boroughs, 30 to 53.
    Registration of, for Counties, 54 to 71.
               for Boroughs, 72 to 96.

VOTES, tender of, at Elections, 110.

W.

WALES,
    Counties in which will return Two Members, 4.
                       One Member, *ib.*
    Contributory Boroughs in, Classification of, 12, 13.
    Boundaries of Boroughs and Contributory Boroughs in, how
      settled, 14.
    Polling for Boroughs in, 104.

WAREHOUSE will give Vote for Borough to Occupier, when,
    30, 162.

WIGHT, ISLE OF.—See Isle of Wight and Newport.

WRITS for the Election of Member, to be framed and expressed
    so as to carry the Provisions of the Act into effect, 90.

Y.

YORK, City of, and Ainsty, to be included in North Riding of
    Yorkshire for purposes of County Elections, 2.

YORKSHIRE,
    to return Six Members, 1, 2.
    North Riding of, what it will include, 2.
    East Riding of, what it will include, *ib.*
    Wakefield, principal Place of Election for West Riding of, 91.
    York, principal Place of Election for North Riding of, *ib.*
    Beverley, principal Place of Election for East Riding of, *ib.*
    Sheriff of, Duty of, as to Proclaiming Day of Election, *ib.*
    Polling Places in, appointed by the Boundary Act, *ib.*

London: C. Roworth and Sons, Bell Yard, Temple Bar.

UNIVERSITY OF CALIFORNIA LIBRARY
Los Angeles
This book is DUE on the last date stamped below.

AUG 2 6 1958

10m-9,'66(G5925s4)

1005
1832

ImTheStory.com

Personalized Classic Books in many genre's

Unique gift for kids, partners, friends, colleagues

Customize:

- Character Names
- Upload your own front/back cover images (optional)
- Inscribe a personal message/dedication on the inside page (optional)

Customize many titles Including
- Alice in Wonderland
- Romeo and Juliet
- The Wizard of Oz
- A Christmas Carol
- Dracula
- Dr. Jekyll & Mr. Hyde
- And more...

WS - #0009 - 260424 - C0 - 229/152/24 - PB - 9781314522952 - Gloss Lamination